# HODDER GCSE HISTORY FOR E

# CRIME AND PUNISHMENT THROUGH TIME

## c.1000–present

**Alec Fisher • Ed Podesta**

The Publishers would like to thank the following for permission to reproduce copyright material.

**Photo credits**
**p.4** *A* © Mary Evans Picture Library, *B* © David Crausby / Alamy Stock Photo, *C* © INTERFOTO/Alamy Stock Photo, *D* © Mary Evans Picture Library; **p.19** © Neil Setchfield/Alamy Stock Photo; **p.25** © Angelo Hornak/Alamy Stock Photo; **p.26** © Granger, NYC/Alamy Stock Photo; **p.29** © Geoffrey Morgan/Alamy Stock Photo; **p.36–37** © Mary Evans Picture Library/Alamy Stock Photo; **p.40** © Pictorial Press Ltd/Alamy Stock Photo; **p.41** *t* © Mary Evans Picture Library/Alamy Stock Photo, *b* © Fotosearch/Getty Images; **p.43** 'Beggars All': Beggars Bush, a Wandering Beggar and a Gallant Beggar, title page of 'The Praise, Antiquity and Commodity of Beggary, Beggars and Begging' (woodcut), English School, (16th century)/Private Collection/The Stapleton Collection/Bridgeman Images; **p.46** © Three witches hanging. After the title page of a contemporary pamphlet on the third Chelmsford witch trial of 1589/Ken Welsh/Bridgeman Images; **p.47** © Mary Evans Picture Library; **p.48** © Mary Evans Picture Library; **p.50** © National Archives; **p.58** © GL Archive/Alamy Stock Photo; **p.62** © Chronicle/Alamy Stock Photo; **p.66–67** © Mary Evans Picture Library/Alamy Stock Photo; **p.68** © GROSVENOR PRINTS/Mary Evans Picture Library; **p.71** Classic Image/Alamy Stock Photo; **p.72** "Black-eyed Sue and Sweet Poll of Plymouth taking leave of their Lovers who are going to Botany Bay", 1792 (engraving) © National Library of Australia, Canberra, Australia/Bridgeman Images; **p.75** *b* © World History Archive/Alamy Stock Photo; **p.76** © INTERFOTO/Alamy Stock Photo; **p.77** *t* © The Granger Collection/ TopFoto, *b* © Pictorial Press Ltd/Alamy Stock Photo; **p.78** *t* © Chronicle/Alamy Stock Photo, *b* © Mary Evans Picture Library/Alamy Stock Photo; **p.79** *both* © Mary Evans Picture Library/Alamy Stock Photo; **p.80** *t* © Chronicle/Alamy Stock Photo, *b* © Mary Evans Picture Library/Alamy Stock Photo; **p.88** © Jack Sullivan/Alamy Stock Photo; **p.90** © ONSLOW AUCTIONS LIMITED/Mary Evans Picture Library; **p.91** © Imperial War Museum; **p.93** © Justin Kase zsixz/Alamy Stock Photo; **p.95** © Terry Harris/Alamy Stock Photo; **p.97** © Reyaz Limalia; **p.99** © Paul Doyle/Alamy Stock Photo; **p.101** © Shirley/ullstein bild/Getty Images; **p.101** *t* © Popperfoto/Getty Images, *b* © Bettmann/Getty Images; **p.114** *t* and **p.126** © Peter Higginbotham Collection/Mary Evans Picture Library, *b* and **p.144** © Mary Evans Picture Library/Alamy Stock Photo; **p.115** © The Execution by Hanging of Henry Wainwright at Newgate Gaol on 21st December 1875, published in *Police News*, 1875 (wood engraving), English School, (19th century)/London Metropolitan Archives, City of London/Bridgeman Images; **p.119** © Chronicle/Alamy Stock Photo; **p.122** © Maddy Podesta; **p.123** and **p.125** © Wellcome Library, London/http://creativecommons.org/licenses/by/4.0/; **p.124** © Mansell /Getty Images; **p.127** © Carol B London; **p.128** © Hulton Archive/Getty Images; **p.130** © Jewish Encyclopaedia; **p.134** © Print Collector/Getty Images; **p.135** *l* © Illustrated London News Ltd/Mary Evans Picture Library, *tr* © Illustrated London News Ltd/Mary Evans Picture Library, *br* © Mary Evans Picture Library; **p.136** © Mary Evans Picture Library/Alamy Stock Photo; **p.139** © National Archives; **p.143** © Illustrated London News Ltd/Mary Evans; **p.150** © Mary Evans Picture Library/Alamy Stock Photo; **p.152** © DAVID LEWIS HODGSON/Mary Evans Picture Library; **p.153** *l* and **p.169** © Lordprice Collection/Alamy Stock Photo, *r* © DAVID LEWIS HODGSON/Mary Evans Picture Library; **p.156** © Mary Evans Picture Library; **p.157** © Historical Images Archive/Alamy Stock Photo.

**Acknowledgements**
To B5 tutor group at Mill Chase Academy for making Mr Fisher smile.

**p.100** 'Let Him Dangle', Words & Music by Elvis Costello © Copyright 1989 Universal Music Publishing MGB Limited. All Rights Reserved. International Copyright Secured. Used by Permission of Music Sales Limited.

Every effort has been made to trace all copyright holders, but if any have been inadvertently overlooked, the Publishers will be pleased to make the necessary arrangements at the first opportunity.

Although every effort has been made to ensure that website addresses are correct at time of going to press, Hodder Education cannot be held responsible for the content of any website mentioned in this book. It is sometimes possible to find a relocated web page by typing in the address of the home page for a website in the URL window of your browser.

**Note:** The wording and sentence structure of some written sources have been adapted and simplified to make them accessible to all pupils while faithfully preserving the sense of the original.

Hachette UK's policy is to use papers that are natural, renewable and recyclable products and made from wood grown in sustainable forests. The logging and manufacturing processes are expected to conform to the environmental regulations of the country of origin.

Orders: please contact Bookpoint Ltd, 130 Milton Park, Abingdon, Oxon OX14 4SB. Telephone: +44 (0)1235 827720. Fax: +44 (0)1235 400454. Email education@bookpoint.co.uk Lines are open from 9 a.m. to 5 p.m., Monday to Saturday, with a 24-hour message answering service. You can also order through our website: www.hoddereducation.co.uk

ISBN: 9781471861727

© Alec Fisher and Ed Podesta 2016

First published in 2016 by
Hodder Education,
An Hachette UK Company
Carmelite House
50 Victoria Embankment
London EC4Y 0DZ

www.hoddereducation.co.uk

Impression number    10 9 8 7 6 5 4

Year        2020 2019 2018 2017

**Cover photos** *left* © APIC/Getty Images; *right* Harl 4375 f.140 Victims tortured to decide on Innocence or Guilt, from 'Dicta et Facta Memorabilia,' c.1475 (vellum)/British Library, London, UK/© British Library Board. All Rights Reserved/Bridgeman Images

Illustrations by Aptara, Barking Dog Art, Oxford Designers and Illustrators, Peter Lubach, Richard Duszczak, Tony Randell

Typeset in ITC Legacy Serif 10/12pt by Melissa Brunelli Design

Printed in India

A catalogue record for this title is available from the British Library.

# CONTENTS

## How much do you know about crime and punishment?

Crime sells. It sells newspapers, magazines, books, films and video games. It is often featured in the news. People seem both shocked and fascinated by crime and it can lead to heated debates.

- Is crime becoming more violent?
- Should punishments be harsher or easier?
- Does prison make a difference?
- Should we send criminals to prison for longer?
- Should we bring back **capital punishment** (the death penalty)?

Attitudes have had a huge effect in shaping the history of crime and punishment. So let's find out about the attitudes of the different people in your history class. Work through the survey below and share any differences of opinion you might have. You might find that you have your own heated debate!

---

### What are your attitudes to crime and punishment?

**1. What should be the main reason behind punishing criminals?**

- ☐ a) Retribution – revenge to satisfy the victim or their families
- ☐ b) Deterrence – to warn others not to commit the same crime
- ☐ c) Reform – to help the criminal improve their behaviour
- ☐ d) Removal – to keep criminals off the streets

**2. Should capital punishment (the death penalty) be brought back?**

- ☐ a) Yes, for all murders
- ☐ b) Yes, for some murders
- ☐ c) Yes, for certain types of serious crime
- ☐ d) No

**3. Should physical punishments, such as whipping, be used against criminals?**

- ☐ a) Yes
- ☐ b) No

**4. Should the police carry guns?**

- ☐ a) Yes, all the time
- ☐ b) No, unless there is a dangerous situation to deal with
- ☐ c) Only in some areas
- ☐ d) Never

Often people simply voice their ideas and opinions without really knowing the facts about something. This course should help you to avoid that. By studying the ideas and attitudes of people in the past, you can come to a better informed view of the issues surrounding crime and punishment that affect us today. So what do you know, or think you know, about crime and punishment today? Carry out the crime survey below. Then check the answers on page 182 to see if you were correct.

## Crime survey

**1. In the last ten years crime has:**

- [ ] a) Risen dramatically
- [ ] b) Stayed roughly the same
- [ ] c) Fallen

**2. Who is more likely to be the victim of a mugging?**

- [ ] a) A female pensioner
- [ ] b) A male pensioner
- [ ] c) A female under 29
- [ ] d) A male under 29

**3. Yearly numbers of murders and killings are:**

- [ ] a) Slightly higher than they were ten years ago
- [ ] b) Considerably higher than they were ten years ago
- [ ] c) Slightly lower than they were ten years ago
- [ ] d) Considerably lower than they were ten years ago

**4. In the last ten years, car crime (theft of cars and possessions from cars) has:**

- [ ] a) Increased dramatically
- [ ] b) Increased a little
- [ ] c) Decreased
- [ ] d) Decreased dramatically

**5. Women are more likely than men to be attacked by a stranger.**

- [ ] a) True
- [ ] b) False

**6. Burglary is:**

- [ ] a) Increasing dramatically
- [ ] b) Increasing a little
- [ ] c) Decreasing
- [ ] d) Decreasing dramatically

**7. What percentage of crimes are violent?**

- [ ] a) 50 per cent
- [ ] b) 35 per cent
- [ ] c) 10 per cent
- [ ] d) 3 per cent

Societies and law makers have struggled with the issues of crime and punishment for thousands of years – it is no wonder that you may not be sure about things at this early stage! When you get to the end of this book, try answering these survey questions again. You may find that you have changed your mind about some of your earlier answers.

# 1 Crime and punishment in Britain: The Big Story from c.1000–present

There is over a thousand years of history in the next 160 pages. But don't worry – by the end of this chapter you will be able to tell, in outline, the whole story of crime and punishment from AB 1000 until the present day. Once you have that clear outline in your mind, you can start to build up more detailed knowledge as you progress through the book.

The history of crime and punishment reveals a tremendous amount of information about what people in different societies in the past thought and how they lived. On the one hand, things seem to have changed. Today, you are far less likely than someone living in medieval England to be a victim of a violent crime. You can also decide your own religious beliefs (or lack of them), without running the risk of being burnt at the stake.

On the other hand, some things seem to stay the same. You, or perhaps someone you know, may have had a mobile phone or a laptop stolen. Although these particular items were only invented in the late twentieth century, petty theft has remained the most common type of crime for the last thousand years! So, it would appear that the story of crime and punishment is one of both dramatic change but also significant continuity.

## 1.1 Becoming a master of chronology

Lots of things you learned in Key Stage 3 history lessons are going to be useful during your GCSE course. One example is your knowledge of chronology – the names and sequence of different historical periods. As you are going to study such a long period – a thousand years – you will have to talk and write confidently about a variety of historical periods.

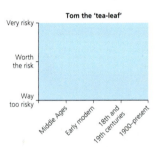

### IDENTIFYING HISTORICAL PERIODS

1 Place the four historical periods below in chronological order:

The twentieth century · The Middle Ages · The early modern period · The eighteenth and nineteenth centuries

2 Roughly what dates does each period cover?

3 Look the pictures on this page. Which picture (A–D) comes from which chronological period? Give one reason for each choice.
   a) What seems to be happening in each picture?
   b) What can you work out from each picture about crime and punishment at that time? Think about what they might reveal about one or more of the following:

   – different types of crime
   – methods used to enforce the law
   – methods used to punish criminals.

4 Part of learning about history is having the confidence to come up with your own hypothesis, which you later test against the evidence. Look at the graph above. Based on what you know so far, when do you think was the best time to be a criminal? Plot your thoughts on your own copy of the graph. Don't worry if you are not sure – we will come back to this later on!

## CHRONOLOGY

**1** Look at the timeline below and work out the missing dates.

| 11th | 12th | 13th | 14th | 15th | 16th | 17th | 18th | 19th | 20th |
|---|---|---|---|---|---|---|---|---|---|
| | 1100–99 | | | 1400–99 | | | 1700–99 | | |

**2** Is 1829 in the eighteenth or nineteenth century? Can you explain why?

**3** The tabards below are in the wrong sequence. What is the correct chronological sequence?

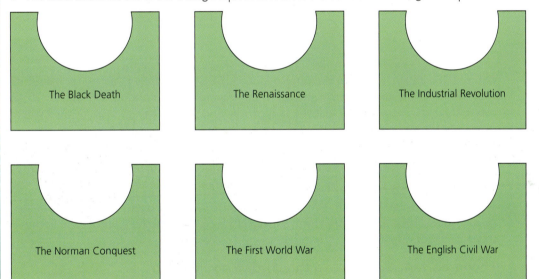

The Black Death

The Renaissance

The Industrial Revolution

The Norman Conquest

The First World War

The English Civil War

**4** Look at the two boxes below – Period A and Period B.

Tudors and Stuarts     The Renaissance     The age of the Black Death     Early modern period

The Victorian age     The twentieth century     The Industrial Revolution     The nineteenth century

a) One name in each box is the odd one out. Explain which is the odd one out in each box, and why.

b) The three remaining names in each box are given to roughly the same historical period, but they mean slightly different things. Explain the differences between them. You can use dates to help you and check the timeline above if it helps.

# Getting better at history – why we are making learning visible

We'll come back to chronology later on – if you take a look at the activity box on page 7, you'll see plenty more chronology activities. However, these two pages are only partly about chronology, and are actually part of a much bigger topic – what do you have to do to get better at history?

You have to build up your knowledge and understanding of the history of crime and punishment. That might sound straightforward, but you will keep meeting new information and sometimes you are going to feel puzzled, maybe even totally confused.

What do you do when you feel puzzled and confused? You have two choices:

> Muddle on, try to ignore or hide the problem and don't tell your teacher. You may lose confidence and stop working hard.
>
> The result – you make mistakes in your exams and do badly.

**Choice A**

> Think about why you're puzzled and **identify** the problem. Then admit there's something you don't understand and tell your teacher.
>
> The result – your teacher helps you sort out the problem, your confidence increases and you do well in your exams.

**Choice B**

## Visible learning

It's OK to get things wrong. We all do. And often the things we get wrong initially and then correct are the things we remember best because we've had to think harder about them. Saying 'I don't understand' is the first step towards getting it right.

Choice B is a lot smarter than the Choice A! With Choice B you are taking responsibility for your own learning and your own success. It may sound strange, but one crucial way to get better at history is to admit when you're confused and getting things wrong – then you can start to put things right.

We emphasised one very important word in Choice B – **identify**. You cannot get better at history unless you and your teacher identify exactly what you don't know and understand. To put that another way, you have to make that problem **visible** before you can put it right.

Throughout this book we will identify common mistakes that students make and make them visible so that you can see them. Then you have a much better chance of avoiding those mistakes yourself.

## The importance of getting the chronology right

One of those very common and very important mistakes – an issue that confuses students **every year** – is chronology. It's so important that we decided it had to be made visible at the very beginning of this book. If you get the chronology wrong you can end up writing about completely the wrong things in an exam. There are plenty of examples of students being asked about developments in one period of history but writing about an entirely different period of history because they've confused the name or dates of the period. As an example, lots of students have been asked about changes in crime and punishment in the nineteenth century and written about events between 1900 and 1999. That's a big mistake and a lot of marks to lose.

Why is the chronology confusing? It's because the history of crime and punishment covers a thousand years and so includes a number of different periods of history. What you need to do is:

- get the periods of history in the right sequence
- know the approximate dates and centuries of the periods
- know that some periods have more than one name.

So the purpose of the activity on page 7 is to help you **identify** [that word again!] what you know, what you get wrong and what confuses you. That makes those mistakes **visible** and you can put them right as soon as possible.

# 1.2 The Big Story of crime and punishment

On the next two pages you can read about the entire history of crime and punishment! We are starting the book with this Big Story to help solve another problem some students have. Those students know the detail of individual events and periods but they cannot 'see' the whole story – the overall pattern of changes and continuities in the history of crime and punishment.

The four boxes outline the Big Story. Each box has the same sub-headings – and these sub-headings are in the triangle. The triangle is hugely important because it shows the link between what people thought about crime and how they tried to enforce the laws and punish criminals. Ideas about the causes and threat from crime are very important, because they influence the methods used to enforce the law and punish criminals.

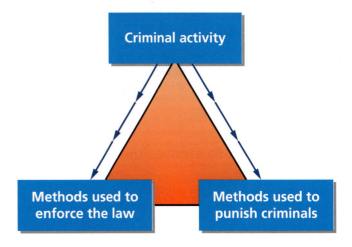

**IDENTIFYING THE KEY FEATURES OF CRIME AND PUNISHMENT**

1 Read the four boxes on pages 8–9 telling you about each time period to get a first impression of the overall story.

2 Create a new document for each of the four periods, then note down the major features of crime in each period under the three bold headings below. Think about the questions underneath the headings to help you:

## Criminal activity

What was the nature of crime in each period?

- Crimes against the person – for example: murder, assault, rape.
- Crimes against property – for example: theft, robbery, burglary, poaching, smuggling.
- Crimes against authority – for example: heresy, treason, illegal protest.

## Methods used to enforce the law

What was the role of authority and local communities in law enforcement?

- What policing methods were used?
- What trials were used to establish guilt or innocence?

## Methods used to punish criminals

What was the main idea or purpose of punishments?

- Retribution – revenge to satisfy the victim or their families.
- Deterrence – to warn others not to commit the same crime.
- Reform – to help the criminal improve their behaviour.
- Removal – to keep criminals off the streets.
- Compensation – the victim or society is paid back for the trouble caused by the criminal.

3 Across the top of each page write down two or three short phrases that sum up crime and punishment in that period. Use at least one of these words in your phrases for each period:

change · continuity · turning point · progress

4 **This is the core activity on this page.** You have up to two minutes to tell the outline story of crime and punishment. Work in a group of three to plan and tell your story.

5 After you have told your story, write it down. This is important to help it stick in your mind. Think about how to make it memorable by:

using headings · using colours to identify changes and continuities · adding drawings

## CRIME AND PUNISHMENT IN MEDIEVAL ENGLAND, C.1000–C.1500

### Criminal activity

Most crime was petty theft – the stealing of money, food and belongings. Violent crimes against people were just a small minority of cases. The crimes regarded as most serious were those that were a direct threat to the king's authority such as rebellion, protest or attacking royal officials.

### Methods used to enforce the law

There was no police force. Law enforcement was based around the local community. Victims of crime called on their fellow villagers to help catch the criminal – they raised the **hue and cry**.

Adult men were grouped into tens called **tithings**. If one of them broke the law then the others had to bring him to justice.

At first, local juries decided guilt or innocence. If the jury could not agree, then God was asked to decide using the method of **trial by ordeal**.

As time went on, **parish constables** were chosen from leading villagers to help keep order. Major crimes were investigated by **coroners** and **sheriffs**, and the accused would be brought before royal judges who travelled around the country. Each manor had its own court held by the local lord, often once a week, dealing with less serious cases.

### Methods used to punish criminals

At first, only a few offences carried the death penalty. Criminals paid **compensation** to their victims or their families. This was called **wergild**. By 1100, punishments were more about **retribution** and **deterrence**, with executions and **corporal punishments** used more frequently. Prisons were not used and people were only locked up while awaiting trial.

## CRIME AND PUNISHMENT IN EARLY MODERN ENGLAND, C.1500–C.1700

### Criminal activity

Tudor Times

Vagrant menace

Most crime was petty theft. Violent crimes against people remained a small minority of cases. Religious changes made by Henry VIII in the 1530s led to protest and rebellion against the authorities. People who disagreed with the religious views of the monarch were persecuted, accused of **heresy** or **treason**, and sometimes killed. **Witchcraft** also became a criminal offence.

Despite a drop in the late 1600s, most people believed crime was increasing, and concern about **vagabondage** increased. Some crimes and criminals became well-known due to publicity from pamphlets and broadsheets (a type of newspaper that had not existed in the Middle Ages).

### Methods used to enforce the law

There was still no police force. The use of parish constables and the hue and cry continued. In the early 1700s **thief-takers** earned a living from the rewards they received for bringing criminals to justice. However, their efforts were mainly confined to London, so criminals had little fear of being caught by them.

The court system was made more efficient and the speed at which cases were heard was improved. Royal judges continued to tour the country hearing serious cases and **manor courts** still dealt with local, minor crimes.

### Methods used to punish criminals

Nearly everyone believed that the best way of deterring criminals was to have savage, terrifying punishments that would frighten people away from crime, so corporal and capital punishment were still widely used.

## CRIME AND PUNISHMENT IN EIGHTEENTH- AND NINETEENTH-CENTURY BRITAIN, C.1700–C.1900

### Criminal activity

There was a rise in crime from 1750 to 1850, which is explained by the huge increase in the population from 11 million in 1750 to 42 million in 1900. By 1851, the majority of the British population lived in urban areas, where there was more opportunity for crime. Petty theft remained the most common type of crime. However, the authorities were now less concerned about vagabondage, witchcraft and heresy. Instead they became more worried about crimes that disrupted trade such as **highway robbery** and **smuggling**.

### Methods used to enforce the law

The growth of towns created new opportunities for crime, which challenged existing policing methods. A huge change came in 1829 with the setting up of the **Metropolitan Police** – the country's first professional police force. Although unpopular at first, by the 1850s the police played an important role in capturing criminals and investigating crimes.

### Methods used to punish criminals

The idea of reform – that criminals could become law abiding – became more widespread in this period. However, there were some who believed in a recognisable 'criminal type', who had certain physical characteristics and were somehow less evolved than other people. Another big change in this period was the increasing use of prisons. This generated much debate throughout the nineteenth century. Some felt the purpose of prisons was to deter others from turning to crime. Others wanted to reform convicted criminals through making inmates work hard.

## CRIME AND PUNISHMENT IN MODERN BRITAIN, C.1900–PRESENT

### Criminal activity

There was a big increase in crime from the 1950s to 1995. Since then, the overall crime rate has slowly declined. New technology has helped to create new types of crime, such as driving offences. **Race crime** and **drug crime** have also emerged as new types of crime. There are also new opportunities for old crimes, including new forms of theft and smuggling.

### Methods used to enforce the law

Finger printing was introduced in 1901 and more recently the use of DNA samples has helped the police to investigate crimes and track down criminals. The use of radios and cars has allowed the police to respond more quickly to events. Specialist units within the police force concentrate on different types of crime. At a local community level, **Neighbourhood Watch** developed to encourage communities to work together to help deter crime and anti-social behaviour.

### Methods used to punish criminals

Fines are the most widely used punishment, especially for driving offences. Prisons are used for more serious crimes and for repeat offenders, and different types of prison have developed such as **open prisons** and **young offenders' institutions**. Debate has continued over the purpose of and effectiveness of prisons. Since the 1990s electronic tagging has been used as a way of monitoring a criminal's movements and as an alternative to prison. The death penalty was abolished in 1965.

**THIS IS A SIMPLE OUTLINE. IT IS NOT THE COMPLETE STORY. YOU WILL LEARN MORE IMPORTANT DETAILS LATER IN THE BOOK.**

# 1.3 Why changes happened – and didn't happen

The Big Story on pages 7–9 gave you some idea of the changes and continuities in the history of crime and punishment. However, it did not say much to explain those changes and continuities. This page introduces the factors that explain them.

Each factor is shown in one of the factor diamonds below. You will see and work with these diamonds throughout the book because explaining why crime and punishment has changed or stayed the same is central to its history. It is also central to doing well in your exams!

In the diagram below we have shown two groups of factors:

**a)** The factors above the triangle have had the most impact on crime and punishment throughout history.

**b)** The factors below the triangle have been important in particular periods of history, but not so consistently through time as the factors above the triangle.

> **Factors**
> Factors are the reasons or causes of changes in crime and punishment or of crime and punishment staying \ the same.

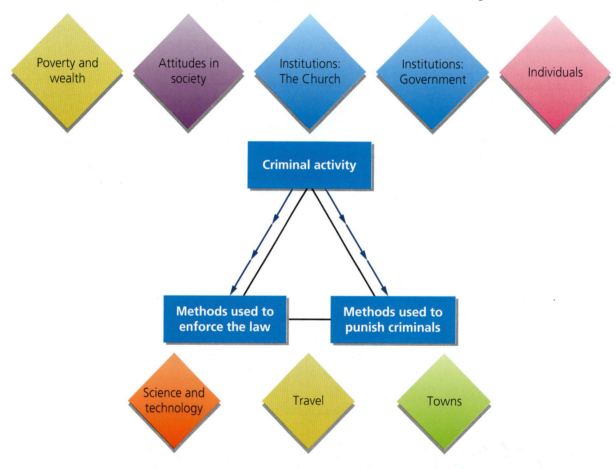

## STARTING TO THINK ABOUT THE ROLE OF FACTORS

1 It's time to make good use of your Key Stage 3 history knowledge again.

   a) Work with a partner and choose two of the factors in the diagram.

   b) For each factor, decide when you think it had the most effect on crime and punishment. Choose from:
   - The Middle Ages, c.1000–c.1500
   - The early modern period, c.1500–c.1700
   - The eighteenth and nineteenth centuries, c.1700–c.1900
   - c.1900–present.

   A good way to do this is to brainstorm what you already know about each period in general. For example, who governed the country, what you know about living and working conditions, etc.

   Make sure you are clear about crime and punishment in each period (see pages 8 and 9) and whether each period saw a little or a lot of change.

   c) Now suggest when each of your factors probably had the most impact and whether they helped crime and punishment change or stay the same.

2 Below are three important moments in the history of crime and punishment. Which factors are influencing the people and events described in each one? (Don't worry if you're not certain – you will find out exactly why each one took place later in the course.)

3 Now you have an idea of the big picture, let's return to Tom the 'tea-leaf' who we met back on page 4. You already plotted how risky it was to be a criminal in each different period. Look back at your choices. Do you want to revise the graph in any way?

## THE GUNPOWDER PLOT, 1605

Many Catholics had hoped that the King James I would be tolerant of their religion, but instead he declared his 'utter detestation of [the Catholic] superstitious religion'. In 1605, a group of Catholic plotters attempted to blow up King James I and his ministers during the opening of Parliament. The plotters were angry that James had not allowed Catholics freedom of worship and made them pay heavy fines. The plotters were captured and publicly punished in the most brutal way possible. They were hanged, before being taken down alive and then **castrated** and **disembowelled**. Their bodies were cut into quarters and sent to different towns to be displayed.

## THE FIRST POLICE FORCE IS SET UP IN LONDON, 1829

In 1829, the government established the first police force in London for several reasons. There was a widespread belief that crime and especially violent crime was out of control. In London there were too many people crammed into closely packed houses and streets. This made the old system of parish constables and watchmen seem inadequate. Moreover, in the years after 1815 there were many protests about unemployment and high bread prices, so the government and rich landowners wanted to prevent the possibility of riot becoming revolution. Finally, the government had been raising more money in taxes which made a full-time police force affordable.

## CAPITAL PUNISHMENT IS ABOLISHED IN BRITAIN, 1965

By 1965 many people wanted an end to capital punishment. Opinion had been divided but the topic was regularly debated on television and in the newspapers. Opinion polls were run to measure the views of the public. One argument was that execution was barbaric, uncivilised and un-Christian; another was that execution was not really a deterrent as most murders happen on the spur of the moment.

# 2 Crime and punishment in medieval England, c.1000–c.1500

## 2.1 Understanding medieval England, c.1000–c.1500

To understand crime and punishment in the Middle Ages, and the factors affecting it, we need a clear picture of medieval society, as shown in the boxes below.

### The king

Medieval people believed their kings were chosen by God. The king was the most important person in the country as he controlled the land and decided how to share it out. The main tasks facing medieval kings were defending the country from attack and ensuring their subjects were protected by the law.

### The nobles

The nobles were the king's main supporters and advisers. In return for land, the nobles provided the king with knights and military service in times of war. They were also expected to keep law and order in their own lands.

### The Church

People in the Middle Ages saw this life as preparation for the eternal afterlife after death. They believed firmly in Heaven and Hell. Therefore, the Church was an important organisation because it offered ways to help a person's soul get to Heaven. There was a priest in every village and everyone was expected to attend church and live by its rules. The Church ran its own courts for churchmen and offered sanctuary to criminals who took refuge in a church building. This sometimes brought the Church into conflict with kings who wanted to enforce royal justice on everyone without interference.

### The peasants

Most people in medieval England were peasants – farmers who worked the land and lived in villages. For part of each week they worked on the land of the local lord. In their remaining time peasants worked on their own land to feed their families. People lived in close-knit communities and knew their neighbours well. As there was no police force, they were expected to look out for one another and ensure the village was a lawful place.

### Medieval society

1 Who was responsible for upholding the laws in medieval England?
2 Why might the Church and the king have argued over upholding the law?
3 What advantages do you think criminals had in medieval England?

### Visible learning

**When were the Middle Ages?**

This book deals with a thousand years of history. By far, the biggest chunk of this time was taken up by the medieval period. Although the medieval period began around c.400, when the Romans left Britain, we focus on the years c.1000–c.1500. However, 500 years is still a long time! Therefore, to make things clearer, we divide the period into Anglo-Saxon England (before 1066), Norman England (c.1066–c.1100) and the later Middle Ages (c.1100–c.1500). And one more thing – historians also call the medieval period the Middle Ages!

## ASKING QUESTIONS ABOUT CRIME AND PUNISHMENT IN THE MIDDLE AGES

Learning to ask good questions is an important historical skill. Some questions are 'bigger' – more important – than others.

1   Which of these four questions are the bigger ones for understanding the history of crime and punishment? What makes them bigger?
   a)   Who was the most powerful person in medieval society?
   b)   How can we explain the increase in harsh punishments during the early modern period?
   c)   What year was the first police force set up?
   d)   Why did it take so long for the first police force to be set up?

2   Make a list of the questions you want to ask about crime and punishment in the Middle Ages. Divide your list into 'big' and 'little' questions. Use the question starters below to help you.

| | | | | |
|---|---|---|---|---|
| When ...? | How ...? | What effects ...? | Who ...? | What ...? |
| What happened ...? | How significant ...? | Did they ...? | Why ...? | |
| Where ...? | Did it really ...? | | | |

## Your Enquiry Question

Like you, we thought of lots of questions about crime and punishment in the Middle Ages. However, the one we settled on was:

We chose this question for three reasons. First, it's a 'big' question because it helps you understand a period of 500 years, half of all the chronology we cover in this course. Second, it helps you to understand how medieval society functioned and the different roles people played.

> Who had the most influence on law and order in the Middle Ages – the Church, the king or local communities?

Good historians usually start answering a question by suggesting an initial hypothesis – a first draft answer. A hypothesis helps you to stay on track as you continue working, but remember that you can change it or add to it as you learn more.

1   Based on what you have found out *so far* using pages 4–12, who do you think would have had the most influence on law and order in the Middle Ages – the Church, the king or the local community?

The next step is to research this topic and collect evidence that helps you to answer the Enquiry Question. We are going to use a Knowledge Organiser. This is to help you avoid the common mistake of making notes so detailed that you cannot see the main points that you need.

2   Make your own large copy of the chart below. You will be instructed to add detail to it as you work through the rest of this section on the Middle Ages.

| | Influence from the Church | Influence from the king | Influence from local communities |
|---|---|---|---|
| Enforcing the law: policing methods | | | |
| Enforcing the law: trials | | | |
| Punishment of criminals | | | |

## 2.2 Criminal moment in time: Saxon village, c.1000

After the Romans withdrew from England in c.400, waves of settlers from Germany began to settle. These Angles and Saxons brought their own laws and customs as they established local kingdoms across England. These early Anglo-Saxon kings allowed victims of crime to punish the criminals themselves. If someone was murdered, the family of the victim had the right to track down and kill the murderer. This system, known as 'blood feud', was all about retribution and often led to more violence. Furthermore, it offered no justice for those unable or unwilling to use violence themselves.

Your GCSE study begins in c.1000, by which time England had been united into a single Anglo-Saxon kingdom and blood feud had long been replaced by more effective ways of upholding the law. Anglo-Saxon society was based on close-knit farming communities who shared responsibility for maintaining law and order in the village. By far the most common crimes were against property, usually in the form of petty theft.

Maybe this will teach you to stop stealing. This is the fifth time you have been caught! May this be a lesson to all of you not to steal.

There was no evidence in this case, so God will decide. Bandage his hands and we will see if God has helped them heal in three days' time.

Saxons sometimes used trial by ordeal.

I drank too much and insulted my neighbour.

Stop, thief!

### Saxon law and order: An overview

1 Work in pairs or small groups. You have five minutes. What evidence can you find in the picture of:
   a) different types of crime (against the person, property or authority; see page 7)
   b) different punishments
   c) different forms of policing and/or crime prevention
   d) different trials.

2 Let's return to the Enquiry Question we came up with on page 13. Revisit the hypothesis you made in answer to the Enquiry Question. Do you want to make any changes to it in light of the evidence you have found?

3 List any questions that these two pages raise about the nature of Anglo-Saxon law enforcement and punishment. You will be able to answer these as you work through the next few pages.

If someone shouted 'Thief!' they raised the 'hue and cry' and everyone in the village had to stop what they were doing and chase after the criminal or they would have to pay a fine.

Sorry I killed your brother. Here is the last wergild payment that I have to make to you for the cost of his life.

Saxons practised trial by jury. The members of the jury came from the local village and knew the accused.

You have been found guilty. You ploughed some of Alfred's land. You must pay him five chickens as compensation.

Thank you. Now I hope that this will be an end to this sad affair.

Now he's twelve he could join our tithing. He seems old enough to take his responsibilities seriously.

I am only to be locked in this 'prison' until my trial – thank God.

Each man over the age of twelve had to belong to a group of ten men. They were responsible for keeping each other out of trouble. If one of them broke the law, they all had to make sure he went to court.

# 2.3 Was Anglo-Saxon justice violent and superstitious?

Novels, films and television often depict medieval justice as violent, cruel and superstitious, based only around retribution and deterrence. They give the impression of savage punishments based on 'an eye for an eye' and terrifying public executions to set an example. On these pages you will investigate Anglo-Saxon methods of enforcing the law and punishing criminals. Once you have made a judgement about whether these were violent and superstitious, we can return to the Enquiry Question on page 13 and use the information to formulate an answer.

## MAKING A JUDGEMENT

You are going to use a judgement matrix to help you decide how harsh and superstitious Anglo-Saxon justice really was. This is another effective Knowledge Organiser which helps you summarise important information and show your thinking in a visual way.

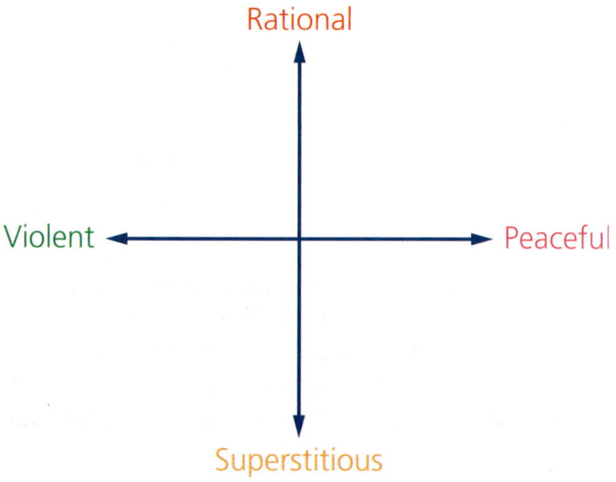

1 Draw your own larger copy of the matrix on the right.

2 Use the information on pages 17–19 to make your own summary cards on each of the methods the Anglo-Saxons used to keep law and order (tithings; hue and cry; trial by local jury; trial by ordeal; wergild; capital and corporal punishment). Summary cards are meant to be clear and to the point. Look at the example below for guidance.

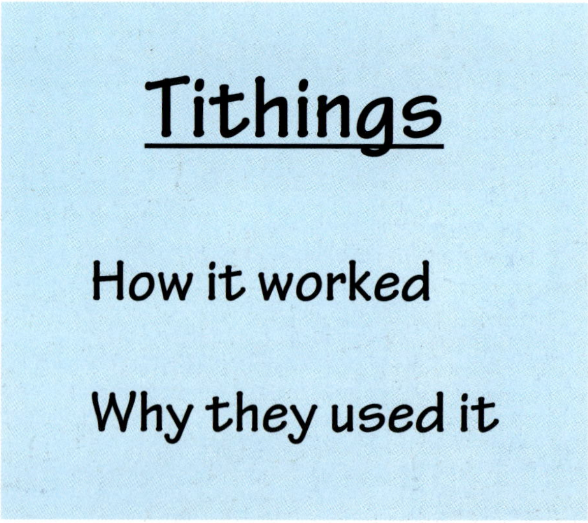

Rational

Violent ← → Peaceful

Superstitious

# Tithings

## How it worked

## Why they used it

3 Discuss each card carefully with a partner. Where should it be placed on the judgement matrix?

## Tithings

Anglo-Saxon England lacked anything that we would describe as a police force. People lived in small villages and knew their neighbours well. Law enforcement was based around the local community.

By the tenth century, Anglo-Saxon kings had set up a self-help system known as a tithing. Every male over the age of twelve was expected to join a tithing. This was group of ten men who were responsible for each others' behaviour. If one of them broke the law, the other members of the tithing had to bring him to court, or pay a fine.

## Hue and cry

If a crime was committed the victim or witness was expected to raise the 'hue and cry'. This was more than just calling out for help. The entire village was expected to down tools and join the hunt to catch the criminal. If a person did not join the hue and cry then the whole village would have to pay a heavy fine.

## Trial by local jury

The Anglo-Saxons used two types of trial. The first of these relied on the local community and used a form of trial by jury. The jury was made up of men from the village who knew both the accuser and the accused.

The accuser and the accused would give their version of events and it was up to the jury to decide who was telling the truth. If there was no clear evidence such as an eyewitness to the crime, the jury decided guilt or innocence based on their knowledge of the people concerned. If the jury felt that the accuser was more honest than the accused, they would swear an oath that the accused was guilty. This oath taking was called **compurgation**.

> **?** What do you think the advantages and disadvantages of the tithing system were? Why might it be difficult to use such a system today?

▲ The tithing system in action

## Trial by ordeal

The Saxons were a very religious society. If a local jury could not decide guilt or innocence, then the Saxons turned to trial by ordeal in the hope that God would help them. The diagram below helps you understand the different types of trial by ordeal and the role religion played in the process.

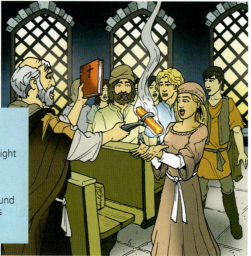

**Trial by hot iron**
- Usually taken by women.
- The accused picked up a red-hot weight and walked three paces with it.
- The hand was bandaged and unwrapped three days later.
- The accused was innocent if the wound was healing cleanly or guilty if it was festering.

**Trial by ordeal**
- All ordeals (except cold water) took place inside a church.
- The accused had to fast for three days and then hear Mass as preparation.
- A priest was always present, as it was believed God would judge guilt or innocence.

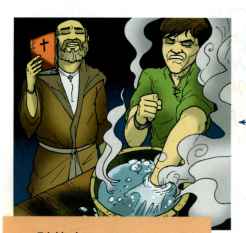

**Trial by hot water**
- Usually taken by men.
- The accused put his hand into boiling water to pick up an object.
- The hand or arm was bandaged and unwrapped three days later.
- The accused was innocent if the wound was healing cleanly, but guilty if it was festering.

**Trial by blessed bread**
- Taken by priests.
- A priest prayed that the accused would choke on bread if they lied.
- The accused ate bread and was found guilty if he choked.

**Trial by cold water**
- Usually taken by men.
- The accused was tied with a knot above the waist and lowered into the water on the end of a rope.
- If the accused sank below God's 'pure water' then he was judged innocent. If the accused floated, then he had been 'rejected' by the pure water and was found guilty.

## Wergild

The Saxons relied heavily on a system of fines called wergild. Wergild was compensation paid to the victims of crime or to their families. The level of fine was carefully worked out and set through the king's laws.

Wergild, unlike blood feud, was not about retribution and so made further violence less likely. However, it was an unequal system. The wergild for killing a noble was 300 shillings; the wergild for killing a freeman was 100 shillings; while the fine for killing a peasant was even lower. Perhaps most outrageously, the wergild paid for killing a Welshman was lower still!

Wergild was also used to settle cases of physical injury, with different body parts given their own price. For example, the loss of an eye was worth 50 shillings, whereas a broken arm could be settled with payment of only 6 shillings to the victim.

## Capital and corporal punishment

Some serious crimes carried the death penalty in Anglo-Saxon England – treason against the king or betraying your lord. This harsh capital punishment was intended to deter others and show people the importance of loyalty to the king, who Saxons believed was chosen by God.

Re-offenders were also punished harshly if they were caught. Corporal punishment for regular offenders included mutilation, such as cutting off a hand, ear or nose or 'putting out' the eyes. This was intended to deter them from further offences.

### ? USING YOUR KNOWLEDGE ORGANISER

Well done so far! You have learnt a lot about Anglo-Saxon justice but that does not mean you can forget about our Enquiry Question. Use your completed judgement matrix and the information on pages 17–19 to start to add key points to your Knowledge Organiser. You may want to reconsider or revise your original hypothesis.

▶ Prisons were rarely used in Anglo-Saxon England because they were expensive to build and to run. Gaolers would have to be paid and prisoners fed. This was impossible at a time when kings only collected taxes for war. Therefore, prisons were only used for holding serious criminals before trial so that they could not escape.

# 2.4 How far did the Normans change Anglo-Saxon justice?

Put yourself in the shoes of William, Duke of Normandy. It is 1066 and, victorious after the Battle of Hastings, you have replaced King Harold as ruler of England. The diagram below gives you an idea of the main issues that you, as the new king, have to consider.

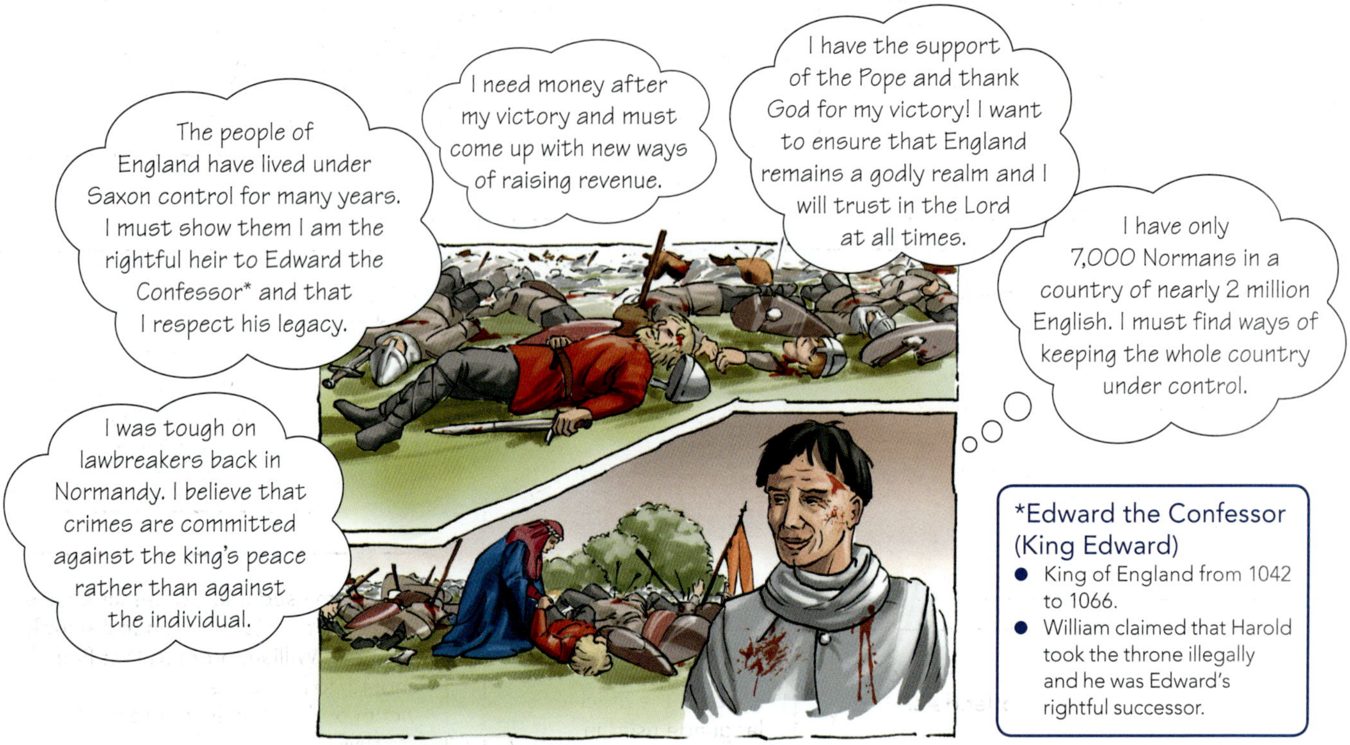

The people of England have lived under Saxon control for many years. I must show them I am the rightful heir to Edward the Confessor* and that I respect his legacy.

I need money after my victory and must come up with new ways of raising revenue.

I have the support of the Pope and thank God for my victory! I want to ensure that England remains a godly realm and I will trust in the Lord at all times.

I have only 7,000 Normans in a country of nearly 2 million English. I must find ways of keeping the whole country under control.

I was tough on lawbreakers back in Normandy. I believe that crimes are committed against the king's peace rather than against the individual.

**\*Edward the Confessor (King Edward)**
- King of England from 1042 to 1066.
- William claimed that Harold took the throne illegally and he was Edward's rightful successor.

## WHAT SHOULD THE NORMANS DO? ?

How might the issues facing William have affected the way the Normans dealt with justice?

1  Look back at the cards and judgement matrix that you made on page 16 showing the Anglo-Saxon system of justice. Discuss what William might have wanted to change and what he might have wanted to keep the same. Give your reasons.
2  Make a prediction (you will find out if you were right later on) about the amount of change the Normans made to Saxon justice:
  a)  Complete change: the Normans wiped out the old system.
  b)  Some change but also some important continuities.
  c)  Complete continuity: the Normans left the old system unchanged.
  d)  Your own more detailed theory.

## What did the Normans actually do?

There is no doubt that the Normans made lasting changes to England. Castles sprung up all over England and many churches were built or rebuilt in the Norman style. Even the language changed. However, when it came to crime and punishment things were not quite so clear.

> **Source A:** From the Laws of William the Conqueror, 1066
>
> *I command that all shall obey the laws of King Edward with the addition of those decrees I have ordained for the welfare of the English people.*

The following boxes 1–10 give an outline of the Norman approach to justice. So how far did the Normans change existing definitions of crime, adapt law enforcement and alter punishments? Read the information carefully to help you with the tasks on page 22.

How does Source A on page 20 give the impression of both change and continuity?

**1.** The Normans built many castles to help control the land. Sometimes Anglo-Saxon homes were destroyed to make room. There was much anger and some Saxons fought back, killing Norman soldiers. William made a law that if a Norman was murdered, all the people of that region had to join together and pay an expensive **Murdrum fine**.

**2.** William decided to keep the majority of Anglo-Saxon laws as they were. The traditional laws of previous Saxon kings were retained.

**3.** Local communities were already effective at policing themselves. Therefore, the Normans kept the tithings and the hue and cry.

**4.** William introduced the much-hated **Forest Laws**. This changed the definition of crime and made previously legal activities into serious offences. Trees could no longer be cut down for fuel or for building and people in forests were forbidden to own dogs or bows and arrows. Anyone caught hunting deer was punished by having their first two fingers chopped off. Repeat offenders were blinded.

**5.** The Normans kept the religious ritual of trial by ordeal, but also introduced **trial by combat**. The accused fought with the accuser until one was killed or unable to fight on. The loser was then hanged, as God had judged him to be guilty.

**6.** William used capital punishment for serious crimes and for re-offenders.

**7.** Norman-French became the official language used in court procedures and all court records were kept in Latin. Most English people understood neither.

**8.** William used fines for lesser crimes. However, the Normans ended wergild – instead William ordered that fines should no longer be paid to the victim or their family, but to the king's officials.

**9.** The Anglo-Saxons gave women almost equal rights in law with men. Norman law was much harsher on women. A Norman legal text said, 'Women's authority nil. Let her in all things be subject to the rule of men.'

**10.** The Normans introduced Church courts (see page 28). These were separate courts used for churchmen and tended to be more lenient.

**11.** Medieval chronicles say England was a safer and more law-abiding place after the Norman Conquest. However, many ordinary people were prepared to break the Forest Laws. This is what historians call a '**social crime**'. The local community were willing to turn a blind eye to people hunting or collecting fire wood from the King's forests as they regarded the law as unfair.

## IDENTIFYING CHANGES AND CONTINUITIES

1 Draw your own large version of the Venn diagram below. Read the boxes on page 21 and make notes on the diagram showing the things the Normans did. Be careful, some of the things they did were partly change and partly continuity. Put these in the overlap.

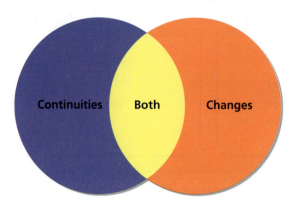

2 Now it is time to weigh-up the overall amount of change versus continuity. This is not as easy as simply counting the number of examples in each part of your Venn diagram. Some examples are more important than others. Put another way, some examples carry more 'weight'.

   a) Draw your own large copy of the scales below.

   b) Look again at your completed Venn diagram. Underline the different examples on your diagram using the key below:

   laws · policing methods · trials · punishments

   c) Now you must decide how much weight you will assign to the four areas above. For example, the Normans kept the traditional laws of previous Saxon kings. This was a big and important continuity so you might give LAWS a weight of 5 before placing it on the left side of the scales. However, some laws such as the Forest Laws were new. How much weight would assign to LAWS on the change side of the scales? Make sure you annotate each weight on each side of the scales to explain your thinking.

   d) Write a short conclusion to the question: How far did the Normans change Anglo-Saxon justice? Use your annotated weighing scales to help you make a decision. Don't sit on the fence!

## USING YOUR KNOWLEDGE ORGANISER

What key details about the Normans could you add to the Knowledge Organiser you started on page 13 to help you with the Enquiry Question?

## 2.5 How far did kings change justice during later medieval England?

As we have seen, Anglo-Saxon and Norman kings had two main responsibilities during the Middle Ages. These were to keep the country safe from invasion and protect the people from lawbreakers. During later medieval England (c.1100 to c.1500), medieval kings took an even closer interest in laws, policing, trials and punishments. Let's start with a murder and find out what happened next …

### Murder in a medieval village

John the Shepherd's house looked empty. Roger Ryet had already walked past it once, glancing through the shutter, just out of curiosity. There wasn't much to see – a well swept floor, a couple of benches, a table. Hanging over the benches was a piece of cloth. 'Nice piece of cloth,' thought Roger. 'It will make someone a nice tunic.' He continued his journey, hoping that today he would get work on the lord of the manor's land and be able to buy his own new tunic.

Roger failed to find work that day. There were many idle hands in his village that year, all clamouring for work. By the time he arrived, others were already turning away disappointed. Roger cursed, knowing that his own scrap of land did not produce enough food for him to live on.

Now Roger was walking back past the John the Shepherd's house. The shutter stood invitingly open, the cloth still hung on the bench. There was no one nearby. The cloth was within arm's reach. Roger leant in, grabbed the cloth and started running.

'Thief!' shouted a man's voice. Roger reeled in shock. Where had the man come from? He had been sure there was no one about.

The man blocked Roger's path, and now he heard the footsteps of a woman at his heels. Roger hesitated as he gripped the cloth tightly. He had to move. He had to get away. In his other hand he held his knife. He moved forward, desperate to escape …

Seconds later, John the Shepherd lay dead. His wife, Isobel, knelt screaming by his side.

### WHAT HAPPENED NEXT? ?

1 This story above is based on a real murder that took place in Norfolk in the early 1300s. Your first task is to speculate on what happened after Roger Ryet killed John the Shepherd. The statements below list some possible ways that Roger might have been caught, put on trial and punished. Only some of them are correct. Make your prediction by choosing the statements you think are true. Keep a note of these, as the next few pages will reveal if you were right.
   a) The local men chased Roger in the hue and cry led by the parish constable.
   b) The Norfolk coroner held an inquiry into the death and the jury decided there was enough evidence to accuse Roger in court.
   c) A message was sent to the local sheriff who took Roger off to prison.
   d) When the king's judges arrived in Norfolk, Roger went before the court.
   e) Roger faced trial by ordeal, plunging his hand into boiling water.
   f) Roger paid Isobel the wergild of 200 shillings for her husband.
   g) Roger was hanged by order of the judges.

## FINDING OUT ABOUT THE LATER MEDIEVAL ENGLAND

1 Extracting detail from written accounts is an important skill for GCSE. You can make this easier by working in groups of three and deciding who is responsible for finding information in the story about:
   - ☐ policing methods
   - ☐ trials
   - ☐ punishments.

   As you read through the rest of the story on pages 24–27, write each piece of relevant information you find on a separate slip of paper or sticky note.

2 Compare your group's findings with others in the class. Who extracted the most information in the time available?

## Escape

'Keep running, don't stop, can't breathe … must breathe, got to keep on running,' thought Roger. He didn't know how long he'd been running, but it seemed like a very long time. Looking down he saw the cloth, still gripped tightly in his hand, but now spattered with the drying blood of John the Shepherd. He stopped to catch his breath in the woods north of the village. How had it come to this?

### Hue and cry

Roger already knew what would be happening back in the village. Isobel's screams would have alerted others and the hue and cry would have been raised. Every villager would have downed tools immediately in order to join the hunt for him. No one wanted to risk the fine for not joining in. They all knew Roger. These people were his neighbours; they lived and worked alongside both Roger and John.

### The parish constable

Now deeper into the woods and leaning against a large oak tree, Roger stopped to catch his breath. He could hear the sounds of the villagers now, the crack of branches underfoot and voices raised in anger. One voice could be heard above the rest – it was Walter, the parish constable. Walter was a blacksmith by trade but had volunteered to be constable for that year. He was well-respected in the village and people looked up to him – the right man for the job. Walter had to keep the peace in his spare time, keeping an eye out for any crime that might take place, leading the hue and cry when it was needed. Roger's spirits sank. Walter took these responsibilities seriously, even though constables were unpaid. Roger knew it was only a matter of time before he would be caught.

But Roger was lucky. He heard the hue and cry start to move off in the wrong direction. He relaxed a little and sensed, for the first time, the deep hunger that had been with him these past few days. How could he have been so stupid? If only he hadn't acted in haste, he might be sitting down to a modest meal at home.

### The coroner and the sheriff

Back at the village, eating was not a priority for Walter. The hue and cry had failed to track down Roger so now he had to inform the coroner about John the Shepherd's death (since 1190 all unnatural deaths had to be reported to the coroner). In this case it was clear what had happened and the coroner would be able to confirm events with Isobel, who had witnessed the whole thing. The coroner would then have to inform another royal official, the sheriff of the county, that a man had been murdered. If the hue and cry had still not found Roger then the sheriff would organise a **posse** to track down and capture him.

◀ A painting thought to be of King Edward I, c.1300. Edward I introduced parish constables in 1285. The parish was the smallest unit of local government in the country. Every parish was centred on a church.

## Sanctuary

The sun was beginning to set and the daylight sounds of the woods gave way to the hoots of owls and other signs of approaching darkness. Roger had a plan. His best hope of escape was to reach the cathedral in Norwich. He would reach the church door and bang on the sanctuary knocker. Once a criminal had reached sanctuary, even the sheriff could not take him by force from a church. Roger would then have the choice to stand trial for his crime or leave the country within 40 days. He'd go to France he thought. Yes, that is what he'd do.

## Sleep

On the second day Roger hid until nightfall. He moved slowly so no one could hear him, avoiding the country paths, crossing ditches and fields under the cover of darkness. The landscape seemed unfamiliar on this moonlit night and Roger soon felt himself hopelessly lost. Regrets flooded his mind. If only he had more land to grow enough food. If only he hadn't drawn his knife. If only he hadn't seen the damned cloth in the first place. There in the bracken Roger drifted off into a fitful sleep.

## Rude awakening

'Get up cur! On your feet! He's over here – come quick!' Roger woke with a start. Looking up, he saw a finely dressed man, who must be the sheriff, towering above him. He was accompanied by several other men who had been summoned as part of the sheriff's posse to track Roger down. He recognised one of them as his cousin, a lanky boy of 15. Roger smiled to himself. He couldn't blame the lad – all men of that age could be summoned to join a posse.

It was light as they took Roger away, his hands bound with rope. On the horizon Roger spotted the tell-tale spire of Norwich Cathedral. He'd been so close to claiming sanctuary!

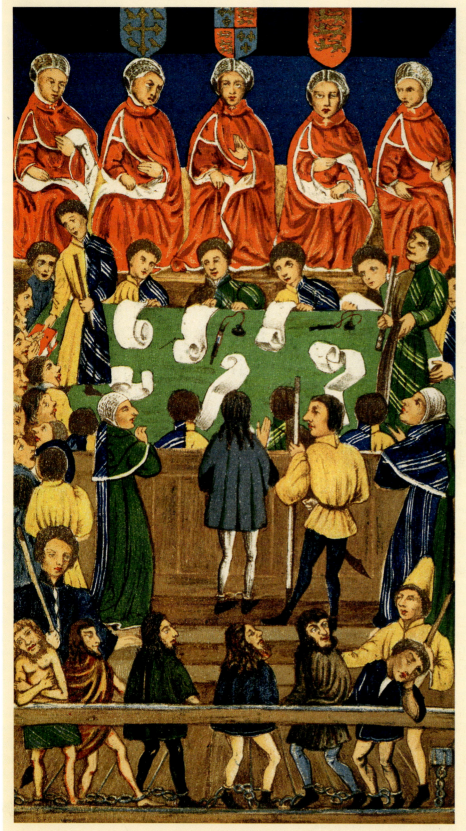

Royal courts like this one would have been similar to the one Roger attended. Royal judges were appointed by the king and visited each county two or three times a year to hear the most serious cases. Most other cases continued to be heard in manor courts before local juries who usually set fines as punishment (see page 8).

## The royal court

Roger was accused of murder. After a week in the local gaol he was taken, by his tithing, before the royal court. The royal court dealt with the most serious crimes. As he walked in he saw a row of five judges raised up high and dressed in fine red robes. Just below them were the **scribes**, writing everything down on long scrolls of parchment. To his left Roger spotted the jury. Their faces were known to him as they had been selected from the villages in the local area.

'If only she'd not seen me,' thought Roger as he spotted Isobel weeping in the courtroom. Roger had been well-liked and trusted by his fellow villagers. Without any evidence against him they might have sworn an oath of innocence based on his good character. Isobel now stood and gave her eyewitness testimony. It was not surprising that the jury trusted Isobel's description of events. Some of them even recalled hearing Isobel's screams when Roger had stabbed her husband. The jury swore an oath that Roger was guilty.

## The noose

As a boy, Roger had listened to his grandfather scare him with stories of boiling cauldrons of water and God's divine judgement. Trial by ordeal had finally been abolished in 1215. 'At least I avoided that,' thought Roger. Then reality came crashing back into Roger's thoughts. Just last year he had witnessed one acquaintance being whipped and another placed in the **pillory** just for being drunk! Selling weak beer could land you a night in the **stocks** so what hope did he, a murderer, have? Roger knew he was bound to swing for his crime, to set an example and serve as a warning to others.

Of course, there were some ways of avoiding death but Roger could not afford to buy a pardon from the king. Nor was he able to read, which made claiming **benefit of the clergy** (see page 28) impossible. That would have involved him reading a verse from the Bible and being tried by the Church courts, who never executed people. 'If only there was a war on. I could avoid all of this by fighting in the army as my punishment,' thought Roger as the hangman tied the noose around his neck.

It was his very last thought before he convulsed, legs kicking into thin air at the end of the rope.

## CHANGES AND CONTINUITIES IN LATER MEDIEVAL ENGLAND

1 Look back at the predictions you made on page 23. Were you correct?

2 Law enforcement and punishment clearly did change during the later Middle Ages. Using the information that you collected from the activity on page 24, sort these into changes and continuities and use them to fill in your own copy of the table below.

|  | Situation by 1100 | Changes made by kings | Continuities |
|---|---|---|---|
| Policing | • No police force<br>• Tithings were organised to bring accused to court<br>• Hue and cry used to catch criminals |  |  |
| Trials | • Local juries decided guilt or innocence<br>• If jury could not decide then ordeal was used – God was judge<br>• Royal courts for serious cases. Manor courts for others |  |  |
| Punishments | • The Normans ended wergild and fines were paid to king<br>• Serious crimes and re-offenders were punished by death |  |  |

3 Which of the statements below do you think best sums up how far law enforcement and punishment changed during the later Middle Ages?
  a) By the end of the Middle Ages law enforcement and punishment had changed very little since 1100.
  b) Key parts of law enforcement and punishment had remained the same since 1100. However, trials and policing methods had been improved.
  c) By the end of the Middle Ages law enforcement and punishment had been almost totally changed. They were unrecognisable.

4 What key details about the late Middle Ages could you add to the Knowledge Organiser you started on page 13 to help you with the Enquiry Question? Refer back to your initial hypothesis and decide whether you need to revise it in any way.

## 2.6 Case study: Did the Church help or hinder justice in the early thirteenth century?

You have already begun to discover how the Church and religious beliefs played an important part in medieval law and order. God was firmly at the centre of trial by ordeal (see page 29) but this was not the only way in which the Church influenced justice. This influence had previously brought the Church into conflict with the king. The most infamous example of this came in 1170 with the brutal murder of Archbishop of Canterbury Thomas Becket. Becket had fallen out with King Henry II over the issue of Church courts, which Henry believed were allowing criminals to get off too lightly.

**A description of events in July 1174, written a few years later by the monk Ralph Diceto:**

*King Henry made a hasty journey across England. When he reached Canterbury he leaped from his horse and took off his royal clothes. He put on simple clothes and went into Canterbury Cathedral. There he lay down and prayed for a long time. Then King Henry allowed each of the bishops to whip him five times. And after that the monks who were there (and there were a large number) each whipped the king three times.*

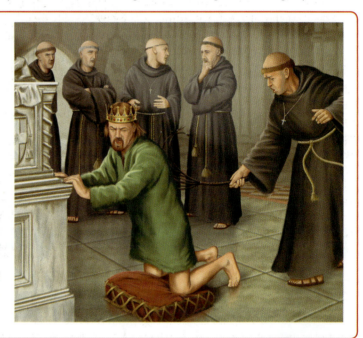

As you can see from the illustration above, Henry was eventually forced to seek forgiveness for the death of Becket and the power and influence of the Church continued. In the eyes of Henry and some later kings, this challenged royal authority and hindered effective justice. How far was this still true in the early thirteenth century?

### Church courts

The Church claimed the right to try any churchman accused of a crime in its own courts. This would be presided over by the local bishop. Unlike ordinary courts, Church courts never sentenced people to death, no matter how serious the crime committed. Church courts also dealt with a range of **moral offences** including failure to attend church, drunkenness, adultery and playing football on a Sunday.

### Benefit of the clergy

Benefit of the clergy was when an accused person claimed the right to be tried in the more lenient Church courts. In theory, this right was intended only for priests. In practice, anyone loosely connected with the Church, such as church doorkeepers or gravediggers, used it to escape tougher punishments. To get around this problem, the Church used a test requiring the accused to read a verse from the Bible. The idea was to weed out the non-churchmen who, unlike priests, were usually unable to read. However, others learnt the verse by heart and it soon became known as the 'neck verse' because it could literally save your neck from the hangman's noose!

## Sanctuary

If someone on the run from the law could reach a church, he or she could claim sanctuary. Once a criminal reached sanctuary, they were under the protection of the Church. Even the county sheriff could not remove them by force. The criminal then had 40 days to decide either to face trial or to leave the country. Those choosing to leave had to make their way, barefoot and carrying a wooden cross, to the nearest port and board the first ship heading abroad.

## Trial by ordeal

Although it was ended by Pope Innocent III in 1215, trial by ordeal had long been used to judge guilt or innocence in the eyes of God (see page 18). It was used when juries could not reach a verdict and was based on the legally unreliable idea that God would decide a case. As such, it was possible that some guilty men and women escaped punishment while some innocent people were found guilty.

◀ The sanctuary knocker at Durham Cathedral. A criminal would grasp the knocker and hammer on the door to be let in. A church bell would be rung to alert the townspeople that someone had claimed sanctuary.

---

### HELPED OR HINDERED? ❓

Draw your own copy of the spectrum below to show how much of a help or hindrance to medieval justice each type of Church involvement was. We have done **trial by ordeal** for you as an example to get you started. Use the information on these two pages to mark and annotate **Church courts**, **benefit of the clergy** and **sanctuary**.

Trial by ordeal

HINDERED ————————→ HELPED

Trial by ordeal provided an outcome if a local jury could not reach a verdict. However, this outcome seemed to be based on luck rather than real guilt or innocence. Therefore, guilty criminals sometimes escaped punishment while innocent people could be punished.

---

### USING YOUR KNOWLEDGE ORGANISER ❓

What key details about the Church could you add to the Knowledge Organiser you started on page 13 to help you with the Enquiry Question?

# 2.7 Communicating your answer

Now it's time to write your answer to the Enquiry Question and ...

STOP! We have forgotten something very important.

Revise your hypothesis and get your summary answer clear in your mind before you begin writing.

This is a vital stage because a big mistake students make is starting to write without having the answer clear in their minds. The activities below help to clarify your thinking and work better if you do them with a partner.

1   Compare the information in your Knowledge Organiser (page 13) with your partner's. Make any necessary additions.
2   Rank the Church, kings and local communities in order of the influence they had in each of the following areas:
    ● enforcing the law: policing methods
    ● enforcing the law: trials
    ● punishing criminals.

## Now it's time to write your answer

Now it's time to write an answer to our question.

**Who had the most influence on law and order in the Middle Ages – the Church, kings or local communities?**

Use the following plan to help you structure your answer:

Paragraph 1 – Describe how policing methods worked and explain what, *if any*, role the Church, kings and local communities played.

Paragraph 2 – As above but consider trials.

Paragraph 3 – As above but consider punishments.

Paragraph 4 – Your conclusion should weigh up which group had the most influence overall.

## Word Wall

A Word Wall identifies words that are useful for writing an answer. They also help you to think and talk about your answer. Add to your Word Wall each time you finish studying a new time period. This helps you to:

● understand the meaning of technical words and phrases
● communicate clearly and precisely when you describe or explain historical events – this definitely helps you do well in your exams
● spell these important words correctly (marks are lost in exams for poor spelling).

Here are some words and phrases to help you think about the Enquiry Question and medieval England. Make your own copy on a large sheet of paper and leave plenty of space so you can add to it.

**Red – words related to the history of crime and punishment.**

**Blue – historical periods.**

**Black – words that make your arguments and ideas answers clear to a reader**

**Golden** – words that help you to use evidence, explain and link your answer to the question being asked.

### Practice questions

1   Explain why the Church sometimes hindered justice in the period c.1000–c.1500.
2   'The Norman Conquest saw little change to law enforcement and punishment in England.' How far do you agree? Explain your answer.

Some of your exam questions (such as question 4, 5 and 6 in the exam paper) will suggest two topics you could use in your answer. You can see examples on page 165. We have not included topics in the practice questions in this book to give teachers the opportunity to change these from year to year.

Anglo-Saxon     tithing     trial by ordeal     sanctuary     constable     coroner

Norman     hue and cry     Church courts     benefit of the clergy     manor court     sheriff

medieval     Middle Ages

little     very     important     continuity     factor

quite     change     influential     reason

for example     moreover     this meant     this led to     overall

secondly     furthermore     this suggests     this resulted in

# 2.9 Visible learning: Revise and remember

Just when you thought you might relax after answering the Enquiry Question, you discover there is something just as important still to do! The most successful students realise that revision is not something that you only do towards the end of the course and the start of your exams. By getting ready for revision now, you make life much easier for yourself later on. Here are some ideas how to revise so you can get started.

## Technique 1: Using memory maps

A memory map is another form of Knowledge Organiser that helps you focus on the key features without getting lost in too much unnecessary detail.

**Step 1:** Use plain A3 paper (or bigger if you have it). Turn it landscape to allow some space and to stop the whole thing looking cramped.

**Step 2:** Add information to the map using your notes and looking back at pages 12–29 if necessary. Use pencil so you can make corrections later. Remember:

- Use key words or phrases. Do not write in full sentences.
- Use pictures/images/ diagrams to replace or emphasise words. This helps the information to 'stick'.
- PRINT important words to make them stand out.

**Step 3:** When you have finished, redraft your memory map to make sure everything is clear.

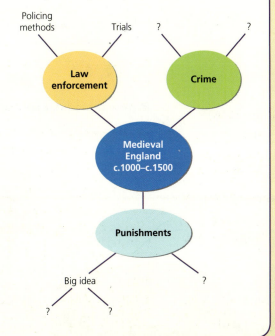

## Technique 2: Test yourself

Making a memory map is itself a way of revising, but you can also use it to test yourself. Try covering up parts of the memory map. Then try to draw that missing part of the memory map from memory. Check this against the original and see what you have missed.

## Technique 4: Writing the Big Story

It's really important that you keep the Big Story of crime and punishment clear in your mind, as this is a great help in the exam. Use the notes in your book or look back over pages 12–29 and write a brief story of crime and punishment in the Middle Ages. You should include the words used in Technique 3 as well as the following:

Change · Anglo-Saxons · This meant that … · Continuity

## Technique 3: Playing a game

In this game the contestant is given an answer and their task is to come up with the matching question. We have provided some answers below but it is your job to come up with suitable matching questions. Try to make each question as detailed as possible so that you are using your knowledge to help you word it.

| Tithing | Benefit of the clergy | Sheriff | Trial by ordeal | Coroner |
|---|---|---|---|---|
| The Normans | Wergild | Oath of compurgation | 1100 | Sanctuary |

# 3 Crime and punishment in early modern England, c.1500–c.1700

The period 1500–1700 saw some important changes to society, the way the country was ruled and in people's religious beliefs. First, this was a time of increasing wealth but also of increasing poverty for different groups of people. Second, rich landowners wanted a bigger say in the way the country was being run and had a growing influence on the making of laws. Consequently, there were tougher laws for crimes against property. Third, England became a Protestant country and this caused much conflict and confusion – having the wrong religious beliefs could lead to execution. As a result, tougher laws emerged dealing with crimes against royal and Church authority. As you work through the chapter you will understand how and why these changes had a big effect on crimes, punishments, trials and policing.

## 3.1 Criminal moments in time, 1600

My best cow has died. She did it! That witch cursed my family and used devil magic to strike down my herd.

Justices of the Peace (local magistrates) dealt with minor crimes and local regulations. Quarter sessions were held four times a year so that visiting royal judges could deal with more serious crimes.

The law of treason had been strengthened. It was treasonable to rebel, speak out or write against the monarch. The punishment for treason was hanging, drawing and quartering. The victim's body parts were displayed as a warning.

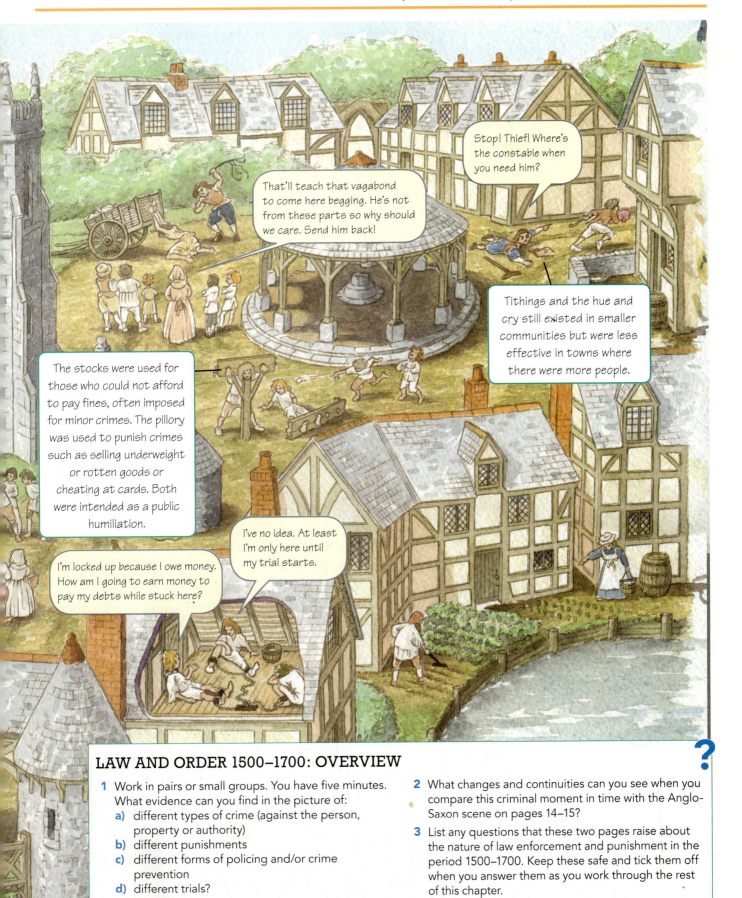

That'll teach that vagabond to come here begging. He's not from these parts so why should we care. Send him back!

Stop! Thief! Where's the constable when you need him?

Tithings and the hue and cry still existed in smaller communities but were less effective in towns where there were more people.

The stocks were used for those who could not afford to pay fines, often imposed for minor crimes. The pillory was used to punish crimes such as selling underweight or rotten goods or cheating at cards. Both were intended as a public humiliation.

I've no idea. At least I'm only here until my trial starts.

I'm locked up because I owe money. How am I going to earn money to pay my debts while stuck here?

## LAW AND ORDER 1500–1700: OVERVIEW

1 Work in pairs or small groups. You have five minutes. What evidence can you find in the picture of:
  a) different types of crime (against the person, property or authority)
  b) different punishments
  c) different forms of policing and/or crime prevention
  d) different trials?

2 What changes and continuities can you see when you compare this criminal moment in time with the Anglo-Saxon scene on pages 14–15?

3 List any questions that these two pages raise about the nature of law enforcement and punishment in the period 1500–1700. Keep these safe and tick them off when you answer them as you work through the rest of this chapter.

# 3.2 Which social changes affected crime and punishment, c.1500–c.1700?

Many aspects of crime and punishment had not changed since the Middle Ages. The theft of food, money or low-value belongings remained the most common crimes. No police force existed and there was a continued belief that savage, terrifying corporal and capital punishments deterred people from committing crime. However, there were also some important changes in the period 1500–1700.

1 The amount of crime seems to have gone up during the 1500s and early 1600s.
2 There was an increased fear of crime. By the late 1600s, there is evidence that crime was actually falling. However, most people continued to believe that crime was rising rapidly.
3 In the 1680s, even minor crimes could result in execution as punishments became even harsher. The number of crimes carrying the death penalty (capital punishment) was greatly increased.

---

### HOW DID SOCIAL CHANGES AFFECT CRIME AND PUNISHMENT?

Read the social changes boxes below and on page 35 and use these to help you answer the following questions.

1 Which changes help explain the increase in crime during the 1500s and early 1600s?
2 Which changes help explain the increased fear of crime in this period?
3 Which changes help explain tougher laws surrounding crimes against property?
4 Which changes help explain the tougher laws surrounding crimes against royal and Church authority?
5 Which changes help explain the increased use of capital punishment for even minor crimes from the 1680s?

---

## Population growth

During the sixteenth and seventeenth centuries there was a steady increase in the population. More people meant it was harder for some to find work.

## Economic changes

England was becoming wealthier overall and some people became richer. However, the overwhelming majority of people remained poor. This made them vulnerable to rises in the price of food caused by bad harvests. A fall-off in trade could lead to unemployment and hardship for many.

## Printing

After printing was invented in the fifteenth century, more books, broadsheets and pamphlets started to appear. A favourite topic for pamphlets was crime, particularly witchcraft and vagabondage. Pamphlets were usually illustrated and frequently read out loud to others. Even those unable to read could still understand the general message they contained.

## Religious turmoil

Religious changes made by Henry VIII during the 1530s caused much unrest and confusion. This was followed by a period of religious upheaval as the country switched from Protestant to Catholic monarchs and back again. As religious argument continued, both sides accused the other of being in league with the Devil. This helped increase public belief in evil and supernatural explanations for events.

## Political change

This period also saw the greatest rebellion of all – the English Civil War (1642–1649) in which Parliament fought and beat the King's forces. This culminated in the execution of King Charles I. To many people the war and the death of the king felt like the 'world turned upside down'. This created a feeling of insecurity and fear that lasted decades.

## Landowners' attitudes

Landowners were becoming richer and growing in influence during this period. They encouraged laws that defended their rights, power and property against those they regarded as a threat. Increasingly landowners regarded the poor with suspicion. They felt threatened by their growing numbers and wanted to keep the poor firmly in their place.

## KNOWLEDGE ORGANISER: FACTOR CARDS

You are going to make some factor cards to get the big picture of the period 1500–1700 and to help you with your revision. Here are some factors you should consider:

Make your own copy of the card below and for any other factors you think were important during 1500–1700. Don't worry if you have to leave parts of your cards blank – you should be able to add more information as you work through this chapter. AND don't worry if you can't use all of the factors, they might not be important in this period but they will crop up later!

Attitudes in society

Institutions: The Church

Institutions: Government

Individuals

Science and technology

Poverty and wealth

Travel

Towns

| Factor: *Science and technology* | | |
| --- | --- | --- |
| **Effect on crimes:** | **Effect on law enforcement:** | **Effect on punishments:** |
| *New technology of printing increased fear of crimes like vagrancy and witchcraft as more people were reading about it.* | | *Printing increased fear of crime so government introduced harsher punishments to deal with it.* |

# 3.3 An execution: Early 1600s

The main picture on this spread shows a particularly grim execution that took place in the early 1600s. You found out in Chapter 1 that good historians pose their own big questions or enquiries. On these pages we would like you to pose much smaller questions about the picture below. By posing and then answering your own small questions, you will understand a big change that took place in the period 1500–1700.

## POSING USEFUL QUESTIONS

Questions like, 'What is it all about?', are too big. Focus instead on the basics and the details within the picture. Avoid questions that can be answered with a simple yes or no.

1. Work in pairs or small groups to compile a list of questions about this picture. Then come together as a class to make a list of all of the questions you have come up with.

2. Read Clues 1–3. Discuss which questions they might help you begin to answer. Don't worry if you are not sure! Use the tentative language at the bottom on these pages to help you.

3. Note any further questions that arise from Clues 1–3 and add these to your list.

**Clue 1** A description of the savage punishment for traitors, taken from an Act of Parliament in 1800.

*That the offender be dragged to the gallows; that he be hanged by the neck and then be cut down alive; that his entrails be taken out and burned while he is yet alive; that his head be cut off; that his body be divided into four parts and that his head and quarters be at the King's disposal.*

**Clue 2** An eighteenth-century description of the symbolic meaning of the execution.

*He was dragged to the scaffold because he was 'not worthy any more to tread upon the earth whereof he was made'.*

*He was hanged 'by the neck between heaven and earth, as deemed unworthy of both, or either'.*

*He was drawn [disembowelled] because he 'inwardly had conceived and harboured [hidden] in his parts such horrible treason'.*

*He was beheaded because here he had 'imagined the mischief'.*

**Clue 3** Part of an anonymous letter sent in 1605.

*My lord, I have care for your safety. Therefore, I would advise you devise some excuse to miss your attendance at this Parliament. For God and man have come together to punish the wickedness of the time … they shall receive a terrible blow this Parliament – and they shall not see who hurts them.*

| Possibly | Perhaps |

SUPPLICIUM

De octo coniuratis sumitur in Britannia, diebus 30. et 31. Ian. Styl. vet. Anno CIƆ. IƆ.CVI. Sumitur quidem separatim de quaternis, Sed tamen propter eandem omnino Supplicy rationem, hac tabella coniunctim expressum.

Fama

**Probably** | **Very likely** | **Definitely**

## Why were the Gunpowder Plotters punished so harshly?

### Months before the execution

When James I (r.1603–1625) became king, many Catholics were hopeful that they would be allowed to worship more freely. However, many powerful members of James' council were strongly anti-Catholic and believed that more than one religion caused disunity. Therefore, in 1604 James declared his 'utter detestation' for the Catholics! Laws against them were tightened and more harshly enforced than before. Although disappointed, most Catholics had little choice but to accept the changes. However, a few determined gentlemen had ideas of their own.

▲ 1. Robert Catesby hatched a plan to blow up Parliament in order to kill the King and put a Catholic on the throne.

◄ 2. One of the thirteen plotters, Guy Fawkes, filled a vault beneath the Houses of Parliament with 36 barrels of gunpowder, more than enough to destroy the building and everyone in it.

▲ 3. An anonymous letter warned Lord Monteagle not to attend the opening of Parliament as it would, 'receive a mighty blow'. He took it straight to Robert Cecil – the King's Chief Minister.

4. The vaults beneath Parliament were searched and Fawkes was arrested. He was tortured until he revealed the names of the other plotters and signed a confession. ▶

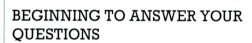

▲ 5. The rest of the plotters escaped. However, 200 government soldiers caught up with them at Holbeach House. Catesby and a number of his fellow plotters were killed in the fighting. The others were returned to London before being found guilty and sentenced to be hanged, drawn and quartered.

### BEGINNING TO ANSWER YOUR QUESTIONS

1 Look back at the list of questions you and your classmates came up with. Which questions can you now answer or begin to answer? Use the tentative language at the bottom of page 37 to help you.

2 Are there any further questions that arise from the information on this page? Here is a question to get you started: Why were Catholics not allowed to worship freely, even before James became king?

## Years before the execution

In the early sixteenth century everyone in England belonged to the Catholic Church and followed the authority of the Pope in Rome. This had been the case for hundreds of years. If you did not have the same religious beliefs you were called a heretic and could be punished or even executed for heresy.

In 1534, after the Pope refused to approve his divorce, Henry VIII (r.1509–1547) split with the Catholic Church and made himself Head of the Church in England. Those who refused to accept the split with the Catholic Church were executed. Henry used Protestant ideas to justify his divorce, but in his heart was still a Catholic.

Henry's son Edward (r.1547–1553) continued the split with the Catholic Church and, during his reign, laws were made requiring the people of England to worship in a much more Protestant way. Even the way churches were decorated became a matter of law.

**Religion Swingometer**

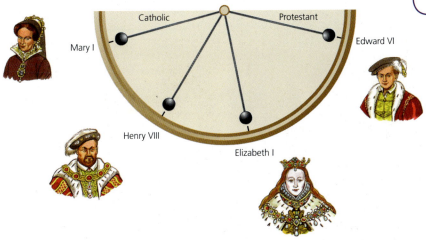

When Edward died he was succeeded by his elder sister Mary (r.1553–1558). She was determined to make England a Catholic country once more. She ordered the execution of nearly 300 Protestants who refused to change their beliefs. Mary regarded them as heretics and the traditional punishment for heresy was to be burnt at the stake.

Elizabeth (r.1558–1603) restored England to Protestantism. Catholics were fined for not attending church and could be locked up for taking part in Catholic services. These laws were intended more to frighten Catholics, and were not too strictly enforced. As her reign continued, England became involved in conflict with Catholic Spain. The Pope declared that Elizabeth was not the rightful ruler and that it was the duty of Catholics to rebel against her. There were various plots to kill her and replace her with a Catholic ruler. Elizabeth's advisers believed that Catholics posed a serious danger to her government. Altogether, around 250 Catholics were executed as traitors during Elizabeth's reign.

## ANSWERING YOUR QUESTIONS

1 You should now be able to answer most of the questions you and your classmates came up with. Use the tentative language at the bottom of page 37 to help you.

2 Write a brief explanation of why the Gunpowder Plotters were punished so harshly and in such a gruesome way. You should include the reasons hanging, drawing and beheading were used and why the plotters were punished for treason rather than heresy.

3 Look back at the factor cards you made on page 35. What information can you add to your existing cards, or what new factor card can you make?

# 3.4 A 'rascally rabbalage'? Were vagabonds really a threat to respectable society?

In the Middle Ages people usually lived and worked close to where they were born. By the 1500s, a rising population and fewer jobs meant more people were moving around looking for work. Therefore, people started to become very concerned about vagabonds, or vagrants as they were sometimes known. These were tramps, beggars and others who wandered the country without a settled job. Concern about vagabondage intensified during times of poverty and hardship, when the numbers of unemployed people increased.

We have been taught that good Christians should work hard. After all, the Bible says, 'the Devil makes work for idle hands' so those not working might be tempted to commit sins.

Vagrants commit many different crimes such as thefts, assaults and even murders. It seems obvious to me that these vagabonds carry out crimes as a way to get their hands on money without working.

Most of us want to help the genuinely poor, the old and the sick, but we get suspicious of outsiders asking for help. Why should we aid those who appear fit and healthy enough to work?

The better-off among us already pay **poor rates** to support the genuine poor from our own parish. They can use this to buy food. I don't want to spend more of my hard-earned cash paying for the poor and idle from other areas. These wandering poor should be made to return to their own towns and villages.

▲ The main reasons people worried about vagabondage in the 1500s.

**Source A** From William Harrison's *Description of England*, published in 1577.

*They are all thieves and extortioners. They lick the sweat from the true labourer's brow and take from the godly poor what is due to them. It is not yet sixty years since this trade [vagabondage] began but how it has prospered since that time is easy to judge for they are now supposed to amount to above 10,000 persons as I have heard reported. Moreover they have devised a language among themselves which they name canting such as none but themselves are able to understand.*

**Source C** Extract from *Crime and Punishment in England*, by John Briggs, published in 1996.

*Plays and chap-books (short, cheap pamphlets widely distributed) about these 'cony-catchers' [vagabonds] were as popular with the Elizabethans and Jacobeans as detective novels and television soap operas about the police are today.*

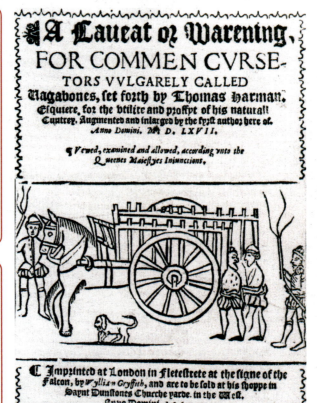

◀ **Source B** The title page of a book by Thomas Harman, warning of the dangers of vagabonds, published in 1567. Harman described 23 different types of vagabonds and described highly organised gangs of criminals who would regularly meet up.

# How did the government treat vagabonds?

Throughout the sixteenth century, the government took different measures against vagabonds. The box below right summarises the main ones.

Many ordinary citizens did live 'in terror of the tramp' and the harshness of the laws against vagabonds tells us landowners and the government also believed they were to blame for many different crimes. Harman, and other pamphleteers, helped stoke government and public fear of vagrancy even further. However, was respectable society really under threat from this 'rascally rabbalage' as Thomas Harman called it?

▲ **Source E** Sixteenth-century print of a beggar being whipped through a town.

**1531:** Unemployed men or women found begging, or vagabonds, were whipped until their bodies 'be bloody' and then returned to their birthplaces or previous residence.

**1547:** First offence – two years slavery. Second offence – slavery for life or execution.

**1550:** The 1547 Act was **repealed** as too harsh. The 1531 Act was revived.

**1572:** First offence – whipping and burning through the gristle of an ear with an inch-thick hot iron. Second offence – execution.

**1576: Houses of Correction** were built in every county to punish and employ persistent beggars.

**1593:** The 1572 Act was repealed as too harsh. Vagabonds were treated as they had been in 1531.

**1598:** Vagrants were whipped and sent home. If they did not mend their ways they could be sent to a House of Correction, be banished from the country or even executed.

◀ **Source D** A vagabond being hanged. Repeat offenders could face execution. Thomas Maynard, Oswald Thompson and John Barres were caught in March 1576 and were severely whipped before being burned through the ear. They were caught again in June and then hanged.

## IDENTIFYING ATTITUDES

1 Look back at the factor cards you made on page 35. Identify which of these factors affected attitudes towards vagabondage and discuss how. To get you started, think about the impact that 'communications and travel' had.

2 Why do you think the authorities viewed vagabondage as such a serious threat? Write a brief explanation in your book.

# Vagabonds – the reality

The information and all of the sources on these two pages will help you decide the truth of Harman's and other pamphleteers' claims about the threat that vagabondage posed to society in the sixteenth century.

## EVALUATING THE THREAT FROM VAGABONDS ?

1 Draw your own copy of the table below and fill it in using the information on pages 40 and 41.

| Fears surrounding vagabondage | Agree/partly agree/disagree | Reason for choice |
|---|---|---|
| Vagabonds were all professional criminals who chose to be idle | | |
| Vagabonds formed highly organised criminal gangs and even spoke their own secret language | | |
| Vagabondage was a big problem that was constantly increasing | | |

## Who were the vagabonds?

Some vagabonds were demobilised soldiers no longer needed in the army after wars ended. No doubt others were hardened criminals, and there is some evidence that **pickpockets**, a relatively skilled group of criminals, did tend to move about. However, the great majority of vagabonds were unemployed people looking for work wherever they could find it, as Source F and other information below shows.

**Source F** Extract from *Crime in Medieval England 1550–1750*, by J.A. Sharpe, published in 1999.

*Most of those arrested for vagrancy [vagabondage] tended to be travelling alone or in very small groups for company. There is no evidence of JPs [see page 48] having to deal with large numbers of vagrants travelling together in an organised group. It is true that some criminals in London spoke in a secret language called the 'canting tongue'. Words like 'nipper' (meaning boy) and 'cove' (meaning man) are still known today. However, this was not the case across the rest of the country and there is little evidence of its use outside of the capital.*

A girl from Cheltenham was going to find work as a servant.

A man from Henley-on-Thames had no skilled trade but had come to Warwick to find labouring work after being unsuccessful elsewhere.

An inn-keeper from Southwark who had fallen into debt and so left London to avoid being locked up in **debtor's prison**.

◄ Explanations given by a selection of vagabonds, adapted from records for the town of Warwick.

A skilled silk-weaver had tried various places to find work and was on the way to London.

## Why did people become vagabonds?

The biggest problem facing those looking for work in this period was the steadily rising population. Simply put, an increased population meant more people with not enough work to go round. The result was rising unemployment.

In medieval England people had not needed, or had not been very free, to move around from place to place. However, by the 1500s, unemployment was forcing people to travel beyond the local area to look for work.

In normal years vagrancy was not a big problem. The city with the greatest number of vagrants was London. It was the only large town in England during this period and so many people thought they might find work there. For some, it also offered better opportunities for crime. Even so, in 1560 the London Bridewell (an early example of a House of Correction) only dealt with 69 vagabonds.

However, periods of hardship could lead to a growth in the number of vagrants. In the 1570s, following a series of bad harvests, the number of vagabonds increased considerably. The late 1590s were years of even greater poverty with wages at their lowest point since the year 1200. It was not surprising that by 1600 the number of vagabonds in London had swollen to 555.

In normal years Oxford Justices of the Peace (JPs) dealt with around 12 vagrants per year. In Salisbury they dealt with 20 or less. However, in 1598 these towns were forced to deal with 67 and 98 cases of vagabondage respectively.

**Source G** Extract from *Crime in Early Modern England 1550–1750*, by J.A. Sharpe, published in 1999.

*Most of those apprehended do not seem to have been professional rogues … but were unremarkable representations of the lower, and hence more vulnerable, strata of society.*

◀ **Source H** Sixteenth-century woodcut illustrating different types of beggar, including a wandering beggar or vagabond in the centre.

**Source I** Extract from *Crime in Early Modern England 1550–1750*, by J.A. Sharpe, published in 1999.

*Once misfortune sent such people on a downward path … begging, stealing and working must have been regarded as equally useful aids to survival.*

### EXPLAINING ATTITUDES TOWARDS VAGABONDS ?

1 If vagabondage was not as big a threat as the government and the public perceived, why was it punished so very harshly?

2 Look back at the factor cards you made on page 35. What information can you add to your existing cards or what new factor card can you make?

# 3.5 Case study: Was Matthew Hopkins the main reason for the witch-hunt of 1645–1647?

**?** Historians can't be sure why Hopkins started on his witch-finding journey. Discuss what you think his motivation was.

Perhaps, when you were younger, you wore a witch, ghost or monster costume to celebrate Halloween. Nowadays we worry less about witches meeting at midnight and more about bothering our neighbours for sweets! However, nearly 400 years ago witchcraft was taken very seriously indeed. Between 1645 and 1647, around 250 cases of witchcraft came before the authorities in East Anglia. This unprecedented number of accusations has been described as a 'witch-hunt.'

At the centre of the majority of cases was Matthew Hopkins, a man who became known as the Witchfinder General due to his 'ability' to spot witches. This is his story and the story of those unfortunate people who crossed his path.

## 1645: Year of the Witchfinder General

> Aye John, there is work for us both here. The Devil abounds these parts.

▲ In 1645, for reasons we do not know, Matthew Hopkins and his assistant John Stearne started searching East Anglia for witches. Hopkins, who had previously been unsuccessful as a lawyer, was just twenty-five years old.

▲ Hopkins named 36 women as witches and collected evidence against them. They were charged with using harmful magic against their neighbours or their livestock. The majority of the women accused by Hopkins were old and poor, the most vulnerable in their villages.

> See there! It is a creature from the Devil to take orders from its mistress. What foul magic is this?

▲ Hopkins exhausted his suspects by keeping them standing and on the move. He also kept them awake for days at a time to weaken their resistance. Both methods were particularly effective on old people. Worn down, many of them confessed.

▲ If a mouse, fly or spider found its way into the room, Hopkins claimed it was a 'familiar', a creature created by the Devil to do the witch's bidding.

▲ Any scar, boil or spot was regarded as proof of a 'Devil's mark' from which familiars sucked the witch's blood. These were not difficult to find as a lifetime of poor diet and hardship usually left marks on people's bodies.

▲ Fear spread and this led other towns and villages across the region to summon Hopkins to rid them of their witches. Hopkins charged for his services, demanding a fee plus expenses for his time.

▲ Most of those accused by Hopkins were women, but at Brandeston, the local vicar was charged with witchcraft and 'swum' in the castle moat (see page 47). 'Devil marks' were found in his mouth, probably ulcers in this time of poor nutrition, and he was hanged.

▲ Hopkins disappears from the records in 1647 and most likely died from an illness. Between 1645 and 1647, East Anglia witnessed at least 100 executions for witchcraft, possibly more. Nineteen of these victims were women from Manningtree.

## ASSESSING HOPKINS' ROLE

There is little doubt Hopkins played a significant role in the 'witch-hunt' between 1645 and 1647. However, the key question remains whether Hopkins created the panic, or was simply taking advantage of beliefs and attitudes already in place at the time.

1 Make your own copy of the radar graph (right) in the centre of a large sheet of paper. Each axis represents a reason for the 'witch-hunts'. We have labelled two of them for you.

2 Read the information on pages 44–47 and decide on headings for the remaining axis. Then add bite-sized chunks of information around the oval of each axis summarising that reason.

3 When you have added all the information you can, discuss what score you would give each reason axis (1: Not important; 3: Quite important; 5: Very important) to show how important you think it was.

4 Was Matthew Hopkins the main reason for the witch-hunt of 1645–1647? Write a brief explanation in your book.

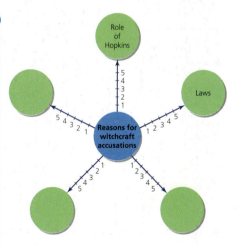

## Village tensions

Accusations were a sign of increased tension between the poor and those richer than them. In times of hardship, the poor would ask for help more often, which sometimes left wealthier villagers feeling threatened by their demands. Poor elderly women, who had once been cared for, were now regarded differently. Most people believed it was possible to injure or even kill others by using harmful magic. This sometimes led to vulnerable women being scapegoated as witches if something went wrong. The cartoon shows a typical scene that may have taken place.

▲ A villager, an old widow, asks for help from a better-off neighbour, but is refused. Often this followed years of suspicion and tension between the widow and the neighbour.

▲ The widow walks away muttering and cursing quietly, maybe even uttering a threat. Both feel angry. The neighbour feels guilty.

▲ Some time afterward, something terrible happens to the neighbour or her family – an illness to her children or animals. Perhaps even a death.

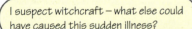
*I suspect witchcraft – what else could have caused this sudden illness?*

▲ The neighbour looks for an explanation of this terrible event. She knows the widow's reputation as a strange woman and the rumours that she is a witch. She suspects these events could be a witch's evil work.

*If she is a witch, we must stop her before she can do any more harm.*

▲ She mentions her thoughts to friends who tell her about other examples of things that have gone wrong when they refused to help the widow. They decide to accuse the widow before any more harm is done.

**Source A** A pamphlet from 1589, showing three women hanging after being accused and found guilty of witchcraft. Printed pamphlets like these were extremely popular and people particularly enjoyed reading about cases of witchcraft.

1 How might pamphlets like Source A have affected ideas about witchcraft? What are the strange animals shown?

2 Do you think witchcraft was a crime against the person or against property?

## Changes to the law

Cases of witchcraft were nothing new in the 1640s. There had been accusations of witchcraft in the Middle Ages, but these were dealt with by Church courts (see page 28) which were more lenient. However, in 1542, during the religious changes that took place under Henry VIII (see page 39), the law changed and witchcraft became a criminal offence. Queen Elizabeth also made tough laws against witches and, in 1590, the future King James I wrote an important book on the horrors of witchcraft. Stricter laws meant witches were tried in ordinary courts and could be punished by death.

There was no sudden flood of witchcraft cases after the laws changed, but over the next 200 years up to 1,000 people (mainly women) were executed as witches. Most accusations were not the work of witchfinders like Hopkins, but of ordinary villagers accusing others of using magic to harm them in some way.

## Uncertain times

There is some evidence that the number of accusations for witchcraft increased during times of uncertainty and unrest. The religious changes that took place under the Tudors (see page 39) meant that old practices and beliefs were being transformed. Protestants preached that the Devil and his servants were tempting good Christians away from God. This heightened talk of the Devil made people fearful and more likely to look for harmful magic as an explanation for unseen events.

The witch-hunt in East Anglia during the 1640s took place against the backdrop of the English Civil War (1642–1649). This had a hugely unsettling effect on the country, and to many people the world felt as if it had been 'turned upside down'. In many areas, there was some breakdown in the proper rule of law. The Civil War meant that assize judges (see page 49) were less able to travel and so locals often took the law more into their own hands.

## How were witches tried?

The accusers would present their charge and bring witnesses to support it. The accused would have to defend themselves. However, around 80 per cent of those accused were elderly widows or unmarried women with no husband to speak up for them. That meant they would be tested further.

**THINKING ABOUT FACTORS?**

Look back at the factor cards you made on page 35. What information can you add to your existing cards, or what new factor card can you make?

◄ **Source B** This woodcut is from a pamphlet in 1600. It shows the 'swim test' used to identify witches. This was similar to medieval trial by ordeal (see page 18). The accused had their hands bound and a rope was tied around their waist. They were then lowered into the water. It was believed the innocent would sink and the guilty would float. If they floated, the accused would be examined for the 'Devil's marks' as a final proof of witchcraft.

# 3.5 How effective was law enforcement 1500–1700?

Between 1500 and 1700 various measures were taken to try to improve law enforcement. Your task on these pages is to make an overview of policing and trials so that you can weigh up whether there was more change or continuity when comparing this period to medieval England.

## Policing

Policing took many forms but still relied largely on the actions of the local community.

### The hue and cry

The hue and cry was still used. If the alarm was raised, citizens still had to turn out and look for the criminal. The constable was expected to lead the hue and cry. The local posse could also be called out to search for criminals.

### Parish constables

Parish constables remained the main defence against crime. This was a part-time job and constables had no weapons or uniform. They spent most of their time dealing with everyday matters such as begging without a licence. They did not go out on patrol. Constables had the power to inflict some punishments, such as whipping vagabonds. They were expected to take charge of suspects and make sure they were held in prison until their trial.

### Town watchmen and sergeants

▼ **Source A** A seventeenth-century image of a night watchman patrolling the London streets, accompanied by his dog and carrying his lamp and bell.

Town watchmen were employed in larger towns to patrol the streets during the day and night. They were poorly paid and often of little use. They were expected to arrest drunks and vagabonds. They were allowed to peer into windows to make sure that people were not breaking the law. Sergeants were employed in towns to enforce **market regulations** by weighing goods and collecting fines if traders were behaving badly.

### Citizens

Citizens (ordinary people) were expected to deal with crime themselves. If someone was robbed it was his or her responsibility to get an **arrest warrant** from a **magistrate**, track down the criminals themselves and deliver them to the constable.

### Rewards

Rewards were offered for the arrest of particular criminals. These tended to be for more serious crimes. The rewards involved could be very high indeed – even the equivalent to a year's income for a middle-class family.

### Justices of the Peace (JPs)

The system of **Justices of the Peace (JPs)** had been set up in the later Middle Ages, but it was during Tudor times that they became a key part of local law enforcement. They were people of local importance, usually a well-off landowner, who took the job for the prestige it offered. JPs judged manor court cases. They could fine people, send them to the stocks or the pillory, and order them to be whipped. They were usually assisted by the constable.

## Trials

Most cases were still dealt with at a local level, much as they had been during the Middle Ages. However, some changes were introduced in order to make the system more efficient.

### Courts

There were a variety of courts in use and all relied on a local jury. Manor courts dealt with local, minor crimes such as selling underweight bread and drunkenness.

JPs dealt with minor crimes on their own but, four times a year, would meet with the other JPs in the county. At these **Quarter Sessions** JPs would judge more serious cases, and even had the power to sentence someone to death.

Royal judges visited each county twice a year to deal with the most serious offences. These were known as **County Assizes**.

### Benefit of the clergy

Church courts remained in use and dealt with crimes committed by churchmen and anyone who could claim benefit of the clergy (see page 28). However, by the 1600s, many more ordinary people were able to read the 'neck verse'. Therefore, the law was changed and prevented those accused of serious crimes from claiming benefit of the clergy.

### Habeas Corpus

The Habeas Corpus (meaning 'you have the body') Act was passed in 1679. It prevented the authorities from locking a person up indefinitely without charging them with a crime. Anyone who was arrested had to appear in court within a certain time or be released. People no longer had to fear being seized and locked up without trial. However, it did not stop governments from making up evidence at trials as an excuse to lock up their critics.

### THE ARMY

The army was used to put down protests, deal with riots and to capture more organised criminal gangs. The use of the army when dealing with protests was very unpopular with ordinary people. It gave the impression the government was ignoring their concerns and silencing them by force.

▲ **Reconstruction of a seventeenth century soldier.**

### WEIGHING UP CHANGES AND CONTINUITIES

1 Draw your own copy of the Venn diagram below and add details using the information on pages 48–49. Use one colour for policing methods and another for trials. You will need to refer back to what you already found out about medieval England on pages 12–29.

2 In which area does there seem to have been the most change in the period 1500–1700: policing methods or trials?

3 Remember Tom the 'tea-leaf' on page 4? Which period do you think he would have preferred to live his criminal life in: the Middle Ages or 1500–1700? Give reasons.

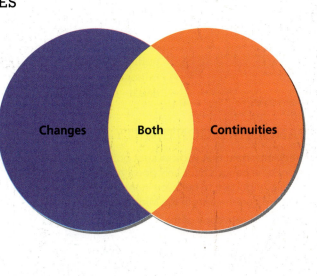

Changes  Both  Continuities

# 3.6 How can we explain the development of the Bloody Code?

**Source A** A public hanging ▶ at Tyburn in London, around 1680. Tyburn had long been used for the execution of London criminals. The Tyburn gallows had three posts and so was known as the 'triple tree'. It could hang up to nine people at a time. It could take up half an hour to die and sometimes relatives or friends would have to pull the condemned man's legs to finish them off. To add insult to injury, London hospitals sometimes claimed the bodies for student doctors to dissect.

In the seventeenth century capital punishment was still used for major crimes such as murder, treason, arson and counterfeiting. Execution was also used for the theft of goods worth more than one shilling. Each year hundreds of people were executed. This was carried out in public to serve as a deterrent to those who might be thinking of committing a similar crime. All of these things were as they had been in the Middle Ages. However, when it came to punishments, some things were beginning to change.

## The Bloody Code

In 1688 there was a big change to the law. The number of crimes carrying the death penalty was increased. There were further increases throughout the eighteenth and into the early nineteenth centuries, a period we consider in the next chapter of this book. In 1688 the number of crimes punishable by death was 50. In 1765 it was 160 and by 1815 it had risen again to 225! Even minor crimes against property such as poaching or cutting down trees were punishable by death – it is no wonder that these laws became known as the 'Bloody Code'.

## CHANGE AND CONTINUITY IN PUNISHMENTS ❓

It is very important that you can spot both changes and continuities between different time periods. Not only does this help you with the big picture, it is also vitally important to help you in the exam! In this section we would like you to compare punishments in the Middle Ages and in the period 1500 to 1700.

1 Make your own copy of the Knowledge Organiser below and use your notes or the information on pages 12–29 to help you fill in the first column.

| Punishments in the Middle Ages 1000–1500 | Changes 1500–1700 | Continuities 1500–1700 |
|---|---|---|
|  |  |  |

2 Use the information on pages 50–51 to help you complete the second and third columns. Add a sentence or two of detail describing each punishment.

## Other punishments

Before we look at the reasons why the Bloody Code began in the 1680s, we need to understand the other types of punishment in use between 1500 and 1700. These ranged from corporal punishment, intended to inflict pain, to public humiliation, fines and even the removal of the criminal altogether.

The pillory was intended to shame and humiliate. It was used to punish crimes such as cheating at cards, persistent swearing and selling underweight bread. If the crowd disapproved of the crime they would pelt the offender with stones. Criminals convicted of sexual crimes were sometimes killed in the pillory.

Fines were perhaps the most common type of punishment and were used for minor offences such as swearing, gambling, drunkenness and failure to attend church.

Whipping was a form of corporal punishment intended to cause great pain. It usually took place on market day when there was a crowd to watch and so had the secondary effect of humiliating the criminal. It was used for a variety of offences such as vagabondage, regular drunkenness and the theft of low-value goods.

By the late 1500s, many towns were building Houses of Correction to punish and reform offenders. These became known as Bridewells after the first one that was built in London. Vagabonds, unmarried mothers and repeat offenders were sent to Bridewells.

Inmates were sometimes whipped but also made to do **hard labour**. The authorities believed some offenders might mend their ways if taught the value of hard work.

Prisons continued to be used for those awaiting trial and for people in debt. However, prisons were very rarely used as a punishment in themselves.

Carting meant being paraded round the streets on a cart for all to see and aimed to shame the criminal. It was used for vagrancy, adultery and running a brothel.

Women who argued with or disobeyed their husbands could be convicted as scolds. The punishment was the ducking stool in the local river or pond. Women who argued in public or swore could be punished in the same way.

From the 1660s, criminals began to be sent ('transported') thousands of miles away to the American colonies. **Transportation** for life was used for murderers who escaped the death penalty. Once in America, some prisoners suffered conditions close to slavery. However, some in England still viewed it as a soft option when compared to the death penalty.

# Crime rate

The introduction of the 'Bloody Code' might give you the impression that England was riddled with crime. It seems logical that punishments became harsher to try to reduce the growing amount of crime by acting as a deterrent. We need to take a look at the overall level of crime in this period and decide if this was really the case.

We should remember it is only possible to know the level of *reported* crimes. Many offences went unreported and so do not show up in the figures. Nevertheless, records from across the country suggest that crime rose in the 1500s, and then fell steadily from the early 1600s (see the graph below). Therefore, it is important to understand that punishments became bloodier at a time when the crime rate was falling! That leaves us the puzzling question – why, then, was the Bloody Code introduced?

**Source B** Figures for Cheshire, 1580-1709, showing number of reported cases of A) theft and other property offences and B) murder.

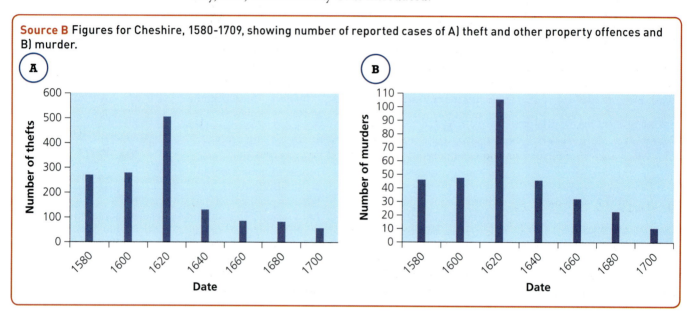

## MAKING A LINK MAP TO SHOW CAUSES

Read the information on pages 52–53 very carefully. Now look at the list of factors below.

1 Which of the factors played a part in causing the introduction of the Bloody Code? Write each one on a large piece of paper and space them out. Add a sentence or two explaining how each factor was a cause.

2 Draw lines between any of the factors that you think link in some way or influenced one another. Write a sentence explaining this link along the connecting line.

3 Look carefully at your completed link map. Is it possible to identify the factor that had the most importance?

4 Look back at the factor cards you made on page 35. What information can you add to your existing cards, or what new factor card can you make?

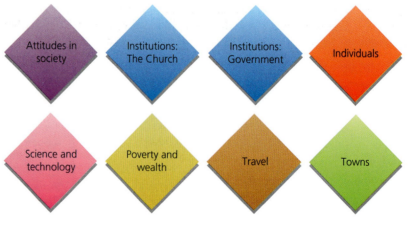

Attitudes in society

Institutions: The Church

Institutions: Government

Individuals

Science and technology

Poverty and wealth

Travel

Towns

## Concerns about crime

Whatever the period, it seems it is human nature to see crime as a serious problem. However, as we saw when we looked at vagabondage (page 40), public perceptions and attitudes do not always reflect the true picture. Even if crime was not rising, there was plenty of evidence around to suggest it was!

Pamphlets often gave horrific and lurid details about robberies, murders, vagabonds and the evil doings of witches. Executions were carried out in public, which had the effect of publicising crime even further. Even the speeches made by those about to hang were published for the public to read. We know today how sensational media reports of just one awful crime can convince the public that crime is out of control.

## People on the move

Since the end of the Middle Ages, towns were growing in number and in size. This made it harder to enforce the law using the traditional methods of the hue and cry and parish constables. Such methods were based around village life and the idea that a person would know all the people in their local area. In towns the streets were more crowded so it was easier for criminals to commit crime and then escape detection.

In the Middle Ages, it was sometimes difficult for ordinary people to travel. By the time the Bloody Code was introduced, better roads and cheaper horses meant more people were on the move. This meant that ideas and news could travel with them and so spread more quickly.

## Protecting property

The MPs who passed the laws that made up the Bloody Code were all wealthy landowners who were keen to protect their lands and privileges. They also felt that they had the most to lose from crimes against property. As a result they passed laws that made punishments for such crimes even harsher. This is not to say that all landowners were acting purely from self-interest. Many of them believed that everyone, including the poor, suffered when laws were broken.

## Traditional views on punishment

For hundreds of years since Anglo-Saxon times, the trend in punishment had been to make it ever harsher. The big idea was always that severe punishments were the most effective way of controlling crime by acting as a deterrent. It was the only method that had been tried and so remained a popular choice throughout this period.

# 3.7 Communicating your answer

It should be clear from this chapter that crime and punishment in the period 1500–1700 shows both change and continuity when compared with the Middle Ages. However, sometimes the exam will ask you to think about crime and punishment across more than just one time period. For example:

**'Punishments were terrifying and harsh in order to deter criminals throughout the period c.1000–c.1700.' How far do you agree? Explain your answer.**

Answering a question like this requires you to select relevant information and to get a 'big picture' of the thinking behind punishments.

## Step 1: Recall – class sticky-note relay challenge

Split into small groups of no more than four. Your task is to work together and come up with a list of all the punishments used between c.1000 and c.1700 that you have learnt about so far.

Write each punishment on its own sticky note and stick it to the board or an area allocated by your teacher. Everyone must take a turn writing a sticky note and sticking it up. Only one member of the group can be out of their chair at any one time. Your teacher will give you a time limit and the group with the most sticky notes (no repeats) wins!

## Step 2: Knowledge Organiser – classifying the ideas behind punishments

Next, you need to organise your knowledge to help you answer the question. If we stop and think about the possible big ideas behind punishments over time, we might come up with a list like this:

- To **deter**
- To **humiliate**
- To **remove** the criminal from society
- To **reform** (try and change the criminal for the better)

1. Come together as a class and make a list of all of the punishments you came up with and write these in your books. Your list will be looking pretty long!
2. Now use the key to classify the different punishments to show the big idea behind each one. Don't worry if you need to underline some in more than one colour and don't worry if you have used one colour more than the others!

## Step 3: Writing your answer

Make sure you mention punishments that were meant to *deter* but also any punishments intended to have *other effects*. Remember that a good answer will make a judgement at the end – was the *main* idea of punishments to deter c.1000–c.1700?

You are now ready to answer the question. We have given you a good deal of help, but you will find more guidance in Writing Better History on pages 164–178. And remember – add to and use your Word Wall!

### Word Wall

Here are some extra words you can add to the Word Wall you made on page 30. They will help you write accurately and with confidence. Look over your notes for the period 1500–1700 and see if you could add some red words of your own.

### Practice questions

1. Explain why the authorities took vagabondage so seriously in the period c.1500–c.1700.
2. 'Landowner's attitudes were the most important factor affecting the development of the Bloody Code in the 1680s.' How far do you agree? Explain your answer.
3. Explain one way in which punishment in medieval England was similar to punishment in the seventeenth century.

Bloody Code    fines    humiliation    capital punishment    whipping

transportation    deterrence    corporal punishment    reform

remove    retribution    stocks    compensation

pillories

early modern    sixteenth century    seventeenth century

# 3.8 Visible learning: Revise and remember

This is the second time you have come across a page to do with revision. We know that it is tempting to skip it and worry about revision later! However, take a look at these two graphs. They should convince you that leaving revision until just before your exam is not the way to success.

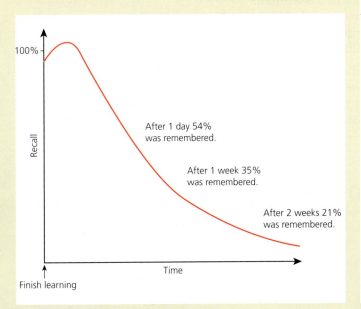

After 1 day 54% was remembered.

After 1 week 35% was remembered.

After 2 weeks 21% was remembered.

Recall

Time

Finish learning

▲ **Graph 1** The Ebbinghaus Curve of Forgetting. That sounds impressive but the graph is alarming. We forget the detail of what we study very quickly.

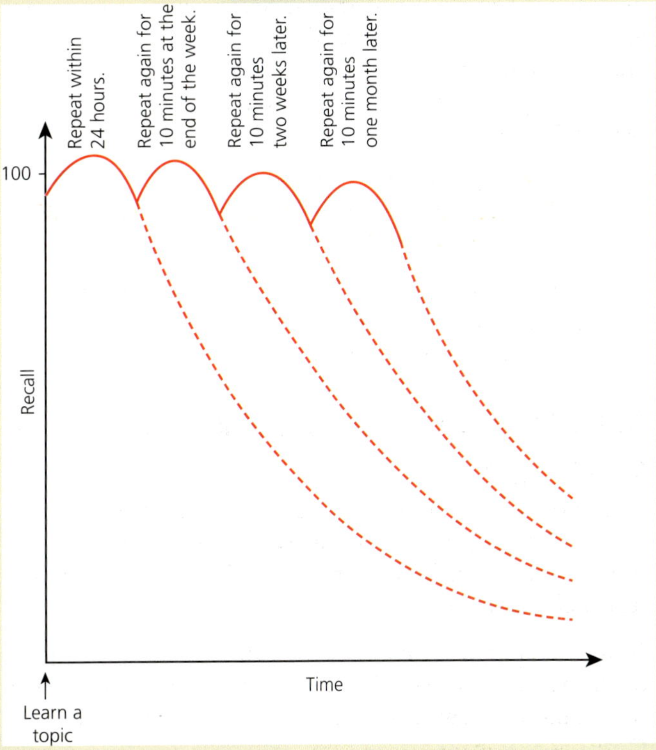

Repeat within 24 hours.

Repeat again for 10 minutes at the end of the week.

Repeat again for 10 minutes two weeks later.

Repeat again for 10 minutes one month later.

100

Recall

Time

Learn a topic

▲ **Graph 2** How do you stop yourself forgetting?

## Technique 1: Repeat your memory map

In Chapter 2 you drew a memory map to help you record the main features of crime and punishment in the Middle Ages (see page 31). Draw a similar memory map for the period 1500–1700. This time, use two different colours to show what were changes and what were continuities.

## Technique 2: Set your own questions and test each other

Go back over the work in your exercise book (and pages 32–53) if necessary. Write ten to fifteen knowledge-based quiz questions for someone else. Make sure that you also record the answers somewhere! Your questions could be multiple choice, multiple select, true or false, or even require short sentences as answers. Use a mix of question types.

Just by composing these questions you are already revising key content. Swap your questions with someone else in your class. Have a go at their quiz and then mark each other's answers.

## Technique 3: Revise your Big Story of crime and punishment

It's really important that you keep the Big Story of crime and punishment clear in your mind. Revise the story you told at the end of Chapter 2 on page 31, but this time make sure you bring it up to date with what you have learned about crime and punishment 1500–1700.

# 4 Crime and punishment in eighteenth- and nineteenth-century Britain

The period 1700–1900 saw some massive changes to crime and punishment. In the years after 1750, Britain became the first country in the world to industrialise. This not only changed the way people worked, but it also had a huge effect on society itself. As you have seen previously, when societies change so do people's attitudes towards crime and punishment.

Centuries-old ideas about using savage corporal and capital punishments to deter were challenged and a discussion began about the best way to deal with criminals. Also, for the first time in history, a full-time and professional police force was established. So what had brought about these revolutionary changes in crime and punishment?

## 4.1 Criminal moments in time: 1840

It's a shame that we don't see executions anymore. I remember a few years ago we'd see them all of the time. Now, hardly any crimes are punishable by death.

I know things aren't like they used to be.

People flocked to industrial cities from rural villages. One of the reasons for the high crime rate was that it was much easier for criminals to go unrecognised in a crowd of strangers.

Charles Dickens described the activities of child pick-pockets in his novel, *Oliver Twist*.

Petty theft was common. It was easy for a thief to disappear in the maze of streets in large towns.

Luckily there is one of those Peelers to hand – a paid policeman who is chasing after the blighter!

## LAW AND ORDER 1700–1900: OVERVIEW

1 Work in pairs or small groups. You have five minutes. What evidence can you find in the picture of:
   a) different types of criminal activity
   b) different punishments
   c) different forms of policing and/or crime prevention
   d) different trials?

2 What changes and continuities can you see when you compare this criminal moment in time with the seventeenth-century scene on pages 32–33?

3 Use your existing knowledge of the nineteenth century from Key Stage 3, to suggest possible reasons for the changes.

4 List any questions that these two pages raise about law and order in the period 1700–1900. Keep these safe and tick them off when you answer them as you work through the rest of this section.

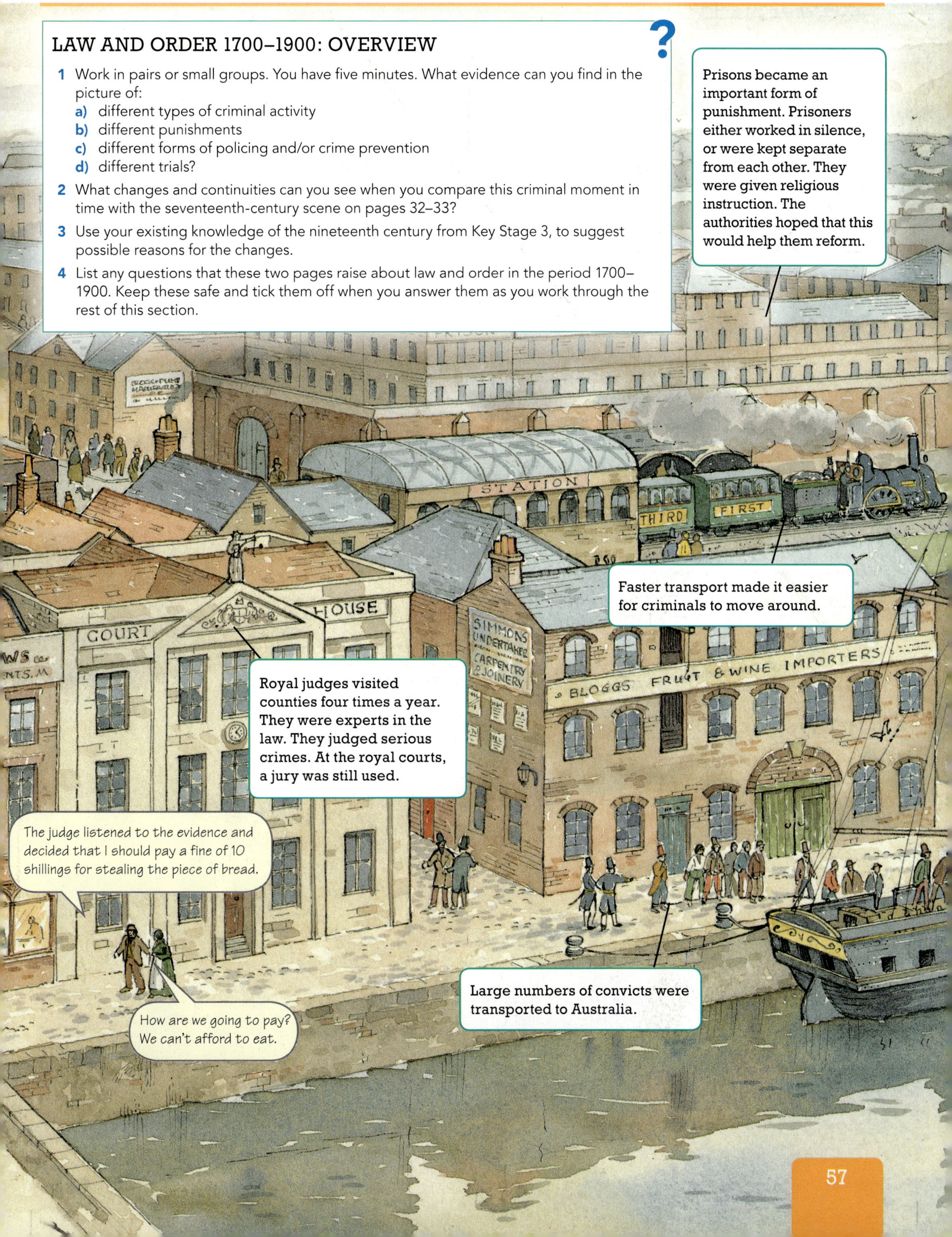

Prisons became an important form of punishment. Prisoners either worked in silence, or were kept separate from each other. They were given religious instruction. The authorities hoped that this would help them reform.

STATION

THIRD   FIRST

Faster transport made it easier for criminals to move around.

COURT

HOUSE

SIMMONS UNDERTAKER
CARPENTRY & JOINERY

BLOGGS FRUIT & WINE IMPORTERS

Royal judges visited counties four times a year. They were experts in the law. They judged serious crimes. At the royal courts, a jury was still used.

The judge listened to the evidence and decided that I should pay a fine of 10 shillings for stealing the piece of bread.

How are we going to pay? We can't afford to eat.

Large numbers of convicts were transported to Australia.

57

## 4.2 Problem crime 1: Why did highway robbery become such a serious crime?

You have already discovered how the authorities feared heresy, vagabondage and witchcraft in the period 1500–1700. By the eighteenth and nineteenth centuries this had changed. First, the religious uncertainty of the Reformation had passed with the last execution for heresy in 1612. Second, the period 1700–1900 saw a general increase in wealth and so fear of vagabondage greatly decreased. Finally, although belief in witches did not totally disappear among ordinary folk, most educated people (who usually judged cases of witchcraft) were less likely to believe such accusations and in 1736 the witchcraft laws were finally repealed.

### Changing definitions of crime

During the eighteenth and nineteenth centuries, the authorities became worried about other types of crime, such as highway robbery and smuggling, which disrupted trade. Any activities that threatened the interests of landowners or employers also came under close scrutiny. The age-old crime of poaching became punishable by death, and even joining a trade union was a risky business.

### Highway robbery: Image versus reality

Highway robbery was not a new crime. It had its beginnings in the chaos caused by the Civil War (1642–49), but by the early 1700s it had become infamous and in some areas reached epidemic proportions.

Highway robbers were greatly feared by ordinary travellers and were regarded by the authorities as a major disruption to trade. The worst areas for highway robbery were around London on the main routes into the capital. Most highwaymen were ruthless and nothing like the romantic image portrayed in the picture below. One highwayman cut out a woman's tongue to stop her reporting him after his mask slipped!

**Source A** William Powell Frith's 1860 painting, *Claude Duval.* Claude Duval, a famous highwayman, was finally caught and hanged at Tyburn (see page 50) in 1670. Duval was reportedly polite and even charming to his victims. His supposed gentlemanly conduct and fashionable clothes made him a hit with the ladies. In this picture he encourages the wife of one of his victims to dance and in return lets her husband keep a small amount of his money. Although this idea of 'gentleman' of the road became popular in printed pamphlets and broadsheets, it was very far from the reality.

# Why did highway robbery grow and then decline?

Highway robbery grew as certain developments created more opportunity for the robbers. However, later developments meant highway robbery declined just as quickly as it grew. The boxes below give reasons for its growth and decline.

Road surfaces began to improve and coaches became more frequent as speeds increased.

More people were travelling in their own coaches.

Handguns had become easier to obtain and quicker to load and fire.

The banking system became more sophisticated over time and the number of banks grew. Fewer travellers carried large amounts of money.

Open land around London and other towns was built on as the population expanded.

**Stagecoaches** were introduced with regular staging posts where tired horses could be changed and travellers could rest for the night.

Mounted patrols were set up around London and high rewards encouraged informers to report on the activities of highwaymen.

There were many lonely areas outside of towns and rough roads where coaches had to slow down.

After wars ended, some demobilised soldiers struggled to find honest ways to make a living.

Highwaymen could hide and sell their stolen loot in taverns.

JPs refused to license taverns that were frequented by highwaymen.

There was no police force and local constables did not track criminals across counties.

Horses became cheaper to buy.

## THE RISE AND FALL OF HIGHWAY ROBBERY

**1** Draw your own copy of the table below.

| Reasons for growth of highway robbery | Reasons for decline |
|---|---|
| **Horses became cheaper to buy.** *Therefore, robbers could afford to set themselves up to ambush moving targets and make quick getaways.* | |

**2** Look at the information boxes on this page and use them to fill in the table. Try to add a sentence of explanation to each one. We have included an example to help get you started.

**3** Look carefully at the reasons in your completed table. Which factors were most significant in bringing about:
  **a)** the growth of highway robbery
  **b)** the decline of highway robbery?

# 4.3 Problem crime 2: Was the law too harsh on poachers?

Many historians describe poaching as a 'social crime' – an offence that many people do not really regard as a crime. In other words, poaching was against the law but widely tolerated by large sections of the community who thought the law unfair. However, the authorities at the time took a very different view. The 1723 Black Act made hunting deer, hare or rabbits a **capital crime** (punishable by death). Anyone found armed, disguised or with blackened faces in a hunting area was assumed to be poaching and could be executed. It is not surprising that during the eighteenth century, some of the most unpopular laws were those dealing with poaching.

> The law is unfair! It is there simply to protect the interests of wealthy landowners.

> Poaching is a harmless sport, a contest to outwit gamekeepers using local knowledge.

> Poachers are just poor folk who take the occasional rabbit or bird to add to the pot.

> What's the harm in a fellow selling the occasional rabbit just to make ends meet?

> The public have sympathy for poachers and regard the death penalty as too harsh.

**Source A** Traditional claims made in defence of poaching.

---

## CLAIMS AND COUNTER-CLAIMS ?

Imagine you are an eighteenth-century judge and have been asked to investigate the crime of poaching, as many people think the laws are too harsh.

Use the information on page 61 to judge the truth of each of the claims made in the speech bubbles above. Make your own copy of the picture and leave space around the outside. In one colour, add supporting evidence, then use a different colour for evidence that challenges the claims.

## The law

Only landowners whose land was worth more than £100 a year could hunt and they could hunt anywhere. £100 was a huge sum of money and would have taken a labourer ten years to earn. Landowners with land worth less than £100 a year and tenants who rented could not hunt, even on their own land. Possessing dogs or **snares** that might be used for hunting was punishable by a £5 fine or three months in prison.

## Why did they poach?

Small landholders and tenants frequently ignored the law and hunted on their own land. Many poached the odd rabbit for the cooking pot or sold the occasional pheasant to supplement their low wages. There was also a minority of better-off poachers who hunted for sport and their own entertainment.

## Who were the poachers?

Most were poor, if only because most ordinary people were poor at this time. The majority of poachers caught by **gamekeepers** were described as labourers, weavers, **colliers**, servants or workers in other low-paid jobs.

## Fear and loathing

Faced with armed gamekeepers and the possibility of the death penalty, some poachers used violence. In 1786, a Staffordshire farm labourer **horsewhipped** a gamekeeper who tried to take his hare. In 1792, two poachers shot a gamekeeper's horse and then aimed their guns up at his window. Fortunately, the keeper failed to wake and look out!

Gamekeepers and those who informed on the poachers for the rewards were generally hated. Villagers frequently provided **alibis** and lied in court to protect poachers from conviction.

## The black market

Court records are full of men such as John Lightwood, a Staffordshire labourer, who killed nearly 80 hares in 1764 before selling them for 3 shillings a piece. Such individuals made more from poaching than they earned in their day jobs.

Lightwood was acting alone and his efforts were small compared to the organised gangs of poachers who supplied the **black market**. These gangs favoured the deer parks and game reserves owned by wealthy landowners. Demand for game grew as the population increased and as people's diet became more sophisticated. By selling their catch in the towns and cities, criminal gangs of poachers could make very high profits.

## WEIGHING UP THE EVIDENCE – ARGUMENT TUNNEL

Historians must be able to see two sides of an argument before reaching a conclusion. Argument tunnels are a fun way of practising this skill.

1 Form an argument tunnel with the people in your class (two seated rows of equal numbers facing each another). One row must argue that poaching laws were too harsh while the other must argue the opposite. After 60 seconds of argument, one side moves to the next seat while the other stays put so each has a new opponent to argue with. Do this as many times as your teacher tells you or until you are back to the beginning.

2 Now make your *own* judgement and decide whether the law was too harsh on poachers.

3 Finally, which factors were most significant in influencing:
   a) the laws surrounding poaching
   b) public attitudes towards poaching?

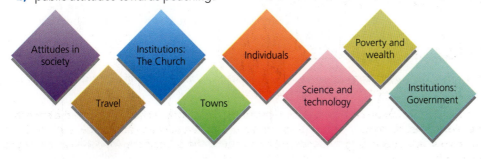

# 4.4 Problem crime 3: Why was smuggling 'a long time uncontrolled' in the eighteenth century?

Smuggling in the eighteenth century was a massive problem in coastal areas. Smugglers brought tea, cloth, wine and spirits into the country without paying any import tax (customs duty) on them. At a time when there was no income tax and duties were the main source of government income, the authorities took smuggling very seriously indeed. Under the Bloody Code (see pages 50–51) smuggling carried the death penalty.

▲ **Source A** Smugglers were often ruthless and were prepared to use violence to hold on to their cargo or to escape capture. This picture shows the Hawkhurst gang seizing back smuggled tea from the customs house at Poole in 1747. In 1748, a gang of smugglers in West Sussex seized and murdered two customs officers. Both were tied to horses and dragged. One of the unfortunate men had his 'nose and privities' cut off before the smugglers broke 'every bone in his body'. The second man was thrown into a well and then stoned to death.

## The government response to smuggling

In 1748, the Duke of Richmond was asked to smash the smuggling gangs. Thirty-five smugglers were hanged for their crimes and a further ten died in gaol. Yet this came nowhere near solving the problem, as it was reckoned there were at least 20,000 active smugglers. Smuggling continued to flourish, partly because of the fear smugglers created to deter any interference. However, there were other reasons why smuggling proved so hard to stamp out.

### WHY WAS SMUGGLING SO HARD TO STAMP OUT?

1 Read the information on pages 62–63 and list as many reasons as you can why the government found it so difficult to stamp smuggling out. Use the headings below to help you organise your notes:

    Fear of smugglers

    The attractions of smuggling

    Organised gangs

    Public attitudes

2 It was clear that the Bloody Code did little to deter the smugglers. What advice would you have given to the Duke of Richmond as the best way to reduce smuggling?

In 1748, 103 people were officially 'wanted' as smugglers. Over 70 per cent of them were labourers; fewer than 10 per cent were small landowners and the rest were tradesmen, such as butchers and carpenters.

Wealthy people also took part in smuggling. Even respectable government ministers were known to have smuggled wine into the country.

For low-paid labourers, smuggling was a quick and exciting way to earn six or seven times the daily wage in just one night. In Sussex, where traditional jobs such as cloth-making and fishing were in decline, smuggling offered an alternative living.

Ordinary people usually turned a blind eye to smuggling. They were happy to pay lower prices for goods and disliked the expensive duties imposed by the government. Locals who helped the smugglers carry goods from ship to shore could expect to earn nearly twice the average labourer's daily wage.

Smuggling gangs could be as large as 50 to 100 men. The gangs were well armed and had little fear of the customs officers or the army.

The gangs could move the goods at speed and supplied a network of traders who were willing to sell tea, brandy and other smuggled goods to the public. It was estimated that 3 million pounds weight of tea was smuggled into Britain each year.

There were very few **customs officers** to enforce the law and the government could not afford to increase their numbers.

## THINKING ABOUT FACTORS

1 Which factors were most significant in influencing:
   a) the growth of smuggling
   b) public attitudes towards smuggling?

2 Why might smuggling, like poaching, have been regarded as a social crime by some historians?

# 4.5 Problem crime 4: Why were the Tolpuddle Martyrs punished so harshly?

After the **French Revolution** in 1789, when the French monarchy was overthrown and thousands of people guillotined, the government became terrified of the same thing happening in Britain. Fearful landowners and politicians viewed every protest as a potential riot or uprising. Therefore, the authorities were on the lookout for signs of conspiracy and for groups whose ideas they considered suspect.

They were particularly anxious about the Grand National Consolidated Trades Union (GNCTU), which aimed to bring all workers together to fight for better conditions. It was not illegal to belong to a union, but employers disliked the idea of working people co-operating. Employers believed that by demanding better pay and conditions, unions threatened their businesses and harmed their interests. The story of the Tolpuddle Martyrs reveals much about these attitudes and how the definitions of crime were changing.

## UNDERSTANDING THE STORY OF THE TOLPUDDLE MARTYRS ?

1 Why did the men of Tolpuddle form a union in the first place?

2 How were the men punished and treated?

3 Which factors do you think were most significant in influencing government attitudes to the Tolpuddle Martyrs?

Attitudes in society · Travel · Institutions: The Church · Towns · Individuals · Science and technology · Poverty and wealth · Institutions: Government

4 Why did the government change the definition of a crime to include the oath sworn by the Tolpuddle Martyrs?

*What nerve! You'll take six shillings and be grateful!*

1. Life was tough for ▶ farm labourers in the Dorset village of Tolpuddle. Local labourers, led by George Loveless, asked their employers to increase their weekly wage after it had been cut several times. The farm owners refused, before cutting wages again!

◀ 2. In 1833, the labourers set up a union, the Friendly Society of Agricultural Labourers. Each man was blindfolded and swore an oath of secrecy and support for the union.

*I swear.*

"We must put an end to this villainy."

"We can't have the workers demanding whatever they like from us!"

▼ 4. Even though joining a union was not against the law, and they had not threatened anyone or gone on strike, Loveless and five others were arrested. They were sentenced to seven years' transportation to Australia (see page 51).

"Guilty!"

"They'll think twice before making any other demands!"

▲ 3. Despite the oath of secrecy, the local farm owners heard about the union and set about breaking it up. They used a law originally meant to keep discipline in the navy. It said that for sailors taking secret oaths was illegal, as it could lead to mutiny. The Government used the law to include all secret oaths, thus changing the definition of crime for its own purposes.

▲ 5. The trade union movement was badly hit by the sentence and the GNCTU was broken up. Speaking up for workers' rights was clearly a risky business. Employers celebrated.

▼ 7. In Britain, there was widespread outcry at sentence. The men were regarded as martyrs for union rights and a campaign was organised against their unfair treatment. At one meeting in London, 25,000 people attended and a petition demanding their release was signed by 250,000 people.

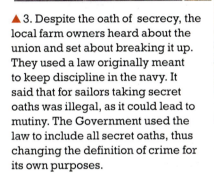

▲ 6. On 17 August, after a voyage of 111 days, the Tolpuddle men arrived in Sydney harbour. They were forced to walk to the farms where they would work. One of the men, Thomas Standfield, was aged over 50 and had to walk 150 miles!

▲ 8. Eventually, in March 1836, the Government granted all six men a pardon. However, it was another two years before all the men were able to return home. It was another 20 years before the trade union movement began to recover.

# 4.6 How did society change in the industrial period?

Britain experienced more social change during the eighteenth and nineteenth centuries than at any other previous time. Although most of these changes were gradual, they completely altered the way people lived their lives. It was only natural that this industrial and social revolution had an effect on punishments and policing. The boxes on these pages summarise these changes.

## Population rise and movement

By 1750 there were around 9.5 million people living in England and Wales. Most lived in villages scattered throughout the countryside. However, by 1900 the population had risen to 41.5 million and was mainly concentrated in towns.

## Work

During the eighteenth century, most people had made a living from farm work. By the end of the nineteenth century, most people found employment in workshops or factories. Work had moved into the towns and cities.

## Voting rights

By the mid-eighteenth century, only one in every eight men could vote. By 1885 nearly all men had this right. Therefore, governments began to make improvements to housing and health, in order to win votes from ordinary people.

## Harvests

By the nineteenth century, there was less chance of poor harvests causing high food prices or starvation. Food could be imported cheaply and quickly from other countries.

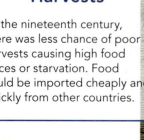

## Travel

Transport underwent huge changes during the eighteenth and nineteenth centuries. By the 1840s, railways had become a major form of travel. These were much faster than the roads and gradually became cheaper so that ordinary people could afford to use them.

## Wealth and taxes

Two centuries of trade and industrial growth made Britain a wealthy country in this period. During the nineteenth century, the government collected higher taxes, which they could use to pay for reforms that would improve people's lives.

## Education

During the eighteenth century, only a small minority of children attended school. Rates of literacy were low. However, by 1850, 70 per cent of the population could read and write. This rose to 95 per cent by 1900, after a law in 1880 said that all children had to go to school until the age of 13.

## Growing acceptance of government involvement

For centuries, British people had resisted any government involvement in local affairs as an interference, which threatened their freedom. However, by the nineteenth century, people began to accept that the government should have some control over certain things.

## New ideas about human nature

During the eighteenth century, new ideas emerged about human nature. Some argued that improving people's education, along with their living and working conditions, might encourage better behaviour. By the mid-1800s, Charles Darwin developed his theory of evolution. This led some people to believe that there was a criminal class that was somehow less evolved than other people.

1 Read the changes in each box carefully. Which of these might have led to:
a) the development of a professional police force
b) different types of punishment?

2 Look again at the boxes. Which of our factors do these changes fit under?

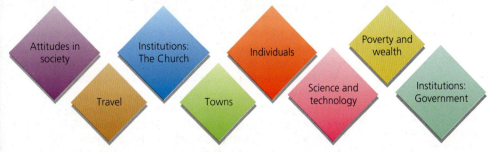

Keep these discussions in mind as you work through the rest of this chapter and see if you were right.

# 4.7 Case study: How far should we thank Sir Robert Peel for the Metropolitan Police Force in 1829?

For hundreds of years, policing had been the responsibility of ordinary people in the local community. However, in 1829, the very first professional and full-time police force was established in London. The man responsible for the introduction of the first police force was Home Secretary Sir Robert Peel (1788–1850). Peel was also a supporter of **penal reform** and was instrumental in making prisons the main method of punishment for serious crimes (see page 76). He also played a significant role in the abolition of the Bloody Code (see pages 70–71).

## The Fielding brothers

Peel was not the first to try to improve policing in the capital. Henry Fielding and his brother John were London magistrates. After taking over at Bow Street Magistrates' Court in 1748, they realised that more men were needed on London's streets to reduce crime.

The Fieldings believed rising crime was the result of breakdown in order as thousands flooded into London to make a living. They also blamed the bad example set by corrupt politicians.

They introduced a **horse patrol** to stop highwaymen. This effectively ended highway robbery around London. When it stopped the robbers returned! In 1805 a new patrol of 54 men was set up.

They established the Bow Street Runners, a team of thief-takers who patrolled the streets of London in the evenings. They also investigated crimes and presented evidence in court.

Their newspaper, *The Hue and Cry*, published information about criminals, crime and stolen goods. Magistrates and gaolers from all over the country passed on the details, which created a national network of information.

▲ Bow Street Runners in action, capturing two muggers, 1806. Thanks to the Fielding brothers a more organised system of preventing crime had developed in London by 1800. However, there was still no overall co-ordination of constables, watchmen and runners. Many feared the cost of a police force and worried the government might use it to limit people's freedoms.

# Why was Peel able to set up the Metropolitan Police Force in 1829?

The Metropolitan Police Act of 1829 replaced the system of watchmen and parish constables. The new Metropolitan Police Force had 3,200 men and opened the way for further changes across the country. The uniform was designed to look civilian rather than military and officers remained unarmed to distinguish them from the army. This was to reduce public fear that the police might be used to limit their freedoms.

## 1. The role of Peel

Sir Robert Peel was appointed **Home Secretary** in 1822. He was determined to improve people's lives by reducing the amount of crime. Peel made use of statistics to paint a picture of rising criminality. He was persuasive and reassured fellow politicians that a police force was no threat to freedom.

## 2. Government and taxation

Governments had become more involved in people's lives. The war with France (1803–1814) forced the Government to raise more money through taxes. Local authorities were also given powers to raise their own taxes that could be used to pay for a police force.

## 3. Increased crime and increased fear of crime

There was widespread belief that crime, especially violent crime, was on the increase. The crime rate had risen quite sharply in the years following the French wars when unemployment was a problem.

## 4. Fear of protest

After the French Revolution governments and landowners feared something similar might happen in Britain. High food prices and unemployment led to many large-scale protests after 1815. Revolution seemed a real possibility.

## 5. London

The rapid growth of towns had made the use of constables and watchmen seem inadequate. These problems were especially serious in London. There were too many people, crammed into closely-packed houses and streets. Fear of crime and revolution was strongest in the capital.

---

### HOW DID POLICING DEVELOP AFTER 1829?

**1835** A new law said towns were allowed to set up their own police forces.

**1839** A new law allowed counties to set up their own police forces. Bow Street Runners and other forces in London merged with the Metropolitan Police.

**1842** The Metropolitan Police set up the first detective force to gather evidence, investigate and solve crimes after they had been committed.

**1856** It became compulsory for all towns and counties to set up police forces. By this time the police were regarded with respect and not suspicion by the public.

**1870** Police helmets were introduced.

**1878** The Metropolitan Police detective force was reorganised into the **Criminal Investigation Department (CID)**. Over the next few years this was rolled out across the rest of the country.

**1884** There were 39,000 police in Britain and over 200 separate forces.

---

### WEIGHING UP THE IMPORTANCE OF REASONS

1  Look at the reasons for the development of the Metropolitan Police Force on this page. Make a graph like the one on the right and show the importance of each reason by adjusting the height of its bar.

   Make sure that you label each bar on your graph with an explanation of *how* that reason contributed to the development of the police in 1829.

2  Why do you think Peel was more successful than the Fielding brothers in establishing London's first police force?

3  Why were 1842, and later 1878, turning points in the history of policing?

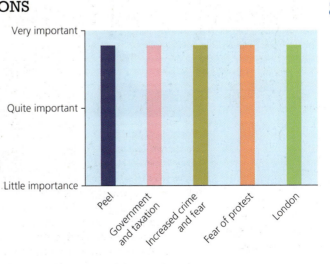

# 4.8 Why was the Bloody Code abolished in the 1820s and 1830s?

You have already solved the puzzle of why the Bloody Code was introduced at a time when the crime rate was falling (see page 52). Now it is time to solve a second mystery. Why was it abolished in the 1820s and 1830s when the crime rate was rising and fear of crime was very high?

The Bloody Code was abolished by the reforms of Sir Robert Peel who was Home Secretary in the 1820s. Peel made key individual contributions to penal reform (see pages 76–77) and the establishment of the first full-time and professional police force (see pages 68–69). However, you know enough about history to realise there must have been further reasons that allowed Peel to end the Bloody Code and make his other reforms.

### KEY DATES IN THE ABOLITION OF THE BLOODY CODE

**1789** Last woman burned for murdering her husband

**1808** Sir Samuel Romilly gets a law passed that abolishes the death penalty for pickpocketing

**1820** Last beheading – of the Cato Street conspirators who had tried to assassinate the entire government

**1820s–30s** Abolition of nearly all capital crimes

**1841** Only murder and treason remained capital crimes

**1868** The last *public* hanging took place

## WHAT REASONS DID PEEL HAVE FOR CHANGING THE LAW?

Peel faced considerable opposition from some MPs when attempting to end the Bloody Code. Make your own copy of the diagram below and use the information on pages 70–71 to add reasons and evidence to each of the blank speech bubbles to help Peel refute these objections.

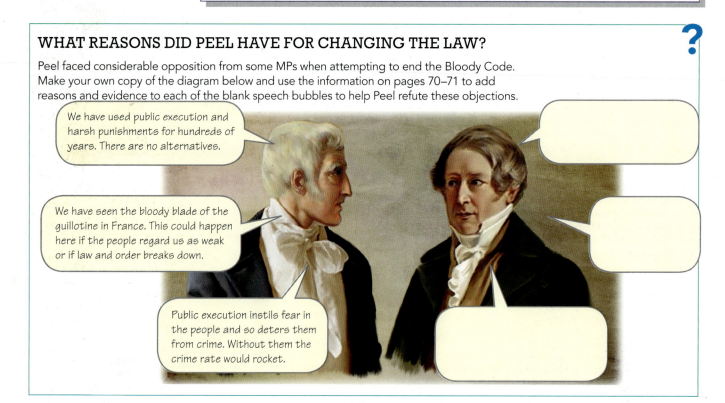

We have used public execution and harsh punishments for hundreds of years. There are no alternatives.

We have seen the bloody blade of the guillotine in France. This could happen here if the people regard us as weak or if law and order breaks down.

Public execution instils fear in the people and so deters them from crime. Without them the crime rate would rocket.

## Juries would not convict

Even in the early 1700s only 40 per cent of those convicted of capital crimes were actually hanged. By the 1800s this had fallen to 10 per cent, despite an increase in the crime rate overall.

Juries were frequently unwilling to find people guilty if they thought the punishment was unfair and out of proportion to the crime. With courts unwilling to convict them, criminals would feel even more confident of escaping punishment, and so were more likely to commit crimes. Therefore, the Bloody Code was actually undermining the law and no longer protected the property of the wealthy landowners and the middle class.

## Public executions were not working

During the 1700s, the crowds at executions grew larger, partly because newspapers publicised them more widely. Some factories even closed on execution day so that the workers could attend what had become cheap entertainment!

As crowds grew, the government felt that it was becoming harder to keep order. There was always the danger of a criminal escaping, especially if the crowd had sympathy or felt them to be innocent. There was also an increased risk of protest riots if there were mass hangings when offenders had been sentenced to death for minor or social crimes.

## Ideas about punishments were changing

Throughout the eighteenth century there had been a growing sense among philosophers and thinkers that punishments were far too brutal. They argued that lawmakers should ensure punishment actually fitted the crime committed.

Politicians had already started to look at different ways of punishing criminals. They hoped that these would be used more regularly, and therefore prove to be more effective. By the 1780s, transportation (see page 51) had emerged as the main alternative to capital punishment. The majority of those transported had originally been sentenced to death and then had their sentences reduced.

▲ **Source A** A public execution at Tyburn (see page 50), printed in 1747. London's magistrates admitted in 1783 that 'all the aims of public justice are defeated. All the effects of example, the terrors of death, the shame of punishment, are lost.' While executions were carried out, the crowds laughed and even drank. Such mass gatherings were perfect opportunities for pickpockets who could escape into the crowd. There was even the occasional risk of the condemned criminal being rescued by a sympathetic crowd.

## THINKING ABOUT FACTORS

Look back at the information on these pages. Which factors help explain the abolition of the Bloody Code?

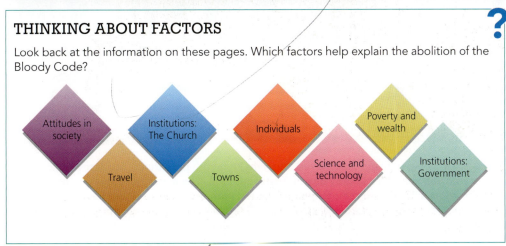

Attitudes in society

Travel

Institutions: The Church

Towns

Individuals

Science and technology

Poverty and wealth

Institutions: Government

# 4.9 Was transportation a success or a failure in the 1820s and 1830s?

Transportation was the system by which convicted criminals were removed from the country by being sent abroad. At first, the authorities had sent criminals to America, but after the American colonies became independent in the 1770s, they had to look for an alternative.

They chose the newly discovered and little known land of Australia. In the early years the voyage was a round trip of eighteen months, and the environment in Australia unforgiving. The idea of sending people to an unknown land at the edge of the world sounded like an excellent deterrent. Lawmakers believed transportation was going to be a success for the following reasons. It would:

- provide a punishment less harsh than hanging so juries will convict
- be harsh enough to terrify criminals and deter them
- reduce crime in Britain by removing the criminals
- help claim the new land of Australia for Britain
- reform criminals through hard work.

## How did transportation work?

Once a criminal had been sentenced to transportation it could still take several months before they finally arrived in Australia and begun a very different life.

> Prisoners were first sent to **hulks** (see page 75) or gaols until enough were gathered for the voyage. They worked in chains while they waited. The voyage itself was unpleasant and cramped, but by the 1830s only around 1 per cent died during the four-month trip.

> On arrival, convicts were assigned to **settlers**. Their sentence became whatever work their master gave them. The masters provided food, clothes and shelter. Good conduct could bring a 'ticket of leave' (early release). This gave prisoners a motive to behave and a sense of opportunity they might not have felt in Britain.

> Prisoners who committed further crimes were flogged or sent to more distant settlements where treatment was frequently harsh.

> Prisoners who failed to complete their sentence and returned to Britain without a 'ticket of leave' were sentenced to death.

▲ **Source A** Sweet Poll and Black-eyed Sue, two Plymouth prostitutes, bid farewell to their lovers who are bound for Botany Bay in Australia, 1792. The majority of those transported were convicted thieves, and most had committed more than one offence. People who had taken part in political protests were a small minority of those transported, but the government regularly used transportation as punishment for such activities (see pages 64–65). Only 3 per cent of those transported had been convicted of violent crimes.

## Transportation: For and Against

Transportation reached its height in the 1820s and 1830s. The peak year was 1833 when 36 ships and 6,779 prisoners were sent to Australia. However, by this time there were doubts about just how successful a punishment transportation really was. The boxes below outline the main arguments on both sides.

By the 1830s, Australia had clearly become an established part of the British Empire. No other country was likely to try to claim control of it.

In 1810, the **Lord Chief Justice** described transportation as 'no more than a summer's excursion to a happier and better climate'.

Many juries failed to convict even the guilty because they felt the death penalty was too harsh for some crimes. In contrast, they were far more willing to sentence people to transportation.

Only a minority of convicts chose to return to Britain once their sentence was up. Many took the opportunity to live peaceful and more respectable lives in Australia. Often they became respected members of the community.

The settlers in Australia had established groups to protest against the 'dumping' of convicts in their country. They wanted to end the idea that everyone in Australia had been transported there as a criminal.

In 1851, gold was discovered in Australia. A **gold rush** began and thousands of people in Britain tried to find the money to pay for the journey there.

Since transportation to Australia had begun, the crime rate in Britain had not fallen. Rather it had increased quite sharply.

By the 1830s, transportation was costing half a million pounds every year – an enormous amount of money at the time. Prisons in Britain were being used more frequently instead, partly because they were cheaper to run.

By the 1830s, wages in Australia were actually higher than those in Britain. Therefore, transportation was seen as more of an opportunity than a punishment once prisoners had won a 'ticket of leave'.

## The end of transportation

Transportation began to decline in the 1840s. Prisons were being used far more widely (see pages 74–75) and in 1857 transportation was finally brought to an end, largely due to pressure from settlers. The government needed to keep them happy to maintain control over this far-flung part of the empire.

### WEIGHING UP THE SUCCESSES AND FAILURES OF TRANSPORTATION

1  Make your own copy of the table below and use the information on pages 72–73 to fill in the second column.

| Reason for transportation | How far was this aim achieved? Give evidence for your judgement |
| --- | --- |
| It would provide a punishment less harsh than hanging so juries will convict. | |
| It would be harsh enough to terrify criminals and deter them. | |
| It would reduce crime in Britain by removing the criminals. | |
| It would help claim the new land of Australia for Britain. | |
| It would reform criminals through hard work. | |

2  Who was transportation more successful for – the government or the prisoners? Explain your reasons.

3  Write a brief explanation summarising the reasons why transportation was ended in 1857.

# 4.10 When was the worst time to be in 'clink', 1700–1900?

During the eighteenth century prisons played only a minor part in the system of punishment. Houses of Correction dealt with vagabonds and prostitutes but generally prisons were only used as a place to house criminals awaiting trial or to lock up people in debt. A survey in 1777 showed there were only 4,000 people in prison in England and Wales and that 60 per cent were debtors. However, over the next 100 years there were three major changes:

1 **Imprisonment became the normal method of punishing criminals**

   By the mid-nineteenth century, prison had replaced capital punishment for serious crimes, except murder.

2 **Prisons became important as the reasons for punishment changed**

   For hundreds of years punishments had taken place in public to terrify and deter others from committing crimes. By 1800 it was clear that public executions did not stop crime. Therefore, punishments began to focus on reforming the criminal.

3 **The huge increase in prisoners led to the government taking over the whole prison system**

   In the 1700s prisons were locally run with no rules about their organisation. By the 1870s government inspectors checked prisoners' work, diet, health and every other aspect of prison life.

---

## KNOWLEDGE ORGANISER: HOW DID PRISONS CHANGE?

Remember our criminal chum Tom the 'tea-leaf' (see page 4)? You are going to find out more about the changes to prisons and decide when would be the worst (and the best) time for Tom to be locked up – or 'in clink' as it was called.

If I was being sent down, when would be the worst time, Guv?

1 Make your own copy of the Knowledge Organiser below.

| Prison system | Positives from Tom's point of view | Negatives from Tom's point of view |
|---|---|---|
| Old prison system | Good place to pick up tips and new criminal skills as convicts were mixed together. | Disease was common. You had to pay to see a doctor. |
| After the first reforms of the Gaols Act, 1823 | | |
| The separate system, 1830s onwards | | |
| The silent system, 1860s onwards | | |

2 Use the information on page 75 to fill in the second row of the table. We have added some examples to help get you started.

# The old prison system

In the early 1800s, most prisons were run along the same lines as centuries before, and conditions had remained largely unchanged.

- All prisoners were housed together. Hardened criminals mixed with first-time offenders, debtors, **lunatics**, women and children. Stories were exchanged and future plans made. There was a concern that prisons were 'schools for crime'.
- **Prison warders** were unpaid. They had to earn their money by charging the prisoners fees. If you were well off you might be able to afford your own cell, good food, beer, tobacco, visitors and even a pet! Prisoners had to pay a fee to be released. Those who could not afford this continued to suffer behind bars.
- The poor relied on local charities to pay their fees and life was grim. While the wealthiest could afford their own rooms, the poorest lived in the most overcrowded conditions. At Newgate Gaol, 275 of the poorest prisoners lived in an area designed for just 150.
- Prisoners even had to pay to see a doctor. This was a problem because prisons were damp, dirty and unhealthy. What was called 'gaol fever' (probably dysentery or typhus) killed many inmates.

**Source A** Reconstruction of a prison cell in Nottingham Gaol. There would be three prisoners lodged in a cell this size. Such overcrowding was typical for all but the wealthiest inmates.

**Source B** Prison hulks were introduced as a short-term solution in the 1770s when transportation to America suddenly stopped (see page 72). These were old and usually rotten former warships. Conditions were as bad as the worst prisons. Prisoners were kept in **irons** most of the time and the death rate from disease was dreadfully high.

## After the first prison reforms, 1820s

It was clear that the harsh punishments of the Bloody Code were not working (see pages 70–71) and that crime was increasing. People began to look at prisons as an alternative and the government began a programme of major penal reform. In 1823, the Home Secretary, Sir Robert Peel (see page 68) passed a new set of laws known as the Gaols Act. Although the Act only applied to around 130 of the biggest prisons, and was ignored in some prisons, it was an important step in improving conditions. The main changes are summarised below.

Prisoners should be separated into groups so that hardened criminals are not mixing with first-time offenders.

Male and female prisoners are to be separated. Women should have female warders.

All prisoners should have proper food, though they can no longer keep pets!

Prison warders and governors are to be paid. They should no longer rely on prisoners paying fees.

All prisoners should attend chapel and receive religious instruction from the chaplain.

Prisons must be healthy, with proper fresh water supply and adequate drainage.

Magistrates have a duty to visit prisons in their area and check up on them.

▲ Robert Peel's Gaols Act, 1823. The new idea behind these changes was to reform the prisoners – to make them into better people so less likely to re-offend.

> **ADDING TO YOUR KNOWLEDGE ORGANISER** ❓
>
> Use the information on this page to fill in the third row on the table you started on page 74.

## The role of the reformers

For the first time in history, the Government had begun to build prisons and take an interest in how these were run. Peel was heavily influenced by the ideas of penal reformers John Howard and Elizabeth Fry. As Home Secretary he was well-placed to finally put these ideas into practice.

## JOHN HOWARD, 1726–1790

- Howard became interested in prisons while he was Sheriff of Bedfordshire. He inspected prisons in Bedfordshire and was shocked by what he found.
- After touring other prisons around the country he published a report in 1777: *The State of Prisons in England and Wales*.
- The report was detailed and highlighted the problems with the old prison system (see pages 74–75). He strongly attacked the fees that prisoners had to pay.
- His proposals for improvement included healthier accommodation, the separation of prisoners, a decent diet and better prison guards.
- However, during his lifetime, Howard was criticised for being too lenient.

## ELIZABETH FRY, 1780–1845

- Fry was a **Quaker** with a strong religious background. Quakers believe that there is something of God in everyone, and so it follows that they can be reformed.
- She visited women in Newgate prison and was horrified at what she found. Three hundred women, some with babies or small children, were crammed into three rooms amid shouting and fighting. Fry witnessed two women tearing clothes from a dead baby to put on a living one.
- She highlighted the poor living conditions and the exploitation of women prisoners by the male prison warders.
- She encouraged other Quakers to visit prisons and offer assistance, and set up prayer groups for the women in order to give religious instruction.
- She set up a school for the children at Newgate and taught them useful work like sewing and knitting to give them a means to survive when released.
- She had a big influence on the 1823 Gaols Act. However, by the 1840s, Fry was criticised by some as being too lenient.

## WHO HAD THE MOST IMPACT ON PRISON REFORM? ?

1 Describe Howard's main ideas.
2 Describe Fry's main ideas.
3 Where can you see evidence of their ideas in the 1823 Gaols Act?
4 Explain which of the two had the most impact on prison reform during their lifetime.
5 Peel clearly played a major part in turning Howard and Fry's ideas into reality. Look back at the social changes on pages 66–67. Which of these do you think made it possible for Peel to implement these reforms?

# Pentonville and the separate system

Between 1842 and 1877 the government built 90 new prisons in Britain. The first of these was Pentonville, which provided the model for the others. Pentonville was built to deal with the increased number of serious criminals who were no longer being transported or executed for their crimes. Pentonville was set up not simply to deter; it aimed to reform the inmates that passed through its doors.

**Source C** A plan of Pentonville prison. The blocks are like spokes from the centre so that fewer guards were needed to supervise the prison. ▶

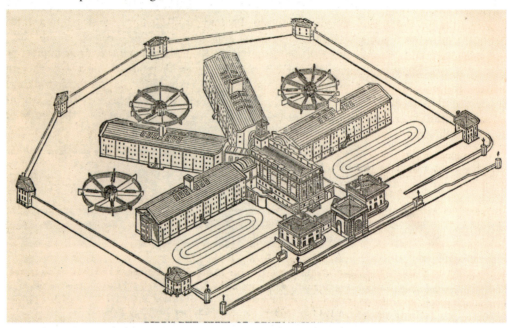

## How the separate system worked

Prisoners spent nearly all of their time alone and in their cells. Contact with other prisoners was made as difficult as possible. The main idea was to keep them away from the wicked influence of other prisoners. By being kept alone prisoners would reflect on their crimes. All this was backed up by religious instruction so that prisoners might live more honest and Christian lives once released. Sources D and F show how the separate system operated at Pentonville.

**Source D** Prisoners exercising at Pentonville. They wore masks so that they could not see anyone and held a rope knotted at 4.5m intervals to prevent them communicating with the other prisoners. ▶

◄ **Source E** Prisoners attending the chapel at Pentonville. The chapel was built so that each prisoner was boxed in. They could not see the other prisoners but could see the chaplain.

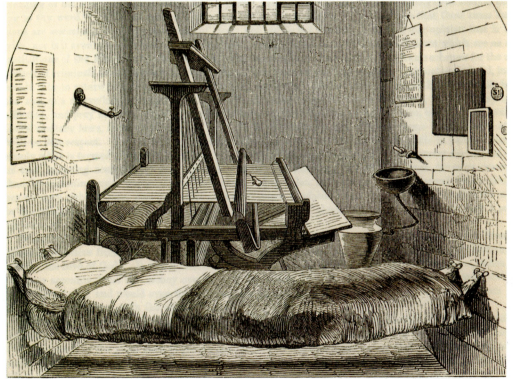

◄ **Source F** A cell in Pentonville, with a hammock for sleeping and a weaving loom for the prisoner to work on. Prisoners were put to useful work to show that hard work and effort could make them productive citizens. It was hoped that once released they would seek honest employment rather than a return to crime.

> **?** Why might the separate system have been bad for the mental health of the prisoners?

## Strengths and weaknesses of the separate system

The separate system effectively isolated prisoners for the whole of their sentence. This ensured prisoners could no longer mix and negatively influence one another. It ended the fear that prisons were acting as 'schools for crime'. However, in practice the separate system effectively placed inmates in solitary confinement. The results of this were quite shocking. In the first eight years at Pentonville, 22 prisoners went mad, 26 had nervous breakdowns and 3 committed suicide.

The separate system also proved costly in other ways. It required inmates to be housed in separate cells and this added to the cost of building and running prisons.

> **ADDING TO YOUR KNOWLEDGE ORGANISER ?**
>
> Use the information on these pages to fill in the third row on the table you started on page 74.

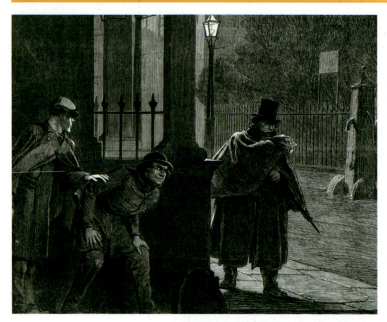

▲ **Source G** Garrotters lying in wait, 1863. Garroting involved partly strangling the victim so that he or she could be robbed easily. There were a few cases, then in 1862 an MP was garrotted near the House of Commons. Newspapers stirred up an outcry, blaming criminals who had won early release from prison for good behaviour. This led the Government to introduce a harsher regime in prisons.

▲ **Source H** A prisoner working the crank in his cell. Prisoners were expected to turn the crank handle up to twenty times a minute, 10,000 times a day, for over eight hours. If a guard tightened a screw, it made the crank harder to turn. This led to guards being nicknamed 'screws'. Some prisoners had to walk a giant treadmill or unpick lengths of old ships' tarred rope to make string.

## Things get tougher: The silent system

By the 1860s, few people were being hanged, and transportation had ended in 1857. Therefore, prisons had become the main method used to punish the most serious offenders.

Although crime was actually falling in this period, certain high-profile crimes created fear among the public. Popular and cheap booklets, known as Penny Dreadfuls, told lurid tales of violent crime and increased public fears that not enough was being done to deter the criminal classes. A good example of this was the panic stirred up by the media over the so called 'garroting crisis' (see Source G).

There was a growing belief that there was an identifiable 'criminal type' who was thought to be physically recognisable and less evolved than the rest of society. These 'criminal types' could not be reformed, only deterred by tougher prisons. The Government responded by introducing much tougher regimes in prison and at the centre of this was the 'silent system':

> Prisoners were expected to be silent at all times. Breaking this rule could result in being whipped or being put on a diet of bread and water.

> Hard wooden bunks replaced hammocks to sleep on. This was known as 'hard board' and was deliberately uncomfortable.

> Food was described as 'hard fare'. It was adequate but monotonous. The same menu every day, year in and year out.

> Prisoners were expected to take part in 'hard labour' – deliberately pointless work for several hours every day.

### FINISHING YOUR KNOWLEDGE ORGANISER AND MAKING A DECISION ?

1 Use the information on this page to fill in the final row on the table you started on page 74.

2 Next, use your completed table to make an overall decision about when the worst and best times were for Tom the 'tea-leaf' to be 'in clink'. Make sure you give reasons.

# 4.11 Communicating your answer

You know that great changes to prisons took place in the nineteenth century, beginning with the Gaols Act of 1823. However, knowing how prison changed is only part of the story. You must also consider the **reasons** why prisons changed. Just listing or describing these reasons is not enough. You must be able to 'prove' why that reason was important by explaining the effect it had. Try answering the following question using the steps below.

**Explain why there was so much change to prisons during the period 1700–1900.**

## Step 1: Describing and explaining

Usually you would organise your answer into paragraphs – each paragraph describing a reason and explaining the effect it had. To help you do this, make a copy of the table and use the statements below it to fill in the blanks.

| Reason | Describe reason | Explain how reason led to a change |
|---|---|---|
| Rising crime | | Therefore, the government began reforming prisons to try to reduce offending. |
| Bloody Code was not working | | |
| Existing prisons were ineffective | Prisoners mixed together. First-time offenders were thrown together with experienced criminals. | This led critics to describe prisons as 'schools for crime'. Changes were needed to stop prisoners committing further crimes when released. |
| Role of the government was changing | | |
| Role of the reformers | | |

**Therefore, public executions were no longer a deterrent. Furthermore, the government feared the risk of riot, which might lead to revolution. An alternative form of punishment was needed.**

**Individuals like John Howard and Elizabeth Fry believed prisoners could be reformed through hard work and religious instruction.**

**This resulted in the government having the necessary funds to improve existing prisons and build new ones.**

**The government was becoming more involved in every aspect of society and higher taxes were being raised.**

**The number of thefts and violent crimes rose between 1820 and 1850. There was also an increased fear of crime.**

**This provided the government with ideas about what changes could be made to help improve prisoners' lives.**

**Public executions had become a form of entertainment. They were rowdy and could attract large crowds.**

## Step 2: Writing a conclusion

A good conclusion makes the overall argument clear – it does not need to repeat everything you have already written. Make it clear which reason you think played the most important role in the changes to prisons.

### Practice questions

1 Explain one way in which the aims of punishment were similar in the late nineteenth century and the later Middle Ages.

2 Explain one way in which policing methods were different in the nineteenth century and the later Middle Ages.

3 Explain why there were changes in methods of punishing criminals in the period c.1700 to c.1900.

4 Explain why there were changes to policing in the period c.1700 to c.1900.

5 'The role of Robert Peel was the main reason for the development of the first police force in 1829.' How far do you agree? Explain your answer.

6 'Reform was the driving force behind the changes made to punishment in the nineteenth century.' How far do you agree? Explain your answer.

## 4.12 Visible learning: Revise and remember

It should be clear by now that the period 1700–1900 saw dramatic changes to crime and punishment. Therefore, this is a good opportunity to revisit the factors affecting crime and punishment.

### Technique 1: Role of individual charts – Robert Peel

You may have noticed that in the period 1700–1900 certain key individuals, including Robert Peel, played a role in the development of crime and punishment. It will be much easier to revise their achievements if you use the same kind of chart for each one. The example below and the questions around it will help you create charts for other individuals, but don't be afraid to think for yourself about what you want to include.

**Make sure you get the basic chronology right.**

**Briefly describe their contribution/activities.**

**Think about what their immediate impact was on crime and punishment. Did it change things at the time?**

**Robert Peel, 1788–1850**

**Time period:** 1700–1900    **Time active:** 1820s and 1830s

**Key contribution:**
- Introduced the first police force in London – the Metropolitan Police – in 1829.
- Reformed and improved prison system.
- Passed laws ending the Bloody Code.
- Contributed to penal reform with the Gaols Act of 1823.

**Short-term impact:**

**Longer-term impact:**
- Police forces established across country.
- Detective force formed.
- Prisons became main form of punishment for serious crimes.

**What other factors played a role?**

**It is important to narrow this down when considering the role they played.**

**Did their contribution lead to other changes later on? What other aspects of crime and punishment changed as a result?**

**Think about any other factors that made the contribution of the individual possible or that also influenced change. For example, other key individuals like Fry and Howard gave Peel the necessary ideas for his prison reforms. Increased revenue from taxation allowed government and lawmakers to pay for a police force.**

Now go back and make similar charts for any other individuals you think were important to crime and punishment. You could consider Fry and Howard on page 77, or go even further back by looking at Matthew Hopkins (pages 44–45) and even William the Conqueror (pages 20–21).

### Technique 2: Repeat your memory map

In Chapters 2 and 3 you drew a memory map to help you record the main features of crime and punishment in the Middle Ages and the period 1500–1700. Draw a third memory map for the period 1700–1900. Once again, use two different colours to show what were changes and what were continuities.

# Technique 3: Tessellate! Appreciate! Accumulate!

Using hexagons can be a great way of recapping and revising previously learnt content. The advantage of hexagons is that they can (get ready to make your mathematics teacher proud) tessellate – fit together. This is a useful way of showing how factors link to changes and sometimes link to each other.

## Step 1

Start with the growth of highway robbery. Write this on a hexagon and add factor hexagons to the outside if they help to explain it. Alternatively, you could make big hexagons and do this as a group. We have started you off to give you some idea. Explain link 1 – how did communications and travel affect highway robbery in this period? Next, explain link 2 in the same way. You'll notice that the outer factor hexagons are also touching – that means link 3 also needs explaining!

## Step 2

Try adding some more factor hexagons, but remember you must explain any links that you make. Here are the factors you could use:

## Step 3

Now see what you come up with when you put each of the following changes in the central hexagon:

- Growth of smuggling
- Harsh laws against poachers
- The abolition of the Bloody Code
- Prison reform
- The creation of a professional police force

You could stick your finished hexagons in your book and write the links around the outside. Alternatively, if using big hexagons and working in groups, use sticky notes to explain the links you make. You could then take a digital photo and stick a copy in your book.

# Technique 4: Play a game

Below are a list of key terms, events and individuals from the period 1700–1900. In pairs, copy these onto individual cards. Swap these with another pair in your class.

Next, divide the cards equally between you and your partner. Sit back to back and take turns at describing what is on the card without using *any* of the words written on it. Move on when your partner successfully identifies what is written on the card.

Finally, retrieve your original cards to add a few of your own before passing them on to another pair and playing the game again.

| The Bloody Code | Gaols Act, 1823 | Elizabeth Fry | Robert Peel |
|---|---|---|---|
| John Howard | Highway robbery | Tea, cloth, wine and brandy | Fielding brothers |
| Silent system | Pentonville | Poaching | |

## 5.1 Criminal moments in time: 2007

There has been more change to crime and punishment since 1900 than any of the previous periods mentioned in this book. Social, cultural and technological changes have led to changing definitions of crime, as well as a revolution in law enforcement and crime detection methods. Perhaps most significantly, the twentieth century saw an end to capital punishment, thus ending a tradition stretching back over a thousand years.

CCTV cameras are used to help prevent crime and to help catch offenders.

In 2007, the Government introduced a new definition of crime – 'hate crimes'. By far the most common of these is race-related crime.

Try this mate, straight off the boat from Amsterdam last week.

Get back to your own country.

What do you mean? I was born here!

Drug offences have become a serious issue and in many cases lead to other types of crime.

OLD WOMAN ROBBED & BEATEN IN OWN HOME

The growth of the internet has made it possible for people to commit online crimes such as hacking into databases to steal people's bank details.

How can I afford to get that fixed now I've got this fine?

Some convicted criminals are electronically monitored and tracked as an alternative to prison.

This is a NEIGHBOURHOOD WATCH AREA

Equipment in the car provides the officer with instant access to computer-held records for all vehicles. All officers have their own radio to communicate with the station and each other.

POLICE

# CRIME AND PUNISHMENT C.1900–PRESENT: OVERVIEW

1  Work in pairs or small groups. You have five minutes. What evidence can you find in the picture of:
   a)  different types of criminal activity
   b)  different punishments
   c)  different forms of law enforcement (policing and/or crime prevention)?

2  What changes and continuities can you see when you compare this criminal moment in time with the nineteenth-century scene on pages 56–57?

3  Use your existing knowledge of the twentieth century from Key Stage 3, to help explain possible reasons for the changes.

4  List any questions that these two pages raise about crime and punishment in the period 1900–present. Keep these safe and tick them off when you answer them as you work through the rest of this section.

85

# 5.2 How far did crime really change during the twentieth century?

The twentieth century saw some dramatic changes in the way people lived their lives in Britain. It was an era of two world wars, economic boom and bust, and tremendous technological advances. Did crime change and grow as a result?

## Better standards of living

By the time this book was written in 2016, the population was better fed, better clothed and better housed than in 1900. The **welfare state** provides a safety net for the most vulnerable, but Britain remains a divided society. The gap between the richest and poorest has continued to grow. Therefore, although **absolute poverty** has declined, many people still feel poor compared with the wealthiest in society.

## Has crime really increased?

Crime has increased since 1900 but not as quickly as the headline figures suggested in the graph below. First, figures show a rise because more people are willing to report crimes. By the second half of the century more households had telephones, making it easier to inform the police. Second, more people report burglaries and theft for insurance purposes. Third, violent crimes and sexual offences are reported more, because the police are better trained and more sympathetic than in the past. Finally, many crimes were previously dealt with informally or 'off the record'. The police now record crime more consistently.

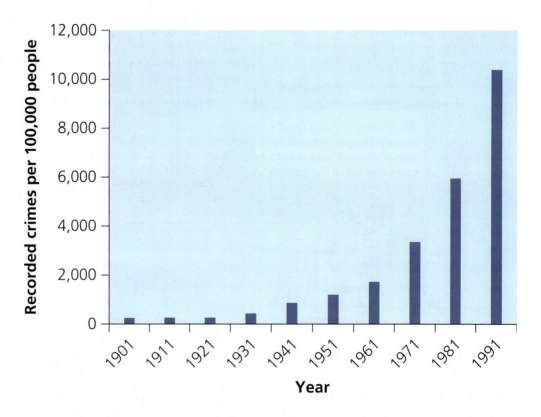

▲ Recorded crimes per 100,000 people in England and Wales during the twentieth century. Recorded crime increased rapidly from the 1950s onwards. However, by the late 1990s it was once again falling. This trend has continued into the twenty-first century with the crime rate at its lowest since 1981.

## NEW CRIMES OR OLD?

1 Draw your own copy of the Venn diagram below **OR** borrow two hula-hoops from the PE department to make a physical diagram. You could add labels and information using sticky notes or slips of paper and take a digital photo of your finished effort to stick in your book.

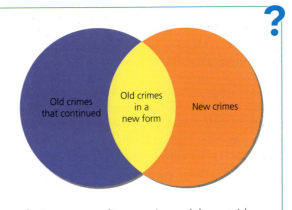

Old crimes that continued · Old crimes in a new form · New crimes

2 Read the information about crimes on pages 86–87. Remember what you found out about crime in earlier periods and then add the different types of crime to your diagram. Around the outside add sentences to explain where you have placed each crime.

## Car crime

In 1900 the motor car was still a new invention. By 1930, cars were cheaper and driving was popular but dangerous. Motorists did not need a licence and in 1934, 7,343 people were killed on the roads. After 1935, all drivers had to pass a test, pay road tax, get insurance and maintain a roadworthy car. Today, driving offences absorb a huge amount of police and court time. Car theft has become one of the largest categories of crime.

## Murder

The number of murders increased after 1900, but not as quickly as other crimes. Throughout history, most murders occur on the spur of the moment and are unplanned. The majority of murderers know the victim and have never committed a serious offence before.

## Hate crimes

In 2007, the Government introduced a new law covering 'hate crimes'. Hate crimes range from criminal damage and vandalism through to harassment or physical assault. Victims are targeted for their race, sexual orientation, religion or disability. The most common type of hate crime is motivated by racism. In recent years, there has been a growth in religiously motivated hate crimes.

## Terrorism

From the 1960s Britain has lived with the threat of terrorist violence. The **IRA** (Irish Republican Army) carried out bomb attacks on buildings in Britain between the 1970s and 1990s, killing and injuring many people. In July 2005, Muslim extremists carried out suicide bombings in London, killing 56 people and injuring many more.

## Violent crime and sexual offences

Violent crimes and sexual offences have always existed, but both showed increases in the later twentieth century, partly due to an increased willingness of victims to report offences.

## Computer crime

Computer crime is mostly theft or online **fraud**. Fraudsters trick people into handing over important details or passwords. This allows fraudsters to steal money from their bank accounts. The internet has also made it easier than ever before to illegally copy music and films without paying for them.

## Theft, burglary and shoplifting

There have always been **opportunistic thieves** and burglars. Today, drug addiction frequently leads to theft as addicts steal to feed their habit. Shoplifting became established in the second half of the century, as more shops placed goods on display. This made shoplifting easier and perhaps more tempting.

## Smuggling and drug offences

Sources A and B describe and show a big problem in modern Britain. However, does that mean this is a totally new type of crime or simply an old crime that has changed and been adapted over time?

---

**Source A** UK Border Force press release, 17 November 2014. Source: https://www.gov.uk/government/news/man-jailed-for-drug-smuggling-attempt

*A man from Germany has been jailed for four years at Canterbury Crown Court after attempting to smuggle approximately one kilo of cocaine into the UK.*

*On 4 October this year Border Force officers stopped and questioned Charles Ukachukwu Imoh after he arrived by coach at the tourist controls in Dover's Eastern Docks. Imoh said he was coming to the UK to visit family in London.*

*After his luggage had been searched Imoh agreed to accompany officers to hospital where he was X-rayed and packages were identified inside him. A total of 83 packages were eventually recovered.*

*The drugs, which were later forensically tested, had a street value of over £215,000 and a purity level of 66 per cent.*

---

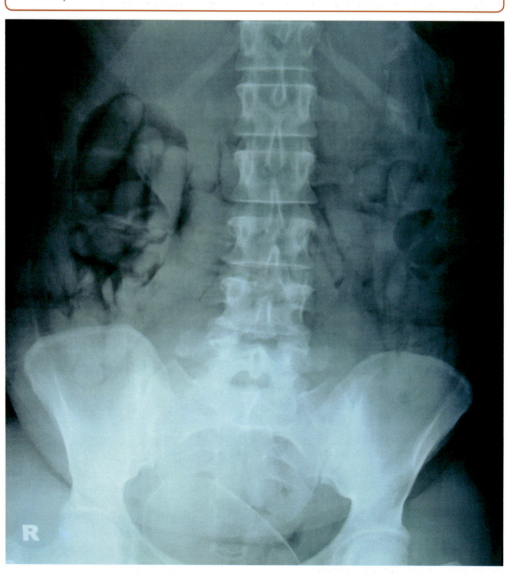

**Source B** An X-ray showing taped up packets that were swallowed by a drug smuggler. So-called 'drugs mules' are an increasing problem particularly at the country's airports. If just one of these packets burst, the person who swallowed them would likely die.

## HOW FAR HAS SMUGGLING REALLY CHANGED? ?

1 Use the information on page 88 to help you compare modern smuggling with smuggling in the eighteenth century. Fill in your own copy of the table below.

| | Eighteenth century | Twentieth century–present |
|---|---|---|
| Items smuggled | • Brandy, tea and cloth | |
| Reasons for smuggling | • To avoid paying duty<br>• Big profits could be made<br>• Public demand for goods at cheaper prices | |
| Methods used | • Fast sailing ships brought in goods from Europe<br>• Moved from coastal areas to towns for distribution | |

2 Decide where smuggling fits on the Venn diagram you started on page 87.

## Modern smuggling

Better transport throughout the twentieth century has made smuggling increasingly difficult to prevent. With millions of people travelling in and out of the country by air, land and sea, the task facing customs officials and border security is huge.

## Legal items

Tobacco and alcohol are smuggled into the country in huge quantities every day. Both are much cheaper on the continent where taxes on such goods are lower. Smugglers purchase large amounts and return to Britain where the goods are sold to make a profit. There is big public demand as smuggled alcohol and tobacco are much cheaper than in the shops.

## Illegal items

Drugs are not the only illegal items smuggled into Britain, but they generate the biggest profits by far. Demand for illegal drugs has continued to rise in the last 40 years and consequently the illegal drug business has become a multi-billion pound industry.

## People smuggling

Tougher immigration controls and conflict in different parts of the world have led to an increase in people smuggling. Immigrants, who might otherwise not be allowed to enter Britain, pay to be smuggled into the country.

The main drug smuggling routes into the UK. Estimates say that 18–23 tonnes of heroin, 25–30 tonnes of cocaine and at least 270 tonnes of cannabis are smuggled into Britain annually. ▼

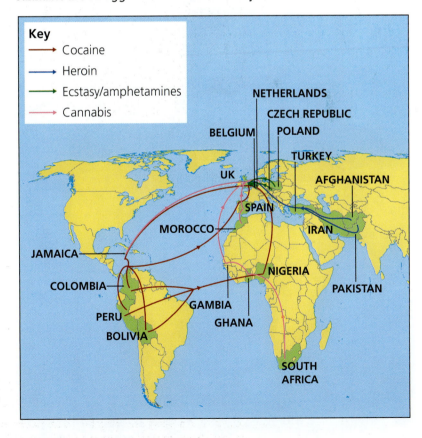

Key
→ Cocaine
→ Heroin
→ Ecstasy/amphetamines
→ Cannabis

# 5.3 Case study: Were conscientious objectors really 'cowards and cads'?

Conscientious objectors (COs) refuse to take part in a war or conflict for moral reasons. This is not usually a problem as professional armies recruit from volunteers. Those who objected to fighting simply avoided volunteering.

## The First World War (1914–1918)

At the start of the war in 1914, the Government relied on volunteers to fight. A massive recruitment drive was launched to encourage as many men as possible to enlist. Over 1 million men signed up, but, in 1916, as the war dragged on and casualties mounted, the Government introduced conscription. This meant all single men aged between 18 and 41 were required to enlist. A couple of months later this was extended to married men. Conscription raised a further 2.5 million soldiers during the course of the war.

Around 16,000 men refused to join because they were COs. The majority of them refused to fight on religious grounds, pointing to the commandment, 'Thou shalt not kill' from the Bible. Others felt that the war was an argument between the ruling classes of Europe rather than the ordinary people. However, majority opinion supported the war and public attitudes towards COs were hostile. They were frequently accused of cowardice and some were even physically attacked.

### ACTIVITY

1 What emotion do you think the man is feeling?
2 Why is the son shown playing with toy soldiers?
3 What other persuasive techniques does the poster use?

Daddy, what did YOU do in the Great War?

◀ **Source A** British recruitment poster, 1915. This clever campaign was used to encourage men to join up.

What impression does this newspaper cartoon give about COs and their reasons for not fighting?

## Treatment of COs

COs had to appear before a local **tribunal** (special court) to state their case. The tribunals were sometimes made up of retired soldiers and other unsympathetic individuals. Some COs were given alternative work supporting the war effort at home. Others took non-fighting roles such as driving ambulances at the front line, which could be incredibly dangerous.

Over 6,000 COs refused to accept the decision of the tribunal and were put in prison where they faced solitary confinement, hard labour and a long sentence. By the end of the war, 73 COs had died as result of their treatment. Even after the war, all COs were stripped of the right to vote until 1926.

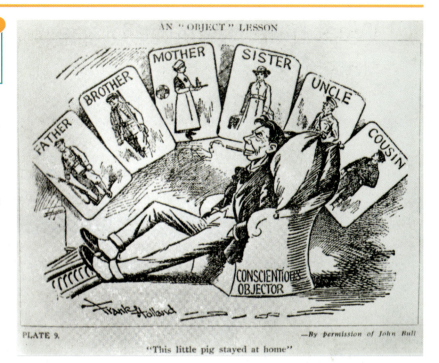

AN "OBJECT" LESSON

FATHER BROTHER MOTHER SISTER UNCLE COUSIN

CONSCIENTIOUS OBJECTOR

*Frank Holland*

PLATE 9.        —By permission of John Bull

"This little pig stayed at home"

▲ **Source C** Newspaper cartoon, 1916. This shows a conscientious objector staying at home while the rest of his family contributes to the war effort.

> **Source B** Extract from *Great Britain's Great War*, by Jeremy Paxman, published in 2013.
>
> *Near Oldham, a tribunal member facing a conchie (CO) ranted that he was ... 'a coward and a cad, and nothing but a shivering mass of unwholesome fat'.*

## The Second World War (1939–1945)

Conscription was introduced again in 1939, and 59,162 people, including women, registered as COs. This time the authorities treated them differently. Tribunals were still held but were no longer allowed to include ex-soldiers. A greater effort was made to give COs alternative work such as farming, or in industries like munitions that were vital to the war effort. COs were sent to prison only as a last resort.

The British public were slower to change their attitudes than the government. COs continued to be attacked in the newspapers and many were sacked from their jobs. Once again, COs were openly accused of cowardice and treason while some were attacked in the street.

### HOW WERE COS TREATED IN THE FIRST AND SECOND WORLD WARS?

1 Make your own copy of the table below and use the information on pages 90–91 to fill it in. An example has been done for you.

| War | Government reaction | Public attitudes |
|---|---|---|
| First World War (1914–1918) | | • Supported the war unanimously<br>• Regarded COs as cowards |
| Second World War (1939–1945) | | |

2 Does the information on these pages prove or challenge the popular view that COs were acting out of cowardice? Explain your reasons.

# 5.4 What have been the biggest changes to policing since 1900?

The powers of the police to question, search or arrest suspects have changed little since 1900. However, there have been some important changes that affect greatly the way officers carry out their duties.

## CHANGES TO MODERN POLICING ?

1 Use the information below and on page 93 to complete your own copy of the table below.

| | 1900 | The situation today |
|---|---|---|
| Numbers and organisation | • Around 200 local police forces – all run differently<br>• Little co-operation between forces<br>• 42,000 officers | |
| Training and recruitment | • Military drill the only training<br>• All police officers were male<br>• Low-quality and poorly paid recruits | |
| Transport | • Officers walked a 'beat' of up to 20 miles a day | |
| Equipment | • Whistle to call for help<br>• Wooden truncheon<br>• Pistols locked up at police station for emergencies | |
| Crime detection tools | • Eyes and ears of the officer<br>• Witness statements | |
| Record-keeping | • Local record-keeping was poor<br>• No national record of criminals | |
| Main duties | • Dealing with crimes, especially petty theft<br>• Dealing with drunkenness | |

2 Which changes had the biggest impact on the effectiveness of the police?

3 Which of the following factors had the biggest influence on the changes to the police force?
   ○ Government
   ○ Attitudes in society
   ○ Science and technology

## Crime prevention

Every force appoints crime prevention officers (CPOs) who advise local people on crime prevention and security, such as fitting locks and alarms to property and vehicles. There is also an emphasis on catching young offenders early and encouraging them away from crime (see pages 98–99). In 1982, the Neighbourhood Watch began. Members of the community report suspicious behaviour to the police who can then follow up and investigate. In 2007, Neigbourhood Watch became a national network that works closely with local police forces.

## Weapons

Ordinary officers do not carry firearms but still have batons or truncheons. **Pepper spray** or **CS gas** can be used to control violent suspects. Some officers are trained in the use of tasers, which temporarily disable a suspect with an electric shock. Specialist officers with firearms training are used when there is a high level of threat.

## Vehicles

Since the 1930s, cars and motorbikes have improved police response speed. By the 1970s these had effectively replaced the foot patrol or 'beat'. Police helicopters track suspects and support officers on the ground. Today, many forces have reintroduced foot or bicycle patrols to build better community relations.

## The science of crime detection

Since 1901, the police have used fingerprints and chemical analysis of blood samples to identify suspects. More recently, DNA samples have been used as evidence with the first murder conviction from this new technology coming in 1988.

## Specialisation

Crime has become more varied and complex. Therefore, there are several highly trained specialist units including the Fraud Squad, Drugs Squad, dog-handlers, counter-terrorist squads, cyber-crime units and others.

## Basic training

Since 1947 new recruits have undertaken fourteen weeks of basic training at the National Police Training College. Local forces have their own specialists to continue the training.

## Communications

In the 1930s two-way radios were introduced to police cars and the 999 emergency telephone number was started. Today, all officers carry a two-way radio for instant communication with the police station or headquarters.

## Computer records

Since 1974, the Police National Computer (PNC) has collected together several databases, including fingerprints, motor vehicles and missing person details. Officers have access to national and local information 24 hours a day.

## Camera technology

CCTV and other security recordings are used to prevent crime, but also to help identify and convict suspects. The police also use Automatic Number Plate Recognition (ANPR). As a vehicle passes an ANPR camera, its registration is read and checked against a database of vehicles of interest to the police. Officers can stop a vehicle, check it for evidence and make arrests.

## Changing roles

Police officers deal increasingly with non-crime related incidents such as anti-social behaviour, drunkenness, missing persons and incidents linked to mental health where someone may be at risk. Officers also keep order at demonstrations, football matches and other large gatherings.

## Numbers

The total number of officers (as of March 2015) is 126,818, spread across 43 local forces in England and Wales. Women officers first appeared in 1920. The proportion of female officers in England and Wales has increased from 7 per cent in 1977 to around 28 per cent (March 2015). The proportion of officers from ethnic minorities is still low but has risen from 1 per cent in 1989 to 5.5 per cent today.

# 5.5 How have prisons changed since 1900?

Since the nineteenth century, prisons have been used as the most common form of punishment for serious crimes. However, the twentieth century saw significant changes to the way prisons operated and the conditions inmates faced.

I've had enough of crime. I'm getting too old for this. Time to turn over a new leaf, Guv. Geddit?!

Remember Tom the 'tea-leaf' from page 4? Well, he's in trouble again. We think it's time that Tom went on the 'straight and narrow' and after a thousand years of history he finally agrees. Tom wants to become a reformed character, so what would he have made of prisons and the alternatives after 1900?

## WHEN WAS THE BEST TIME FOR TOM TO BE IN PRISON? **?**

Use the information on pages 94–97 to help you fill in your own copy of the table below. We have begun adding information to help get you started. **Remember, this time Tom wants to be reformed!**

|  | Positives from Tom's point of view | Negatives from Tom's point of view |
|---|---|---|
| Prisons before 1947 | No more crank or treadmill after 1902 | Prisoners could mix. Tom might fall in with a bad crowd while inside |
| Prisons after 1947 |  |  |
| Non-custodial alternatives |  |  |

## Changes to prisons before 1947

By 1900, prisons had already begun to move away from the separate system (see page 78). The use of pointless hard work such as the crank and the treadmill were greatly reduced and finally abolished by 1902.

The biggest changes came after 1922. Solitary confinement was ended and prisoners were allowed to associate with each other. The broad arrows that marked convict uniforms were abolished, as was the 'convict crop' (shaved hairstyle) that prisoners had worn. Diet, heating and conditions in the cells were improved gradually and more visits were allowed. Teachers were employed in prisons to help inmates have a better chance of finding work when released.

The first open prison was built in 1933. Rules in open prisons were more relaxed and the prisoners were allowed to leave the grounds in order to work. The idea was to prepare inmates for ordinary life back in the community. The use of open prisons was expanded and continues today.

▲ Ford Open Prison in West Sussex. Notice the inmates returning to the prison at the end of a working day in the community.

## Why did it change?

Fear of crime had declined from the heights of the nineteenth century. Therefore, the Government was under less public pressure to make prisons so harsh. There was also a belief that the certainty of arrest rather than prison was the real deterrent.

The old belief that criminals inherited their criminal habits was declining. Instead, many thought poverty or a criminal environment caused crimes. This raised hopes that better treatment and education in prison might reform inmates.

## Changes to prisons after 1947

The prison population began to rise steeply after the 1940s (see the graph below). This trend has continued until the present day, with the number of people in prison doubling between 1993 and 2015. The possible reasons for this are explored below, as are the effects this had on conditions.

### Why have prisoner numbers increased?

The rise in the prison population is due to a number of reasons, not just an increased crime rate. Fear of crime increased after the mid-twentieth century and politicians reacted to public concerns that they were 'soft' on crime:

- The average length of sentences has increased. Prisoners are being locked away for longer as governments seek to be 'tough on crime'.
- There is an increased chance of a prison sentence for certain crimes, particularly sexual, violent or drug-related offences.
- The number of people on remand (awaiting trial in prison) has increased.

### Overcrowding and understaffing

Prison overcrowding peaked in the 1980s and prisons have remained overcrowded every year since 1994. Reduced budgets and difficulties in recruiting have led to fewer staff looking after more prisoners. At the same time, there has been an increase in the number of serious assaults in prison. There are also ongoing problems with deaths in **custody**, reaching a record number in 2014. In recent years there has been a decline in purposeful activity such as work or education for prisoners. In 2014, **Ofsted** judged over half of prisons as inadequate or requiring improvement for learning and skills. This does little to solve the problem that nearly half of all prisoners left school without qualifications and one in five need help with literacy and numeracy.

◄ Prison population 1900–2010. Source: www.parliament.uk/ briefing-papers/SN04334.pdf

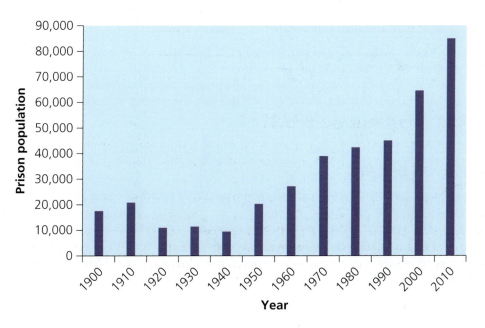

### A recent prisoner's experience

You may have noticed by now that public attitudes have a big effect on crime and punishment. By the 1980s and 1990s, there was growing public feeling that prisons were no longer harsh enough. This remains a popular theme in newspapers and the media, but how far is it really true?

When we were writing this section we were lucky enough to get the following description from an inmate currently serving a prison sentence. The author accurately conveys life inside a typical closed prison.

## A description of prison life in 2016

I'm currently sat in a cell that was built in the late 1840s. The modernisation of the cell is the strip lighting that is running in a reinforced unit along the side of the wall; a TV and FM receiver point plus a TV (that is rented, it isn't just given out to inmates), a kettle and a 'smash-proof' unit that incorporates two desks and drawer units.

Someone who does not do as they are told will soon find themselves on a Basic Regime. That's an hour out of the cells each day. No TV allowed. Fewer visits. Not allowed their own clothes. Conversely, you can engage and get improved conditions. I'm on Enhanced Regime. I'm out of my cell most of the day. I get extra visits. I can spend more money and buy things from approved catalogues. For all, there is a standard 'bang up' time on an evening: 5.30 p.m. at the latest.

TV isn't a right. It's an earned privilege and is paid for. Making phone calls is a right but can be restricted – they are recorded and there is a time limit on them. In short, anything above basic food, water, a blanket and a set of clothes a week, and two envelopes and sheets of paper is a privilege.

Like schools, things run to a timetable. Cells are unlocked for workers at 8 a.m. and at 1.45 p.m. for afternoon sessions. Each work session lasts two and a half hours. Work or education is compulsory for convicted prisoners. Refusal leads to Basic Regime. Some full-time workers can be out of their cells for roughly eight hours a day. A Basic Level prisoner will be out for just over an hour to collect food, have showers, etc.

Fights or suspicion of one will result in a lock down. So will any breach of security and some types of medical emergency. Perhaps the most concerning cause of lock downs is the consequence of using substances (drugs) including legal highs. As these are all banned, they are much more volatile than on the street. The result is more severe reactions to these substances, which include seizures, collapses, hallucinations and violent outbursts.

At least fifteen hours a day is spent locked in a small cell. Each of us has our own way of dealing with that. Newspapers are highly sought after – remember that they cost more than a standard inmate's daily prison earnings. Books are also popular, though lots of the lads need to have them read for them. Other than that it's TV if you have one, talking with cell mate if you share and tidying the cell.

### THE PRISON DEBATE

1 Make a list of all of the things wrong with prisons according to the prisoner's description above.

2 How many of these problems result from overcrowding and understaffing?

3 Discuss as a class whether life in prison today is too harsh or too soft.

4 Does the description challenge or support the view that prison is an effective way of reforming criminals? Give your reasons.

# Non-custodial alternatives

A prison sentence keeps criminals off the street and demonstrates to the prisoners and the public that the government is being tough on crime. However, there are some important drawbacks, as shown in the diagram below.

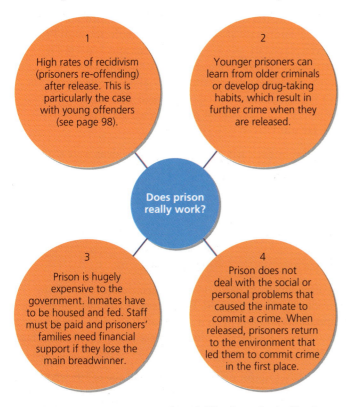

**Does prison really work?**

1. High rates of recidivism (prisoners re-offending) after release. This is particularly the case with young offenders (see page 98).

2. Younger prisoners can learn from older criminals or develop drug-taking habits, which result in further crime when they are released.

3. Prison is hugely expensive to the government. Inmates have to be housed and fed. Staff must be paid and prisoners' families need financial support if they lose the main breadwinner.

4. Prison does not deal with the social or personal problems that caused the inmate to commit a crime. When released, prisoners return to the environment that led them to commit crime in the first place.

### The Effectiveness of Non-Custodial Punishments ?

For each of the non-custodial alternatives in the timeline, explain how it might (or might not) help deal with the criticisms of prisons outlined in the diagram.

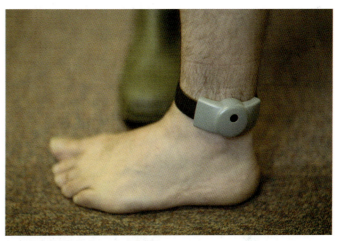

▲ An electronic tag on a released prisoner. These are fitted to the wrist or ankle, to allow a constant watch to be kept, ensuring former inmates are at home during **curfew** hours. If the prisoner breaks their curfew, the electronic tag will alert the contractors and the prisoner may be recalled to prison.

It is easy to criticise prisons, but difficult to find effective alternatives. The timeline below summarises some of the **non-custodial** alternatives different governments have tried since 1900.

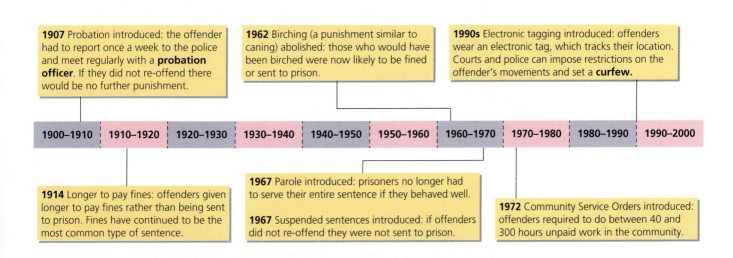

**1907** Probation introduced: the offender had to report once a week to the police and meet regularly with a **probation officer**. If they did not re-offend there would be no further punishment.

**1962** Birching (a punishment similar to caning) abolished: those who would have been birched were now likely to be fined or sent to prison.

**1990s** Electronic tagging introduced: offenders wear an electronic tag, which tracks their location. Courts and police can impose restrictions on the offender's movements and set a **curfew.**

| 1900–1910 | 1910–1920 | 1920–1930 | 1930–1940 | 1940–1950 | 1950–1960 | 1960–1970 | 1970–1980 | 1980–1990 | 1990–2000 |

**1914** Longer to pay fines: offenders given longer to pay fines rather than being sent to prison. Fines have continued to be the most common type of sentence.

**1967** Parole introduced: prisoners no longer had to serve their entire sentence if they behaved well.

**1967** Suspended sentences introduced: if offenders did not re-offend they were not sent to prison.

**1972** Community Service Orders introduced: offenders required to do between 40 and 300 hours unpaid work in the community.

# 5.6 How effectively do we deal with young offenders?

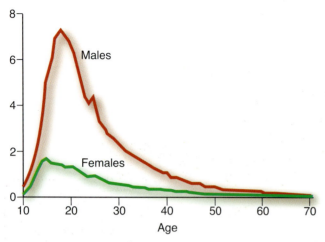

▲ Percentages of all crimes committed by males and females of different ages. The peak age for committing crime is eighteen for males and even younger for females.

## Juvenile delinquents

The Victorian attitude to 'juvenile delinquents' (young offenders) was harsh and children were treated the same as adults. In 1854, after being convicted of minor crime, Edward Andrews was sent to Birmingham Borough Prison. He was placed in solitary confinement and expected to turn a hand crank (see page 80) 10,000 times every ten hours. Andrews refused and was soaked in cold water, put in a straightjacket and fed only bread and water. After two months of this treatment Andrews hanged himself in his cell. He was fifteen years old.

However, by the early twentieth century ideas were shifting away from harsh punishments towards reform. Many believed that young people were ripe for change, as their characters were not yet fixed. With positive influences and a good environment, perhaps they could be turned away from a life of crime.

## Reform begins

The priority was to separate young offenders from hardened adult criminals. In 1902, the first **borstal** opened for offenders under eighteen years old. Borstals were run rather like strict boarding schools, with house competitions and lots of character-building sport. The usual sentence was from six months to two years. Offenders could be released after six months, but only if staff felt they were ready.

In 1932, the first Approved Schools were set up for offenders under the age of fifteen years. These were rather like borstals and offered training in skills such as bricklaying. In 1959, after rioting and large numbers of children **absconding**, there was public criticism and Approved Schools were gradually closed.

In 1948, Attendance Centres were introduced. These non-custodial centres ran compulsory daily or weekly sessions for offenders aged 10–21. These covered basic literacy and numeracy; life skills such as filling in job applications; money management and cooking. Today Attendance Centres deal with offenders aged 18–24 years and encourage an understanding of the impact of their crimes on the community. They also run drug, alcohol and sexual health awareness sessions.

## Short sharp shock!

Borstals were abolished in 1982. Around 60 per cent of those released from borstal went on to re-offend and there was also an increase in youth crime. Public opinion moved towards harsher punishments. In 1982, the Government introduced Youth Detention Centres. Military drill and discipline were intended to provide a short sharp shock. However, this tougher stance failed to deter and re-offending rates actually increased.

# The situation today

Despite changes to youth justice, re-offending rates have remained stubbornly high. Young offenders who have served custodial sentences have the highest rates of re-offending, and in recent years this has continued to rise.

Youth Courts work with agencies such as the police, school, social workers and **probation officers**. The emphasis is on preventing the young person settling into a life of crime.

Custody is seen as a last resort. Offenders under the age of eighteen can be held in a Secure Children's Home, a Secure Training Centre or a YOI. YOIs operate many of the same rules as prisons.

Attendance Centres are the young offender's last chance. If they commit further offences they are locked up in a YOI.

Sentences may start with the parents, fining them if they cannot keep their child under control. Children can be removed from their parents and placed into care.

Non-custodial methods such as tagging and curfews are used to monitor offenders' movements and courts can impose certain activities on youngsters, such as counselling.

▲ Young inmate in his cell, Portland Young Offenders Institution (YOI), England.

## HOW EFFECTIVELY ARE YOUNG OFFENDERS DEALT WITH?

1 Use the information on pages 98–99 to make your own timeline of the ways in which young offenders have been treated since 1900.

2 Add brief notes to explain the thinking (to deter or reform) behind each new development.

3 As a class, discuss how successful treatment of young offenders has been.

4 Finally, a very difficult question: What would you suggest as a more effective alternative?

# 5.7 Case study: Why is the Derek Bentley case remembered today?

In 1953, nineteen-year-old Derek Bentley was hanged for the murder of a policeman. In 1989, the singer Elvis Costello released a song about the case. The case had already inspired earlier songs and in 1991 it was made into a film called ***Let Him Have It.*** So why has the Bentley case remained in the public eye for so long?

## POSING AND ANSWERING QUESTIONS

Read the song lyrics in Source A, but nothing else yet.

1 What questions do the highlighted lyrics raise? Share these with the rest of the class, noting down any new questions.

2 What theories at this stage do you have about why the Bentley case was remembered for so long?

Now read the rest of the information on page 101.

3 Use the information to answer the questions you posed as a class in question 1. Explain the meaning of the highlighted lyrics in your book, taking care to refer to details in the Bentley case.

4 The death penalty in Britain was abolished in 1965. In what ways might public attitudes about the Bentley case have played a role?

---

**Source A** Lyrics to the 1989 song by Elvis Costello, 'Let Him Dangle'.

*Bentley said to Craig, 'Let him have it, Chris'*

*They still don't know today just what he meant by this*

*Craig fired the pistol, but was too young to swing*

*So the police took Bentley and the very next thing*

*Let him dangle, let him dangle*

*Let him dangle, let him dangle*

*Bentley had surrendered, he was under arrest*

*When he gave Chris Craig that fatal request*

*Craig shot Sidney Miles, he took Bentley's word*

*The prosecution claimed as they charged them with murder*

*Let him dangle, let him dangle*

*Let him dangle, let him dangle*

*They say Derek Bentley was easily led*

*Well what's that to the woman that Sidney Miles wed?*

*Though guilty was the verdict, and Craig had shot him dead*

*The gallows were for Bentley and still she never said*

*Let him dangle, let him dangle*

*Let him dangle, let him dangle*

*Not many people thought that Bentley would hang*

*But the word never came, the phone never rang*

*Outside Wandsworth Prison there was horror and hate*

*As the hangman shook Bentley's hand to calculate his weight*

*Let him dangle, let him dangle*

*Let him dangle, let him dangle*

# The story of Derek Bentley, 1933–1953

Derek Bentley had severe learning difficulties and suffered from epilepsy. As a result of his difficulties, Bentley found it hard to hold down even the most basic of jobs and struggled to make friends.

In November 1952, Bentley, along with his sixteen-year-old companion, Chris Craig, were caught burgling a warehouse in London. Craig, who came from a family often in trouble with the law, was carrying a gun. He gave Bentley a sheath knife and a knuckle-duster to carry.

The police arrived while Bentley and Craig were on the roof. Detective Sergeant Fairfax climbed up and managed to arrest Bentley. According to the police, DS Fairfax asked Craig to hand over the gun, at which point Bentley shouted, 'Let him have it, Chris.' Craig fired at Fairfax, injuring him in the shoulder. Bentley did not use the weapons in his pockets and made no attempt to escape.

More officers climbed onto the roof. PC Sidney Miles was immediately shot and killed. After using up the rest of his bullets, Craig jumped from the roof, fracturing his spine and breaking his wrist.

Bentley and Craig were both charged with murder. Craig was under eighteen so too young to hang, but Bentley faced the death penalty if guilty. Bentley and Craig denied Bentley ever said, 'Let him have it.' Even if he had said it, Bentley's lawyer argued, he could have meant 'hand over the gun'. There was also controversy over whether Bentley was fit to stand trial given his low intelligence.

Despite not firing the fatal shot, Bentley was found guilty and sentenced to death, although the jury asked for mercy for him. Craig was imprisoned and not released until 1963. Bentley's lawyers' appeals were turned down.

There was public outcry at the sentence. The decision now rested with the Home Secretary, Sir David Maxwell Fyfe. Two hundred MPs signed a memorandum asking him to show mercy and cancel the execution. Fyfe refused and on 28 January 1953, Bentley was hanged. Afterwards there were angry scenes outside the prison and two people were arrested for damage to property.

Bentley's parents, and later his sister, campaigned for a posthumous (after death) pardon. Finally, in 1998, the Court of Appeal ruled that the conviction for murder be set aside. The ruling also said the original trial was unfair as the judge had put pressure on the jury to convict.

There is no doubt that the public outcry over the Bentley case contributed to the argument against the death penalty. Many believed it was a miscarriage of justice. It also made the law look cruel and caused people to doubt the morality of capital punishment.

Iris Bentley, holding a photograph of her brother Derek ▶ outside her home. Iris campaigned tirelessly to clear her brother's name but sadly did not live to see the 1998 ruling.

# 5.8 Why was the death penalty abolished in 1965?

Throughout the last thousand years you have studied, the ultimate punishment was always the death penalty. Gradually, pressure to end capital punishment increased and in 1965 it was abolished. However, there were strong arguments on both sides of the debate.

## FOR

Those wanting to retain capital punishment argued:

- It had a deterrent effect and criminals would be more likely to carry weapons if there was no danger of them being hanged for murder.
- Life imprisonment was expensive and, in a way, even more cruel.
- Murderers who served a sentence and were then released might kill again.
- Execution showed the proper contempt for murder and avenged the life of the victim.

## AGAINST

Abolitionists argued:

- Other European countries had abolished capital punishment without a noticeable increase in crime.
- Mistakes were made and sometimes the wrong person was executed.
- Most murderers acted on the spur of the moment and without thinking. Therefore, capital punishment did not deter them.
- Execution was against the teachings of different religions and the Christian idea of forgiveness and the sanctity of life.

## A declining trend in executions

By the late 1700s the use of the death penalty was declining. The Government decision to abolish the Bloody Code in the 1820s and 1830s (see page 70) meant that only murder and treason were punishable by death. In 1868 public hanging was ended and after 1840 there were around fifteen executions a year – all for murder.

In 1957 the Government abolished hanging for all murders except:

- murder of a police officer or prison officer
- murder by shooting or explosion
- murder while resisting arrest
- murder while carrying out a theft
- murder of more than one person.

### THINKING ABOUT FACTORS ?

1 Using the information on pages 102–103, find evidence of how each of the factors in the table below contributed to the end of the death penalty in 1965. We have added the two factors we think were most important, but feel free to add any others you think played a role.

| Factor | Evidence of this factor in action |
|---|---|
| Institutions: Government | |
| Attitudes in society | |

2 Can you explain how some of the factors were linked?

3 Which factor played the biggest role in the abolition of the death penalty? Explain your thinking.

As result, executions in Britain fell to an average of only four a year. However, to many the law still seemed unfair – why was murder by shooting worse than strangulation or poisoning?

## The impact of the Second World War

Following the Second World War (1939–1945) and the horrors of the Holocaust, there was a growing feeling that execution was un-Christian and barbaric. The country had been engaged in a life or death struggle against the Nazis. Execution now seemed wrong, the kind of action one associated with Hitler's Germany rather than Britain. In 1948, the United Nations issued its Declaration of Human Rights, which Britain signed up to. The Declaration says, 'Everyone has the right to life, liberty and security of person.' It goes on to add, 'No one shall be subjected to torture or to cruel, inhuman or degrading treatment or punishment.'

## High-profile cases and miscarriages of justice

Two well-publicised cases helped to turn the argument in favour of abolition. The first was the case of Timothy Evans, who was hanged in March 1950. The second was the case of Derek Bentley, executed in 1953 (see pages 100–101).

## After abolition

Capital punishment was abolished in 1965 for all crimes except treason in times of war and piracy. At first this was for a trial period of five years, but in 1969 Parliament voted to abolish it permanently.

## TIMOTHY EVANS

**Timothy Evans was hanged in 1950 and posthumously pardoned in 1966.**

Evans and his wife were lodgers in the house of John Christie, at 10 Rillington Place, London. Christie was a serial killer who had already murdered several women. Evans' wife became pregnant and Christie offered to perform an abortion. He killed Evans' wife and told Evans she had died during a failed abortion. Evans felt guilty and, not thinking rationally, confessed to murder. His story was obviously untrue – he changed it several times – but he was still found guilty and hanged. Three years later, Christie was convicted of eight other murders, making it clear Evans was an innocent man.

## RUTH ELLIS

The last woman to be hanged was Ruth Ellis in 1956. Ellis was found guilty of shooting her lover David Blakely in a 'crime of passion'. It had been an abusive relationship and Blakely often beat Ellis. There was no doubt as to her guilt, but there was tremendous public sympathy for the glamorous Ellis whose photo appeared in many newspapers.

▼ **Source A** Number of murders in the UK, 1900–2010.

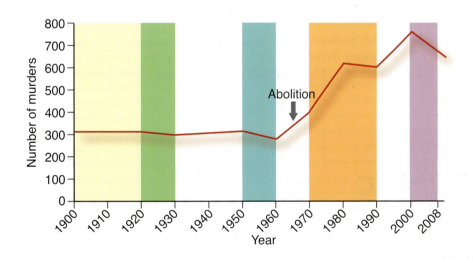

Do the figures in Source A prove that the abolition of the death penalty caused an increase in the number of murders?

# 5.9 Communicating your answer

Now you have completed your research on the period c.1900–present, it is time to answer an enquiry question.

**'Changes to attitudes in society were the main reason for changes in punishments c.1900 to the present.' How far do you agree?**

Before you answer this question you need to think about what to include. That's where the iceberg comes in. It's here to warn you that certain kinds of question may contain hidden dangers lurking beneath the surface. On a first look, this question seems to be just asking you about public attitudes. However, the question also includes the key words – **how far.** This is always a sign that there is more to the question than meets the eye and that you need to consider other factors not mentioned in the question. Remember, you can find additional advice in the Writing Better History section on page 164.

## Practice questions

1 Explain one way in which smuggling in the twentieth century was similar to smuggling in the period c.1700 to c.1900.

2 Explain why there were changes in policing methods of punishing criminals in the period c.1900 to the present day.

3 Explain why there were changes to punishments in the period c.1900 to the present day.

4 'Science and technology has had the biggest effect on policing c.1900 to the present day.' How far do you agree? Explain your answer.

5 'Miscarriages of justice were the main reason why capital punishment was abolished in 1965.' How far do you agree? Explain your answer.

Step 1. Deal with the part of the question which is 'above the surface'. Explain how attitudes in society influenced punishments. You need to think about how public attitudes helped lead to abolition of the death penalty and changes to prisons.

Step 3. Write your conclusion. Don't sit on the fence – reach a judgement. Were attitudes in society the main reason? End with a sentence explaining why you reached this decision.

Step 2. Write about the other factors lurking beneath the surface and explain the effect they had on punishments. You could include:
• Science and technology
• Institutions: Government
• Role of key individuals
• Any other factors you think relevant

## Word wall

Here are some final words you can add to the original Word wall you began on page 30. They will help you write accurately and with confidence. Look over your notes for c.1900–present and make sure that you know what all the words mean. Then add some **red words** of your own.

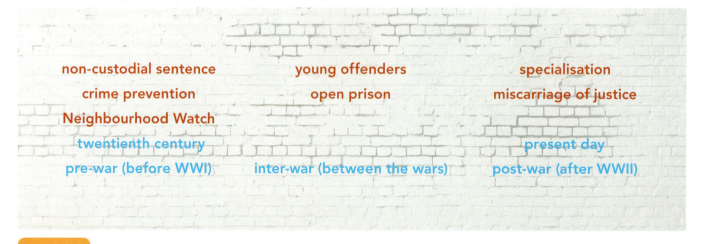

non-custodial sentence    young offenders    specialisation

crime prevention    open prison    miscarriage of justice

Neighbourhood Watch

twentienth century    present day

pre-war (before WWI)    inter-war (between the wars)    post-war (after WWII)

# 5.10 Visible learning: Revise and remember

## Technique 1: The punishment pendulum

In the last two sections you collected a lot of information about changes to prisons since the 1700s. Revision involves taking large amounts of content and slimming it down so it is easier to remember. One way is to make your revision visual. You could view the changes as a pendulum swinging from one side to the other.

**Reform**
Punishments to reform the criminal so that he or she would be less likely to offend again.

**Deterrent**
Punishments should punish criminals so harshly that they would be deterred from offending again.

### Making your own pendulums

As you already know, as governments and the public changed their minds about what prisons should be like, the pendulum for prisons has swung back and forth over the last 200 years.

1   Go back over your notes and decide how far the pendulum swung for each of the following:
    *   the old prison system up until the 1820s (see page 75)
    *   reformed prisons after 1823 (see page 76)
    *   the separate system, 1830s onwards (see page 78)
    *   the silent system, 1860s onwards (see page 80)
    *   prisons before 1947 (see page 94)
    *   prisons after 1947 (see page 95)
    *   non-custodial alternatives (see page 97).
    For each one, list some evidence in bullet point form for your decision.
2   You could use the pendulum idea to analyse other forms of punishment over time. Think about how you would draw a pendulum for each of the following periods. Make sure to add your reasons below each one:
    *   c.1000–c.1500
    *   c.1500–c.1700
    *   c.1700–c.1900
    *   c.1900–present.

## Technique 2: Repeat your memory map

At the end of Chapters 2, 3 and 4 you drew a memory map to help you record the main features of crime and punishment. Draw a similar memory map for the period c.1900 to the present. Use two different colours to show changes and continuities from earlier periods.

## Technique 3: Set your own questions and test each other

Go back over the work in your exercise book (and pages 00–00) if necessary. Write ten to fifteen knowledge-based quiz questions for a partner. Make sure that you also record the answers somewhere!

Your questions could be multiple choice, multiple select, true or false, or even require short sentences as answers. Use a mix of question types. Just by composing these questions you are already revising key content. Swap your questions with a partner. Have a go at their quiz and then mark each other's answers.

## Technique 4: One of your own

Hopefully, we have already given you a fair few ideas about revision and ways of making the information 'stick'. Go back to the Revise and remember pages at the end of earlier chapters. Choose another method listed there and adapt it to help you remember what you covered in this section. You might want to play one of the games, make hexagons or write the 'big story' c.1900 to the present – it's up to you this time!

**Crime and punishment in Britain: Revisiting the big stories**

# How has the nature of criminal activity changed through history?

## THE BIG IDEAS

- There has been great continuity in the types of crime across all periods. Petty crime has remained the main type of offence committed.

- As a proportion of the total crimes committed, violent offences have decreased over time.

- The fear of crime has often been greater than the actual amount of crime has justified.

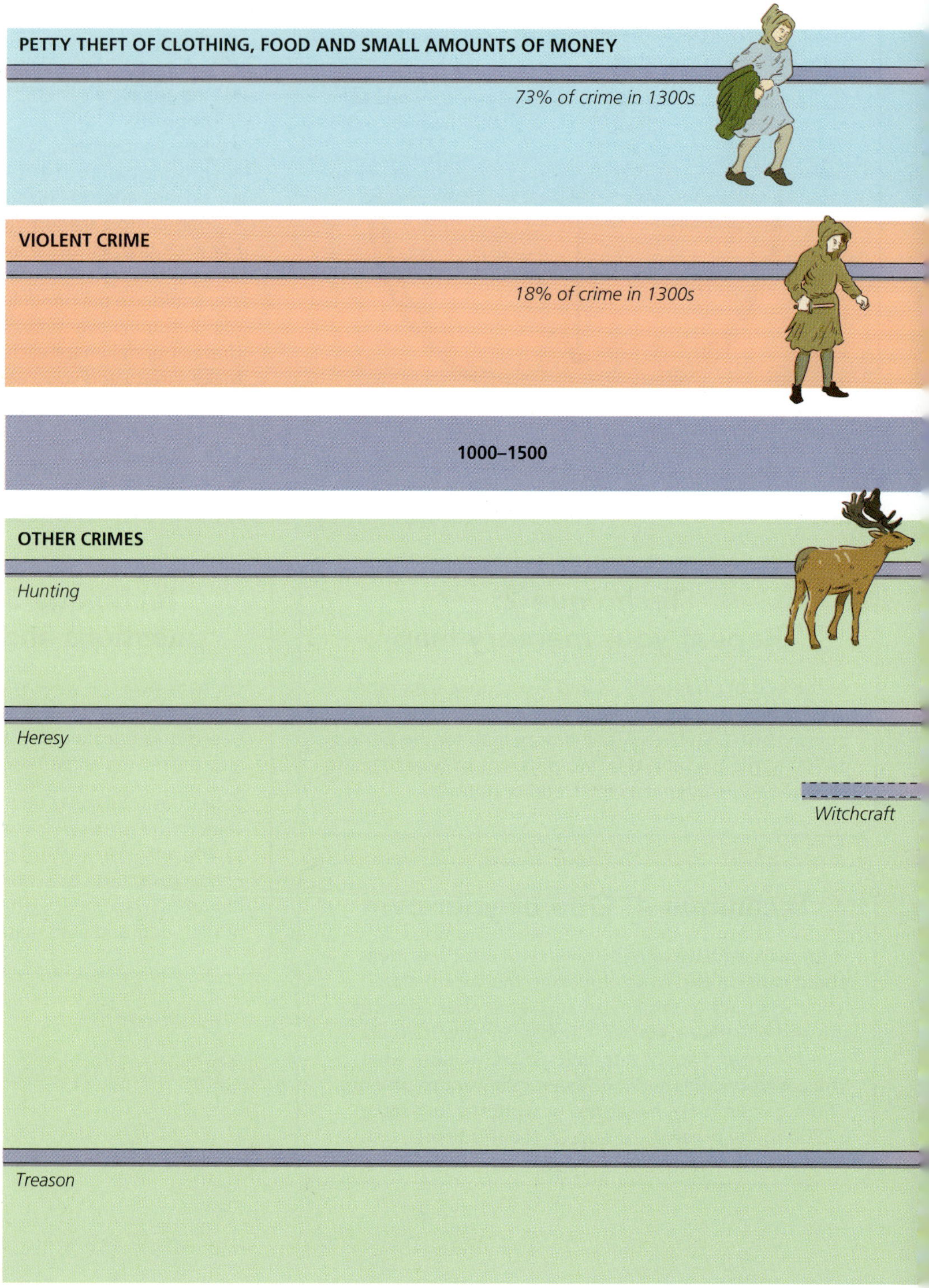

**PETTY THEFT OF CLOTHING, FOOD AND SMALL AMOUNTS OF MONEY**

*73% of crime in 1300s*

**VIOLENT CRIME**

*18% of crime in 1300s*

**1000–1500**

**OTHER CRIMES**

*Hunting*

*Heresy*

*Witchcraft*

*Treason*

These two pages sum up the main types of crime that have been committed across the centuries. Above the timeline are the crimes that have always been committed. The crimes below the timeline are those that have been more common or taken more seriously at different times. Many of these only became crimes because of changing attitudes or new laws made by governments at the time. The dotted lines on the timeline indicate cases where the crime existed but was not regarded as a clear and present threat by the government or local community.

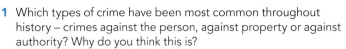

## THE BIG PICTURE OF CRIME

1 Which types of crime have been most common throughout history – crimes against the person, against property or against authority? Why do you think this is?

2 Has the proportion of violent crime increased, fallen or remained the same? Why do you think this is?

3 Which crimes were not committed in earlier centuries but have become common today?

4 a) Which factors do you think help explain increases in crime?
   b) Explain why these factors have made crime more common.

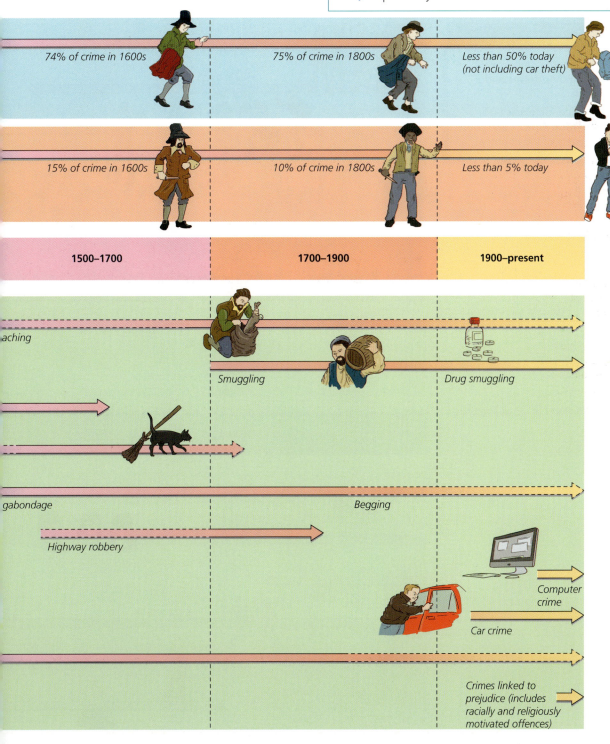

74% of crime in 1600s

75% of crime in 1800s

Less than 50% today (not including car theft)

15% of crime in 1600s

10% of crime in 1800s

Less than 5% today

| 1500–1700 | 1700–1900 | 1900–present |

...aching

Smuggling

Drug smuggling

...gabondage

Begging

Highway robbery

Computer crime

Car crime

Crimes linked to prejudice (includes racially and religiously motivated offences)

# How has the nature of law enforcement changed through history?

For hundreds of years it was the responsibility of individuals and the local community to catch criminals and bring them to justice. However, as society has become more complex, the role of catching criminals, investigating their crimes and bringing them to trial has been taken over by the police. The top part of this timeline outlines the methods that have been used to catch criminals and bring them to court. The lower part outlines the different methods that have been used for trials. The dotted lines on the timeline indicate where the method was in existence but was not a major part of law enforcement.

## THE BIG IDEAS

- For centuries local communities were expected to police themselves and catch any criminals.
- A professional police force was first established in London in 1829 and soon spread to other parts of the country.

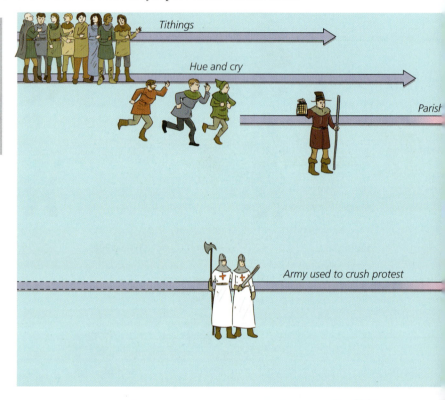

Tithings

Hue and cry

Parish

Army used to crush protest

1000–1500

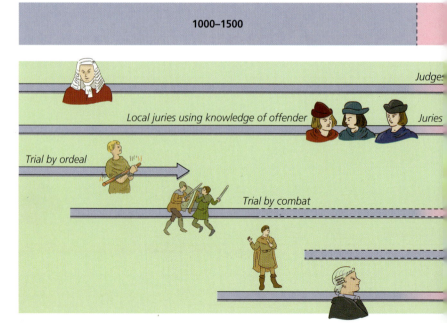

Judges

Local juries using knowledge of offender — Juries

Trial by ordeal

Trial by combat

## THE BIG PICTURE OF LAW ENFORCEMENT

1 Who was responsible for catching criminals and collecting evidence in:
   a) Anglo-Saxon England
   b) the later Middle Ages
   c) Tudor and Stuart England?

2 When did the government rather than local communities first take a serious role in policing?

3 What reasons explain why this change occurred?

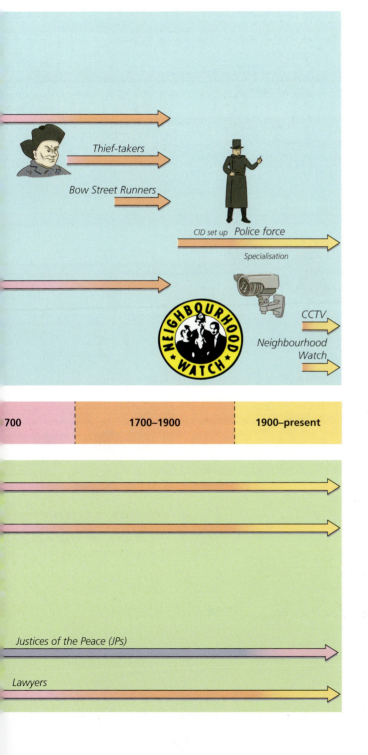

# How has the nature of punishment changed through history?

These pages outline the changes and continuities in punishment through history. Above the timeline shows the thinking behind the different types of punishment. Below the timeline shows the various methods used.

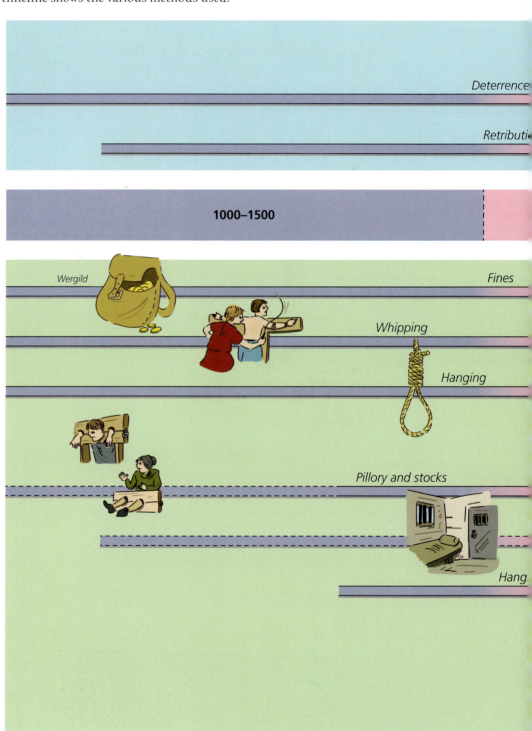

Deterrence

Retributi

1000–1500

Wergild

Fines

Whipping

Hanging

Pillory and stocks

Hang

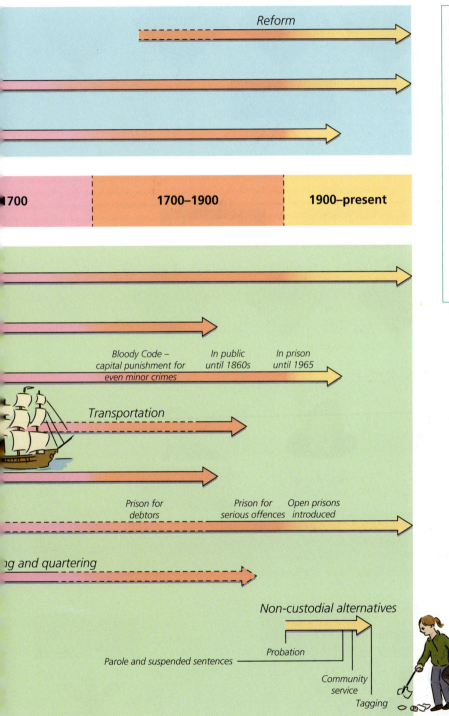

Reform

**700** | **1700–1900** | **1900–present**

Bloody Code – capital punishment for even minor crimes

In public until 1860s

In prison until 1965

Transportation

Prison for debtors

Prison for serious offences

Open prisons introduced

ng and quartering

Non-custodial alternatives

Parole and suspended sentences

Probation

Community service

Tagging

## THE BIG PICTURE OF PUNISHMENTS

1 Which methods of punishment were used for the longest time?

2 Choose one punishment that is no longer used today. Explain why it is no longer used.

3 When was the period of greatest change in punishments?

4 Find examples of punishments that were intended to:
   a) deter
   b) provide retribution (revenge)
   c) reform.

5 How have ideas about the purposes of punishments:
   a) changed
   b) stayed the same?

# Factors for change

Way back in Chapter 1 we introduced you to the different factors affecting crime and punishment.

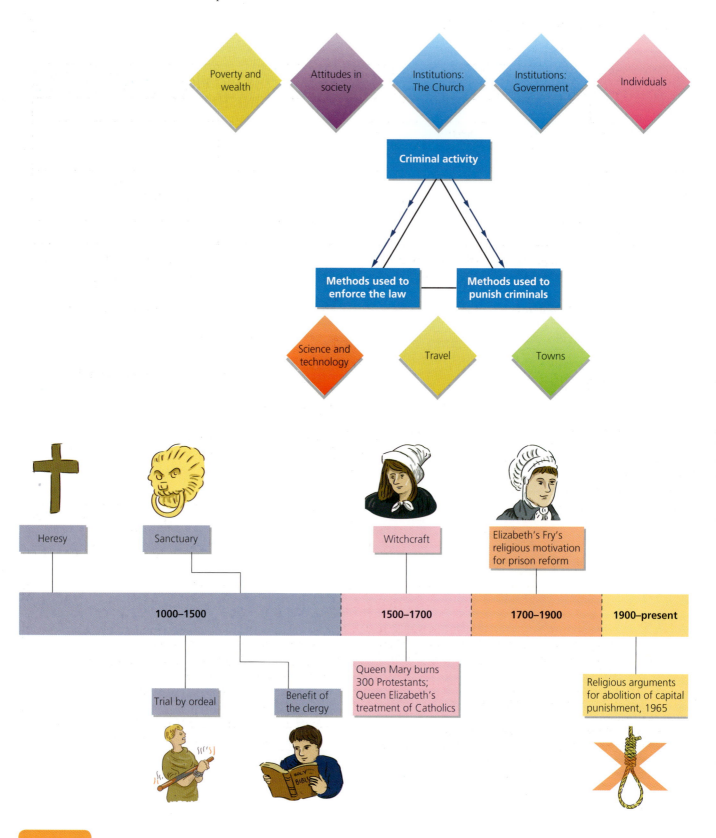

By now it must be obvious that a number of these have kept cropping up again and again. Quite simply, the factors are what made things happen! By focusing on them you will better understand the reasons behind the changes and continuities outlined on pages 7–9. So let's start by looking at one factor as an example – Institutions: The Church.

## FACTORS AND THE BIG PICTURE

**1** Make your own large copy of the table below.

| Institutions: The Church | Effects on amount of crime/ definitions of criminal activity | Effects on law enforcement (policing and trials) | Effects on punishment |
|---|---|---|---|
| 1000–1500 | | | |
| 1500–1700 | Tudor religious changes meant having wrong beliefs could lead to persecution. | | |
| 1700–1900 | | | Elizabeth Fry campaigned for better conditions for women prisoners. |
| 1900–present | | | |

**2** Use the timeline on page 112 to fill in the chart for this factor. We have started this for you, but you will need to add more.

**3** Go back over your notes, using this book if needed, and look for examples of how the other factors have affected crime and punishment. Make a new table for each one. You could do this in small groups, each looking at a different factor, before feeding back as a whole class. Don't worry if there are some blank spaces in your table – this shows that not all factors were important at different times.

# Tom's big picture

Remember Tom the 'tea-leaf'? Well, he's back and he needs your help for the last time. Now that you are an expert in the history of crime and punishment you must help him answer the question he first posed back on page 4: When was the riskiest time to be a criminal?

**Tom the 'tea-leaf'.** ▶

## RISKY BUSINESS?

**1** Use your notes, your own knowledge and this book (where necessary) to plot your own graph showing the risk facing Tom. Remember that 'tea-leaf' is rhyming slang for thief. You should think about:
   **a)** the chances of being caught
   - What policing methods were used?
   - How effective were these?
   **b)** the punishments that Tom would have faced if convicted
   - What was the idea of punishment in each period?
   - How severe were punishments at this time?

Annotate each point with a few sentences of explanation before joining them up with a ruler.

**2** Tom was guilty of theft, a crime against property. How might the graph look different if Tom had been someone who took part in protests or rebellions? When was the riskiest time to commit such crimes?

**3** Would the graph look any different if Tom was a violent murderer – guilty of crimes against the person?

# PART 2: The historic environment: Whitechapel, c.1870–c.1900: Crime, policing and the inner city

## What is this historic environment unit about?

This unit counts for 10 per cent of your GCSE course. It is linked to the Thematic Study on Crime and Punishment in Britain in two ways:

1 You will use your knowledge of crime and punishment in the late nineteenth century in this unit.
2 The enquiry approach you used to study 'Crime and Punishment in Britain' will help considerably because this unit is designed to develop your skills in historical enquiry – from asking questions to communicating your answer. We spent a lot of time on enquiry in 'Crime and Punishment in Britain' to prepare you for this historic environment unit.

There are also three major differences from your work on the Thematic Study on Crime and Punishment:

1 This unit focuses on a single place, a historic site – Whitechapel.
2 It focuses on a short period, the years c.1870–c.1900.
3 It looks much more closely at contemporary sources and how we use them in an enquiry.

This book does not provide all the material you will use for this study. This is deliberate! We have given you the structure for your enquiry and plenty of information and sources, but your teacher will add more sources, perhaps relating to crimes, criminals, victims or policemen, which we have not mentioned in this book.

### Enquiry

Describe in your own words the enquiry process you use to investigate a new historical topic.

# 1.1 Whitechapel: murderers and bad mothers

When we hear the words 'Victorian Whitechapel' we might immediately think of 'Jack the Ripper', the notorious serial killer. This section of the book will look at the Ripper, but it is important to remember that this was just one case among many. We need to think more widely about the types of crime and criminals in Whitechapel.

There were other murders in Whitechapel during our period. Before 1888 the most well-known was the death of Harriet Lane, at the hands of her lover – Mr Henry Wainwright. Wainwright was a fairly successful salesman, and his affair with Harriet was a serious one. He put her and their children up in a flat and paid them a generous allowance. When his business failed he could no longer keep Harriet fed and housed, and she began to call on him at work and to make embarrassing scenes.

Wainwright decided to get rid of her, for good. He asked his brother to write pretend love letters to Lane, under the false name of 'Edward Frieake', so that Wainwright could claim that Lane had run away. He then murdered her, and buried her under the floor of a warehouse in a pit filled with chloride of lime, a bleach which he hoped would destroy the body.

A year later the warehouse was put up for sale because the owner needed the money. Wainwright decided to move the body, so it would not be discovered. However, when he dug up the remains he found that instead of being dissolved by the chloride of lime, the chemical had preserved Lane's body. Wainwright then decided to chop Lane's remains into pieces and put these into sacks. In an inexplicable  decision he also got one of his workers to help transfer the sacks to a waiting cab in the street. This worker, Arthur Stokes, opened one of the sacks to find Harriet Lane's half-decomposed head!

Stokes sent Wainwright and his sacks off in the cab but followed on foot, and shouted for help to the first policeman that he saw. The police stopped the cab, and then opened the sacks to discover Wainwright's ex-lover's remains. Wainwright was arrested, and eventually tried for murder. The sentence of execution by hanging was carried out at the end of 1875. Wainwright's case was big news – as can be seen by the cover of the *Illustrated Police News*.

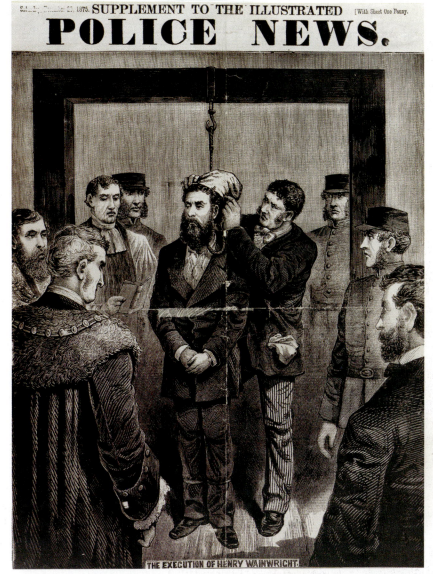

SUPPLEMENT TO THE ILLUSTRATED POLICE NEWS.

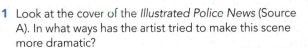

THE EXECUTION OF HENRY WAINWRIGHT.

**Source A** The front cover of a special supplement to the *Illustrated Police News*, 21 December 1875, showing the execution of Henry Wainwright.

## MURDER IN THE MEDIA ?

1 Look at the cover of the *Illustrated Police News* (Source A). In what ways has the artist tried to make this scene more dramatic?

2 What does this tell us about how important Wainwright's crime was?

3 Does this tell us anything about how often murders like this took place?

Gory stories are exciting, but by focusing on stories like these we could be missing learning about other interesting lives, and we might also be distorting our ideas of what crime was like in Whitechapel in our period. The records of the Old Bailey criminal courthouse are available online, and they contain stories just like Henry Wainwright's, but they also let us look at the big picture, at patterns of criminal activity. Using the special search on the Old Bailey website we can find out how many crimes mention the keyword 'Whitechapel' for our period (614) and what different categories these crimes might fit into (see the table below).

▼ Categories of crime

| Theft | 209 |
| --- | --- |
| Violent theft | 132 |
| Deception | 109 |
| Royal offences | 50 |
| Breaking the peace | 48 |
| Killing | 38 |
| Miscellaneous | 16 |
| Damage to property | 11 |
| Sexual offences | 9 |

## CRIMES

### Deception

Dishonestly getting money, property or other benefit.

### Royal offences

Crimes against Royal rights or the country e.g. tax evasion, forging currency, treason and some religious crimes.

### Breaking the peace

Assault, riot, threatening behaviour. Only the most serious examples of these went to trial at the Old Bailey.

## The case of Sarah Fisher's baby

This table tells us that we can easily stereotype crimes and criminals in Whitechapel if we only focus on the high-profile crimes like murder. The Old Bailey records also tell us about lots of different types of crime. A really good example of a very different case is that of Sarah Fisher in 1873.

Fisher was convicted of 'unlawfully exposing' her young child, Lucy. On a frosty night in November 1873, Fisher was begging; her husband was at home unable to work because of injuries to his legs. Her thin and barely clothed 'baby', though really she was eighteen months old, was used to get sympathy and money from passers-by. A solicitor called Sidney Chidley noticed Sarah and the condition of her daughter and found a policeman. Fisher was arrested, and Lucy taken to the Westminster Workhouse. Sadly, Lucy died shortly afterwards, probably from tuberculosis. Sarah Fisher was found guilty of 'exposing' Lucy, and at her trial she pleaded, 'I am very sorry that I was begging. I have lost my baby now.'

### ASKING QUESTIONS ❓

One of the skills you practised in the thematic study on Crime and Punishment in Britain was asking good historical questions. Asking questions is an important part of this unit because it plays a part in your GCSE examination. So we'll pause here and ask you to ask some questions!

1 Make a list of questions we could ask about crime and policing in Whitechapel between 1870 and 1900. These questions could be about famous cases like those of Henry Wainwright or Jack the Ripper. They could also be about the smaller cases like Sarah Fisher's or about crime in Whitechapel in general. Use the question starters below to help.

> When …? What …? Why …? How …? What happened …? Where …?
> What effects …? How significant …? Did it really …? Who …? Did they …?

2 When you have completed your list, divide it into 'big' and 'little' questions. (Look back to page 13 to remind yourself of the differences between them.)

# Asking questions, identifying sources

This page shows you *some* of the questions you could ask about crime in Whitechapel between 1870 and 1900, together with some of the sources you might use to answer those questions. Both questions and sources are here because one aim of this unit is to work out which sources may be most helpful for answering individual questions. You know by now that sources are not 'useful' or 'useless' in themselves – their usefulness depends on which question you are trying to answer. For example, one source may be very useful for learning about the techniques used to try to capture Jack the Ripper, but completely unhelpful if you want to find out about what kinds of punishment people received when they were convicted of theft.

## QUESTIONS AND SOURCES ?

Choose two of the questions below or from your list of questions from the asking questions activity on page 116. Which of the sources below do you think would be most useful for answering each of your two questions? Explain why you think each source might be useful.

We do not expect you to know the 'right' answers at this stage. This task is to get you thinking about what kinds of information *might* be in the sources and which questions they *may* help with. In the rest of this unit you will get to know most of these sources and find out which questions they are most useful for answering.

## Some questions

What kinds of men joined the police force?

Why was Whitechapel a place where lots of crime occurred?

What work did the police do in Whitechapel?

What kinds of trial did criminals have?

Who were the suspects in the Jack the Ripper case?

Who were the Ripper's victims?

Were there many cases of cruelty or neglect of children, like Sarah Fisher's?

What were the injuries to Harriet Lane?

## Sources

| | | | |
|---|---|---|---|
| Records of charities involved in housing | Charles Booth's survey of poverty | Coroners' reports | Reports from London newspapers |
| Old Bailey records of trials | Political cartoons | National newspapers | Local police records |

# Organising your understanding of the sources

Why did we set up the activities on questions and sources? It is because this unit is about how we undertake a historical enquiry and about the kinds of sources we use, as well as being about crime and punishment in Whitechapel at this time. Therefore you are going to use a variety of sources and learn different things from them. The first is the most obvious – the sources will:

- increase your knowledge and understanding of crime in Whitechapel, and the work of the police between 1870 and 1900.

However, other things you learn about the sources are just as important and will be tested in your examination. You will find out:

- the kinds of sources that help us investigate crime in Whitechapel at this time
- which sources are most useful for investigating individual aspects of crime and for answering particular questions.

To keep track of the sources and what you can learn from them, we suggest you use a Knowledge Organiser such as the table below. You could perhaps make a copy of it on A3 paper or in a Word document. You may wish to keep additional, detailed notes to support the summary in your table. Completing the table is an important reminder that this unit is about enquiry and sources, as well as about crime in Whitechapel during this period.

Here is a guide to completing your table over the next few weeks:

1 After you have worked on a section of this unit, identify which sources you have used and fill in a row of this table for each source. Decide which of the categories (see below) the source fits into, for example a personal account, photograph, etc. The text will remind you to do this.

2 Put the category in column 1 and the example such as a photograph of an operation taking place) in column 2.

3 Then complete columns 3–6 for the source.

You may use sources that fit more than one category of source, or you may use other kinds of sources. Don't worry if sources do not fit neatly into categories – historical research is unpredictable and you often find things that you don't expect. That's why it's enjoyable!

It is also important to remember that one source will not tell you everything you want to know. Always try to use a combination of sources. This is because they may each add different information because they were created by different people, at different times, or because they are different types of source – a photograph and a diary perhaps. Using a variety of sources also allows you to check what each is saying as you always need to ask whether the evidence in a source is typical of the evidence as a whole.

## National records

- National newspapers
- Records of crimes
- Police investigations
- Old bailey records of trials
- Cartoons from newspapers and journals.

## Local records

- Housing and employment records, council records and census returns
- Charles Booth's survey and workhouse records
- Local police records, coroners' reports, photographs and London newspapers

| Types of sources<br>N – National<br>L – Local | Examples of this type of source you have used | Which questions can this source help answer? | What information does it provide to help with those questions? | Which questions does this source NOT help with, or why do we have to use it cautiously? | Which other kind of source might you use in combination with this source? |
|---|---|---|---|---|---|
| | | | | | |

## Exploring Sarah Fisher's court record

The reason that we can describe the gruesome discovery of the body in Henry Wainwright's warehouse, and the sad case of Sarah Fisher's dying baby, is that the details of their cases were carefully recorded when they appeared before the judge and jury at the Old Bailey. This was London's most important criminal court between 1673 and 1913.

The Old Bailey's records have been digitised and put online, so that everyone can access them. There is a search tool which means you can home in on particular types of case at particular times. The printed record is also available as a scan – so that you can check the words of the digitised copy.

▲ A photograph of the Old Bailey court taken in 1897. The 'dock' where the accused would have stood is on the left hand side, while the judge's desk is on the right. The seats where the jury would sit are at the back of the photograph.

I'd like to know more about Sarah Fisher, so I think we should study her case report in detail. When you have read through it, see if you can answer some of the questions below. These are supposed to get you started in understanding her case report. You may not be able to work out all the answers straight away, but the report will give you some ideas as to what to study next.

Exposing in this case means taking the baby outside without enough clothes on in the cold weather.

The Workhouse (one of which was the Westminster Union) was the place where very poor Victorians could get food, lodgings and medicine but, as we will see, many refused to go there.

These are the details of the witness against Sarah Fisher.

This is Constable Smith's number. C means the division (Westminster) that he works in. The Whitechapel police were in H division.

The defence part of the record is where the defendant gets to tell their side of the story.

Giving the prisoner in charge means reporting a crime to a policeman.

Tubercular matter means evidence of tuberculosis, a disease which starts in the lungs, and can be deadly. It makes people thin, and used to be called consumption because it seemed to eat away at its victims.

## SARAH FISHER, Miscellaneous > other, 15th December 1873

78. SARAH FISHER (36), Unlawfully exposing Lucy Fisher, a child under the age of two years, whereby its health was permanently injured.

SIDNEY CHIDLEY. I am a solicitor. On 13th November I was in a restaurant in Maddox Street. The prisoner came in with a baby in her arms, and showed it to two females, one of whom exclaimed "Good God! the child is dead!" I looked at it, and thought it was dead, but it moved its arms it looked like a living skeleton. We gave her some money, and I said "You ought not to have that child out; you should take it at once to the workhouse". I watched her from public-house to public-house, stopping everyone she came to. It was a cold, frosty night, and a keen wind. I thought the child would not live the night through, and gave the prisoner in charge for begging, in order that the child might get sufficient food and care.

*Prisoner.* I did not expose the baby; they wished to see it to satisfy themselves that it was alive.

*Witness.* It was not at the request of other people that she showed the baby. She did not ask for money, but she undid the child, and anybody with a farthing in their pockets, must have given her something.

RICHARD SMITH (*Policeman C* 16). On 13th November, the prisoner was given into my custody the child was placed in the cell with her at the station it was comfortably cared for, with wrappers, and had warm milk. I took it to the workhouse next morning and gave it to Dunston. The prisoner gave me an address in Whitechapel, at Sarah King's lodging house. I went there and saw the husband. […]

JOSEPH ROGERS. I am medical officer of the Westminster Union. On 14th November, a female child was brought to me. I ordered it some medicine, a milk diet, and some wine. It only weighed 9lbs. 10oz. where as a child of that age ought to weigh 24lbs. or more. I directed that it should not be brought to me across the yard, but that I would go to it, which I did at some inconvenience. After its death I had it weighed again, and it only weighed 7lbs. 10 11. 2oz. I had given it eggs, brandy, and everything possible, but I was satisfied that it would die when I first saw it. I found no marks of injury, only extreme emaciation. The heart was healthy, in the chest there were old adhesions of the lungs, and the pleura [part of the lungs] and ribs, which had been in existence seven or eight months; I also found deposition of tubercular matter in both lungs. […] It was most improper to take such a child out on a cold, November evening, and to keep it out for several hours, its life was in danger. […]

*Prisoner's Defence.* I am very sorry that I was begging; I have lost my baby now.

GUILTY. *The prisoner's husband stated that he was very poor, and had suffered for years with a bad leg, and was only able to get an uncertain living by penmanship. He was ordered to enter into recognizances for the prisoner's appearance to come up and receive judgment if called upon.*

After the judgment of GUILTY, the court records the judge's decision on sentence. Here Sarah's husband has to guarantee that he will bring her back to court if they decide later to punish her. Really this means that she is being released, with the warning not to commit a crime again.

## SARAH FISHER'S LOST BABY ?

1 What clues are there that Maddox Street was a wealthy place?

2 What was Sidney Chidley's attitude to Sarah Fisher?

3 What do you think drew Sarah Fisher to Maddox Street?

4 How long had the Fishers been living at Sarah King's lodging house?

5 Are there any clues as to why Sarah Fisher needed to beg for money?

6 What seems to be the attitude of the Union medical officer to baby Fisher?

7 What was the baby's name?

8 Did the baby die of hunger or of something else? What does this tell you about her life before 13 November 1873?

There's lots of interesting detail in the report, and some clues as to what to explore next. The first thing to notice is that this crime didn't take place in Whitechapel, but the defendant lived there. Fisher was arrested in Maddox Street, in the West End, a much wealthier part of London. Fisher lived in Sarah King's **lodging house** in Whitechapel, but we are not told where that is. As we will find out, a lodging house was a place where people would pay rent to stay in a room, often sharing with many other people. There were many of these lodging or 'doss' houses in Whitechapel in our period.

## Census frustrations

I used the Census records to try to find out more about King and Fisher. We are given an age for Sarah Fisher, and an approximate age for each of her children. I can use these to try to narrow down the search.

Of the Sarah Fishers living in or near Whitechapel at the time some are older and some younger than the age given for Sarah in the case report. There is one of exactly the right age, but she was living with her mother and father, with no children in 1871. The court case suggests she should have had a child of at least one year old. The closest I can get is a Sarah Fisher living in St Pancras, a good distance north of Whitechapel. She had a son, not one year old at that date. This could be the baby that died in 1873. Frustratingly, I have to admit that I'll never know – there just isn't enough information for me to say that this is our Sarah Fisher. It's a similar story for a search for the landlady, Sarah King. The only person for whom I can find any other record of is poor Lucy. Her death in Westminster is recorded in the register of deaths for that year.

This doesn't mean that the Census will never give me useful information – it just means that I need quite a lot to start with before I can sometimes get more from a Census search. Often, when dealing with the names given to criminal courts, I find that searching the Census is not successful in finding more information. I suspect that this is because many people gave false names to the police and the courts – especially if they didn't want the court to find out about past crimes they had committed, as this would lead to a harsher sentence.

### THE CENSUS

The Census only takes place every ten years. Sarah may have moved regularly each year, let alone in a decade. As we're learning, this kind of community was very mobile so could easily be missing from the Census or living in a different area on the night the Census was taken. It can even be hard to track more stable families, partly because of simple mistakes by the enumerators (the people who wrote out the records). Census records are far from 100 per cent accurate.

The census has told me some useful things. While looking through the Census at all the Sarah Fishers and the Sarah Kings I discovered several things about Whitechapel in this period. One Sarah King lived at 6 Baker's Row in Whitechapel, but so did sixteen other people. On this street there were other houses where families with a married couple, a son or daughter and even a servant lived. This suggests that Whitechapel was a place where the very poor crowded together, but that within a stone's throw we might also find a relatively wealthy middle-class family.

# Visible learning: Planning my enquiry

This is me! I'm the person who's writing this part of the book and planning this investigation. The key word in this situation is to PLAN! I know a little. I want to know a lot – but just starting to read could leave me with a jumble of information. I have been studying history for many years so I know how to work my way through a new topic. This page shows you my plan for my enquiry.

I know a little about some of the types of crime and the types of defendant from Whitechapel that appeared before the Old Bailey, but I have a lot of questions. How do I plan my way from knowing a little and having lots of questions to finding the answers and knowing a lot more?

## Stage 1 What do I know?

This is a summary of my main starting points:

- Between 1870 and 1900 Whitechapel was a place where some people were very poor.
- Poverty made people ill, and made some take desperate measures.
- There was a police force, and it was split into divisions.
- There were high-profile crimes such as those of Jack the Ripper and Henry Wainwright, as well as more ordinary crimes.
- Most crimes were not violent, but were property crimes like theft.

## Stage 2 What do I want to find out?

I need a set of questions as targets when I do my research so I know when I've completed my enquiry:

- Why were some people in Whitechapel living in poverty?
- What different kinds of people lived in Whitechapel?
- What effects did poverty have on people, and on crime?
- What types of crime were committed?
- How did the police do their work?
- Were the police successful?
- Why did the police fail to catch Jack the Ripper?

## Stage 3 Where will I research and find the answers?

There are two kinds of sources I can use.

1 Books, articles and websites written by experts on crime and punishment in Whitechapel at this time.
2 Sources from the time – photographs, accounts written by citizens and government officials, reports from newspapers, court records.

## Visible learning

### Tackling new topics with confidence

I use this plan to help me explore any historical topic that is new to me. Starting to investigate a new topic can feel worrying, like starting completely from scratch, because dates, names and events are different BUT it's important to remember HOW we study every topic is very similar. We use this same plan whether we're exploring Roman history or Crime in Victorian Whitechapel. We have shown you this approach very visibly so you feel more confident whenever you start to tackle a new topic.

**Letting you into a secret**

I have been writing history books as part of my job for more than 10 years. You might think I must know everything there is to know about history but that's not true. The 'secret' is that there are quite a few historical topics I don't know in great detail, because I have never had to study them in detail, or write about them. Though I know quite a lot about the Victorian period, I am not an expert in every aspect of what happened in Whitechapel at this time. I therefore need to find out a lot more about the period, and about Whitechapel in order to start to find the answers for my questions about crime and policing, and about the lives of people like Sarah Fisher.

*Stage 4 How will I do this research?*

I need to:

- Have my questions in mind so I always read with a purpose – to answer those questions.
- Keep careful notes, using my own Knowledge Organisers, so that I don't end up with a heap of disorganised information.
- Make sure the books I read and websites I use are really by experts. This means checking who wrote them and how they know what they're telling me.
- Ask questions about the sources I use. For example: Is a photograph typical of conditions in London at that time? Was the author present at the events he or she was describing? Which are the most useful sources for each question?

- Remember that I may not be able to find exact and complete answers to all my questions so I need to use words such as 'probably', 'in all likelihood', 'possibly' and others we've seen on the Word Walls on pages 30 and 104.
- There may be questions I can't answer at all! And I need to keep thinking! I might find unexpected information which prompts new questions or suggests I look in other books or records. I can't predict exactly what I'll find at the beginning of an enquiry. I need to remember that I'm allowed to change my mind about my answer to a question as I find out more.

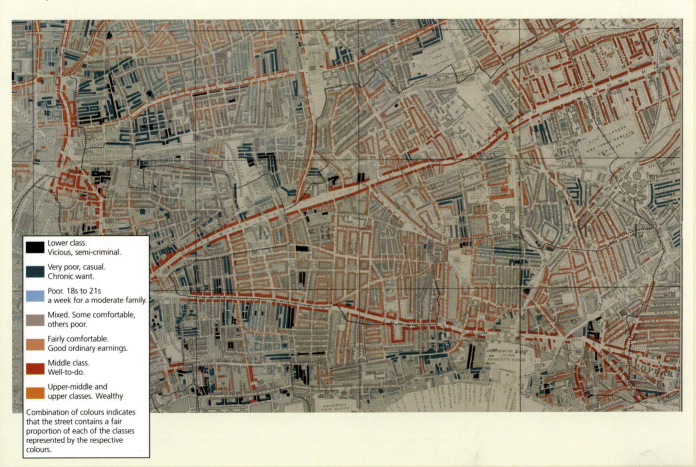

Lower class.
Vicious, semi-criminal.

Very poor, casual.
Chronic want.

Poor. 18s to 21s
a week for a moderate family.

Mixed. Some comfortable,
others poor.

Fairly comfortable.
Good ordinary earnings.

Middle class.
Well-to-do.

Upper-middle and
upper classes. Wealthy

Combination of colours indicates
that the street contains a fair
proportion of each of the classes
represented by the respective
colours.

# 1.2 What was Whitechapel like?

Whitechapel is an area of London's East End, just outside the City of London. In our period it was an inner-city area of poverty – a place where lots of different types of people lived, many of whom were very poor. Some parts were known as '**rookeries**' – an area filled with lodging houses in which some of London's poorest people lived in terribly overcrowded conditions. They spent only one or two nights in a place, each day trying to earn enough money to eat and for the 4d it would cost for their next night's 'doss'. Other parts of Whitechapel were more respectable and during our period, as you will see, parts of the area changed for the better, or for the worse. The work of the police and the crimes that took place in Whitechapel will be covered in more detail later on, so this section focuses on living conditions.

## Three key places in Whitechapel

You are going to get an overview of Whitechapel by looking at three key places. You'll hear about these places again as the unit goes on, but let's explore them a bit first. As you're reading you should record what you find out in a Knowledge Organiser like this one:

| Place | What does this place tell us about housing and overcrowding in Whitechapel? | Does this place give us any clues as to the causes of crime in Whitechapel? | What questions does this place make us ask? |
|---|---|---|---|
| Flower and Dean Street | | | |
| Whitechapel Workhouse and Casual Ward | | | |
| The Peabody Estate | | | |

## THE TEN BELLS PUB

This pub was just north of Flower and Dean Street, on the corner of Fournier Street and Commercial Road. Obviously this was a place where people drank, and as we will see, drink made people more likely to commit crimes and to be victims of crime. Mary Kelly, the last of Jack the Ripper's victims, drank at the Ten Bells on the evening that she was killed. Pubs like the Ten Bells were stop-off points for prostitutes looking for clients, and for thieves and robbers looking for people to steal from.

However, pubs were also places to get warm and to eat a meal, which would have been very welcome for those who were living in doss houses or crowded apartments.

## THE EVIDENCE OF CHARLES BOOTH

**Charles Booth, 1840–1916**

Booth was a successful businessman, who became interested in poverty. He tried to find out the extent of poverty using Census records but, like us, he found quite soon that these records could not answer all his questions, and were sometimes inaccurate. He decided to investigate by setting up what today we might call a **sociological research** project. He employed 80 researchers to explore poverty, living conditions and religious faith across the capital, and used very innovative ways to get at the information that he needed. His team of researchers talked to School Board Visitors, who were employed by local authorities to visit children in the years before they reach the age for school. Booth also asked his researchers to interview many of London's policemen during their 'beats' – their patrols – to find out their views of the areas they were walking through. Booth produced a series of maps which tried to show how poor each area was. There are some extracts from Booth's maps on the following pages.

# Flower and Dean Street

In 1870 Flower and Dean Street was a well-known rookery. The historian Jerry White used the 1871 Census to work out that there were 902 lodgers staying in 31 of the 'doss houses' on this street alone. Some of these houses dated back to late 1600 and they were in a terrible condition. Their yards had been built over to provide more rooms and at the front the street was narrow – only 16 feet at its widest part in the middle. There were outside toilets, but buckets and pots were used indoors, and often spilled. Some lodgings were more settled, but families moved on after a few days or weeks, perhaps because they couldn't afford the rent, or because they moved to find other work. Because of the worst doss houses, Flower and Dean Street had a terrible reputation as a haunt of thieves, drunkards and prostitutes. As you can see, Booth coloured this street in black in 1889, which meant that he saw it as a 'vicious, semi-criminal' area. If we look closely at the map though, it looks like there were middle-class, 'well-to-do' families very nearby. This pattern was repeated across Whitechapel, with very poor and much more comfortably off people living near each other. Overall, however, according to the Medical Officer of Health for Whitechapel's report in 1873, Whitechapel was very densely populated, with 188.6 people living in each acre (about 0.001 square miles), an average 25.6 square foot per person. For London as a whole the figure was 45 people per acre.

## QUESTIONS ON SOURCE B

1 Look again at the different colours. What do they tell us about the spread of different classes of people across Whitechapel?

2 How far away from the better off areas were the poorer people living?

> **Source A** From the Board of Works, Whitechapel district, report on the sanitary condition of the Whitechapel district, for the quarter ended 3 April, 1880.
>
> *I have to state that I have made an inspection of all the private houses, or houses let in apartments, in the undermentioned streets, namely—Flower and Dean Street, Upper Keate Street, and Lower Keate Street. The houses, 38 in number, contain 143 rooms, and are occupied by 298 persons; 210 adults and 88 children [...]. I discovered 4 cases of overcrowding only, 2 in Flower and Dean Street, and 2 in Lower Keate Street. The interior condition of these houses is not good, they are worn out, and many of the walls and ceilings are dirty and dilapidated. The greater portion of these houses have been condemned [...], and three of their number, 5, 7, and 8, Lower Keate Street, should either be taken down, or at once closed, as they are in such a dirty and dilapidated condition.*

▼ **Source B** Whitechapel from Charles Booth's map of poverty in London, 1889.

Lower class. Vicious, semi-criminal.

Very poor, casual. Chronic want.

Poor. 18s to 21s a week for a moderate family.

Mixed. Some comfortable, others poor.

Fairly comfortable. Good ordinary earnings.

Middle class. Well-to-do.

Upper-middle and upper classes. Wealthy

Combination of colours indicates that the street contains a fair proportion of each of the classes represented by the respective colours.

▲ **Source C** A group of men picking oakum in return for a night's stay at St Thomas's Street Casual Ward.

# Whitechapel Workhouse and Casual Ward

I'm starting to understand why Sarah Fisher might be driven to take her young and very sick child out on a frosty and cold night in order to use her to try to earn some money. In the case report I read that the child was taken to the Workhouse, where she was given medicine and food. Why didn't Sarah go to the Workhouse herself, to get help for Lucy?

Those who were unable to afford a bed for the night in a doss house, or who were too young, too old and too unwell to work, could go to the Workhouse. However, people were very reluctant to go for help at the Workhouse because of the strict rules that dictated what people ate, how they worked, the time they went to bed and when they got up. Those with families were segregated from their children and their wives or husbands and for much of the time were not even allowed to speak to one another. Parents were allowed to see their children only once a day.

The Whitechapel Workhouse was at South Grove, to the east, just off Mile End Road. In the centre of Whitechapel at Buck's Row there was a Workhouse Infirmary for the sick, and across the road at St Thomas's Street there was a 'Casual Ward', which could take around 400 inmates. The Casual Ward, for those who wanted a bed for one night, only had spaces for around 60 people. The rules of the Casual Ward were very harsh – inmates were expected to work to earn their bed for the night. They would be made to pick oakum, which means picking apart the fibres of old rope, or they could be asked to work in the kitchens or to clean the Workhouse. It was thought that otherwise the inmates would be tempted to stay on at the expense of the taxpayers, who funded the Workhouse Union.

**?** Make sure you understand the following:
- Workhouse union
- Picking oakum
- Casual ward
- Infirmary
- Sweatshop

**Source D** From *The People of the Abyss*, by Jack London, an American novelist who stayed in doss houses and workhouses to see what it was like. In 1902 he visited the Whitechapel Casual Ward.

*Some were set to scrubbing and cleaning, others to picking oakum, and eight of us were convoyed across the street to the Whitechapel Infirmary, where we were set at scavenger work. This was the method by which we paid for our skilly\* and canvas\*\*, and I, for one, know that I paid in full many times over.*

*Though we had most revolting tasks to perform, our allotment was considered the best, and the other men deemed themselves lucky in being chosen to perform it.*

*'Don't touch it, mate, the nurse sez it's deadly,' warned my working partner, as I held open a sack into which he was emptying a garbage can.*

*It came from the sick wards, and I told him that I purposed neither to touch it, nor to allow it to touch me. Nevertheless, I had to carry the sack, and other sacks, down five flights of stairs and empty them in a receptacle where the corruption was speedily sprinkled with strong disinfectant.*

\* Skilly – a kind of weak broth or soup made from water, vegetables and corn flour.

\*\* Canvas – this means the use of a hammock as a bed for the night.

## THE CASUAL WARD OF THE WORKHOUSE    **?**

1 Make a list of the workhouse rules on this page.

2 Why were many rules of the Casual Ward so harsh?

3 Does this explain why people preferred to take their chances in doss houses?

## The Peabody Estate

To the south of Whitechapel Road, just to the east of the Tower of London, is a street called Royal Mint Street, and just off this street was another 'rookery' like Flower and Dean Street, where there were large numbers of lodging houses. The annual death rate here in the years after 1865 was more than 50 in 1,000. This was double that for the rest of London.

In 1876 the Metropolitan **Board of Works** (a government organisation) bought the area for **slum clearance**. This scheme was very expensive. The Board was supposed to sell the land on, but couldn't find commercial developers to buy it, because of the small profits they would make on the low rents they would be able to charge.

In 1879 they sold most of the site to the Peabody Trust, a charity set up by a wealthy American banker. This trust built blocks of flats which were designed to offer affordable rents. By 1881, 287 flats had been built. Each block of flats was separate from the other and surrounded by a yard, in order to improve ventilation. They were built from brick and had unplastered walls so that lice could not live in the plaster. They also had shared bathrooms and kitchens, and were much more pleasant to live in than the buildings they replaced. However, the rents were probably too high for many of the people who had lived in the area before, and tenants who got behind with their rent were immediately thrown out. So improvements like these caused more overcrowding elsewhere as the poorest people looked for rents they could afford.

### WHY DIDN'T PEOPLE JUST LEAVE WHITECHAPEL?

We might wonder why people didn't move out and find better places to live. The main reason seems to have been that people lived where they could earn money. Between Whitechapel Road and the Thames there were tanneries where leather was cured, **sweatshops** and tailors where clothes and shoes were made, slaughterhouses and butchers' shops and bakeries. All these places needed employees. People had to live within walking distance of their work. This was especially true for the poorest labourers and dock workers. Their jobs were very insecure – they could be taken on for a day's work and laid off the next. These workers had to get to the dock or tannery gates early in the morning to get work before the competition arrived. The low pay – between 6 and 12 shillings a week in good employment – meant that it was hard to save and hard to leave. For those who could not work – either because of sickness like Sarah Fisher's husband, or because of alcohol addiction like most of Jack the Ripper's victims – there were other opportunities to earn money from prostitution, robbery or theft.

▲ **Source E** A picture showing Peabody buildings in Whitechapel in 2012.

### ACTIVITY ?

Find out more about George Peabody and why he decided to donate money for new housing in London.

1 What evidence suggests that people who lived near Royal Mint Street were very poor?

2 Why did the Board of Works find it hard to re-build better houses in this area?

3 What improvements did the Peabody charity bring?

# 1.3 Victorians and the fear of crime in the East End

▲ The French artist Gustave Dore drew pictures like this one of London in 1872. Dore exaggerated many of the features of London life, but can still give us an idea of what conditions in the rookeries were like.

So, I have found out that Whitechapel was a place in which some people who were relatively comfortably off lived close to areas in which very poor people lived. I have also found out that in the poorer areas there was overcrowding caused by high rents and by insecure and low-paid work. It seems many people in Whitechapel were living under threat of homelessness. Sarah Fisher's husband's illness stopped him from getting work, and it seems that her landlady, Sarah King, was running a lodging house like those I found out about on Flower and Dean Street. I have also perhaps found out why Sarah Fisher didn't ask for help from the Workhouse – it seems that only the very desperate would do this. Sarah perhaps thought she would lose her baby if she asked for help from the Workhouse Union. I've made good progress, but I have also opened up some new areas that I might want to follow up. For instance, I might want to know why Victorian newspapers were so interested in crime, why the number of policemen in Whitechapel seemed to be growing, and I might also investigate why wealthy men like Peabody were concerned about living conditions in places like Whitechapel.

> **Source A** From *Tales of Mean Streets*, a novel by Arthur Morrison, published in 1894.
>
> *This street is in the East End [...] an evil plexus of slums that hide human creeping things; where filthy men and women live on penn'orths of gin, where collars and clean shirts are decencies unknown, where every citizen wears a black eye and none ever combs his hair.*

Source A is taken from the first page of a novel by Arthur Morrison. We might be tempted to dismiss it as an exaggeration and say that it offers no useful evidence for us as historians. There is certainly a lot of language of exaggeration – my favourite phrase is 'an evil plexus of slums' – it's exciting stuff and designed to raise the hairs on the back of his readers' necks. However, this source might tell us some important things about the fear of crime and the fear of the East End that many people felt during our period – it could help us to understand why Victorians were afraid of crime.

## A criminal underclass

People had different explanations for crime. Some thought that there was a criminal underclass, sometimes called the '**residuum**' – natural criminals, born to steal, lie and rob. The residuum, it was thought, were attracted to the hard-working people of London and lived off them, like criminal parasites.

> **Source B** From *Crime and its Causes*, a book by W.D. Morrison, a clergyman, published in 1891.
>
> *Habitual criminals are not to be confounded [confused] with the working or any other class; they are a set of persons who make crime the object and business of their lives; to commit crime is their trade; they deliberately scoff at honest ways of earning a living.*

## Lodging houses and pubs

Others, such as Andrew Mearns, a clergyman who visited the East End and wrote a pamphlet called *The Bitter Cry of Outcast London* in 1883, were worried that overcrowding and unhealthy living conditions would spread criminal behaviour. Inevitably, this meant that lodging houses and pubs were seen as places in which crime would be transmitted from habitual criminals to the decent people forced to live alongside them.

---

### RECORDING YOUR RESEARCH ❓

Use five note cards to record the reasons why many Victorian Londoners were worried about crime in Whitechapel, each with one of the following headings:

- A criminal underclass
- Lodging houses and pubs
- Drink
- Immigration
- Difficulties of reform

**Source C** From *The Bitter Cry of Outcast London* by Andrew Mearns, published in 1883.

*That people condemned to exist under such conditions take to drink and fall into sin is surely a matter for little surprise. … One of the saddest results of this overcrowding is the inevitable association of honest people with criminals. Often is the family of an honest working man compelled to take refuge in a thieves' kitchen. … Who can wonder that every evil flourishes in such hotbeds of vice and disease?*

## LODGING HOUSES

1  Read Source C. Why would 'honest' families end up in kitchens full of thieves if they lived in a lodging house?
2  Did Morrison think that drink was a cause or a consequence of harsh living conditions?

## Drink

Drink was one way of coping with the difficulties of life in Whitechapel, and addiction to alcohol was responsible for some committing crimes. The historian Drew Gray in his book *London's Shadows*, published in 2013, made a survey of the seventeen cases before the Thames Police Court on 1 June 1887 for 'disorderly behaviour' and found that all except one mentioned the drunkenness of the accused. Alcohol could also make arguments worse, as in the trial of William Seaman who was convicted of attacking Mr John Simpkin, a chemist, in an argument about his weighing out of an order of alum, which was used in baking (see Source D).

**Source D** From *Old Bailey Proceedings Online*, October 1888, trial of WILLIAM SEAMAN (40).

*JOHN TABARD (Policeman H 85): On 8th September I was in Berner Street when I heard shouts of 'Police'—I went to the prosecutor's shop, and saw the prisoner holding the prosecutor by the left hand by the throat, and punching him in the ribs with his right hand—I caught hold of him, and with the assistance of Smith I pulled him into the street—he was then taken into the back of the shop on account of the crowd—I got this hammer (produced) from McCarthy—I took the prisoner to the station—the charge was taken down by the inspector […]*

### DRINK

1  How did drink increase crime in Whitechapel?
2  Why did so many people drink in Whitechapel?

However, drink was also a factor in making people victims of crime. All of Jack the Ripper's victims were alcoholics, and were probably drunk when they were attacked. There are plenty of other examples of victims being robbed or stolen from while slightly the worse for a drink.

We need to bear in mind that many of the newspapers and other sources are looking at Whitechapel from the outside, and reflect the fears and attitudes of the people 'investigating' the problems that they saw in Whitechapel. However, it seems clear that life in Whitechapel was tough, and that for some, crime was often a way of getting over short-term difficulties. It was also often unplanned and opportunistic, like the case of George Knight, convicted of 'simple larceny' in 1881 (see Source E).

**Source E** From *Old Bailey Proceedings Online*, May 1881, trial of GEORGE KNIGHT (aged 20).

*THOMAS HEWSMAN. I am employed by Messrs. Cook, Sons, and Co., of 22, St. Paul's Churchyard, silk merchants—on 1st April I saw the prisoner about 10 a.m. passing through the warehouse—I knew he was not employed there—he was holding his coat so that it was drawn tightly across the back—I followed him to the back door; there are three steps to go down, so that I could see over his shoulder, and I saw a corner of a parcel inside his coat—I communicated with Mr. Harries, followed the prisoner, and asked him what he had under his coat—he threw the parcel in the road and ran away—this is it—I and Harries ran after him—it was picked up and given to me—Harries caught the prisoner, and he was brought back.*

## Immigration

Whitechapel had long been a place that attracted immigrants – there were jobs, and cheap places to sleep, and for the Irish and the Jews from eastern Europe, there were also communities of similar people who were already settled there. Irish immigration had been happening in large numbers since the early 1800s. By the time of our period there were well-established Irish lodging houses, and Irish workers dominated many of the docks.

After 1881 Russian Jews came to England in large numbers because they were persecuted in Russia following the assassination of Tsar Alexander II. Around 30,000 arrived in London between 1881 and 1891. Jewish immigrants found it harder to integrate than those from Ireland, partly because of language barriers, but also because of cultural factors such as religious holidays and Sabbath rituals. As a result, many recent Jewish immigrants found themselves working for more established Jewish employers, often working in sweatshops making clothing and shoes. All in all this meant that Jewish people were segregated, and a target for prejudice. The map below shows where the Jewish population of Whitechapel mainly lived at this time.

▼ **Source F** Charles Booth's map of the Jewish population of Whitechapel in 1900.

1 This is the area around Flower and Dean Street. Why do you think that the Jewish immigrants of the 1880s and 1890s were drawn to this area?

3 Jewish immigrants tended to cluster in particular areas where they were almost 100 per cent of the population. As you can see in the places around each area, Jewish people were still a minority.

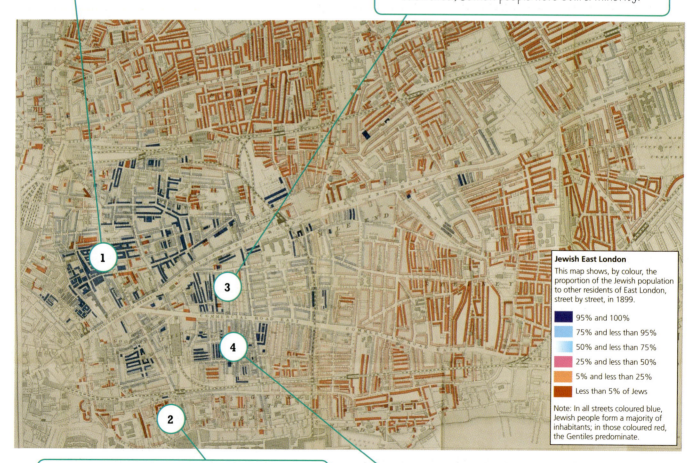

**Jewish East London**

This map shows, by colour, the proportion of the Jewish population to other residents of East London, street by street, in 1899.

- 95% and 100%
- 75% and less than 95%
- 50% and less than 75%
- 25% and less than 50%
- 5% and less than 25%
- Less than 5% of Jews

Note: In all streets coloured blue, Jewish people form a majority of inhabitants; in those coloured red, the Gentiles predominate.

2 This is where the Peabody Estate was built. Why didn't the Jewish immigrants move to these new model apartments?

4 This is where the Berner Street Theatre was, where the *Workers' Friend* newspaper was printed.

## Socialism and anarchism

Adding to the fears of criminal behaviour were worries about political ideas such as socialism and anarchism that these immigrants seemed to bring with them, or which were stirred up by home-grown radical politicians.

The Irish were targets of prejudice because of their Roman Catholic religion, but also because of the rise in 'Fenian' Irish Nationalism. At that time the whole of Ireland was ruled by Britain, but many Irish people wanted at the least 'Home Rule' and preferably independence. Armed protests in Ireland were increasing and in 1884 a small bombing campaign led to an explosion on a train at Gower Street station, and the discovery of a bomb left in Trafalgar Square. Two other bombs did explode in the campaign, though there were only slight injuries in each.

There had been a series of attempted assassinations and bomb attacks on the continent, which newspapers had labelled anarchist 'outrages'. Anarchism was a revolutionary political idea which said that people would be better off without government and without laws, and that left to their own devices people would act honourably and kindly to one another. To the English press this idea was very threatening. The idea of anarchism was developed by Russian revolutionaries, and some politicians emphasised the threat of Jewish immigration and Jewish radicalism from eastern Europe.

Some Jewish immigrants did bring radical political beliefs and set up socialist organisations such as the International Worker's Educational Club and a newspaper – the *Arbeter Fraint* or *Worker's Friend* at a theatre just off Commercial Road in Whitechapel at Berner Street, now called Henriques Street. Many people were already blaming the Ripper murders on a Jew when the body of Annie Chapman, the third victim, was found in the yard of the Berner Street theatre. Rumours were circulated and printed that Nikolay Vasiliev, a Russian anarchist Jew, was responsible for a string of similar murders in France, and was now living in England, though it unlikely that this person even existed. Even though there was never a serious connection found between political anarchists and the Ripper murder, the police were worried about their ability to keep an eye on the activities of the Jews in Berner Street, especially as many of them were carried out in Yiddish – the language that many of the immigrants spoke.

## Difficulty of reform

These ideas and fears led reformers to want to open up the East End and Whitechapel in particular, by widening roads, and by knocking down the rookeries and lodging houses. It was these ideas that led to the calls for laws to knock down the slums and replace them with new housing projects like the Peabody Estate near Royal Mint Street.

However, as we've already seen, these schemes often didn't benefit those people in the greatest need – they found themselves crowding into other lodging houses. Increasingly, they were in competition for rented accommodation with immigrants from Ireland and eastern Europe. This meant that the problem seemed like an intractable one, and efforts to improve the environment and the character of the East End seemed fruitless. This situation seemed to confirm W.D. Morrison (see Source H) in his view that it was character and nature that caused crime, not environment.

**Source G** From Arnold White's book, *The Modern Jew*, published in 1899.

*There are thousands of [Jews] who prefer existence without physical exertion, and who are content to live on others, untrammelled by considerations of honesty or truth [...] [consider] the benefit that the country would derive from the total cessation [stopping] of the immigration of professional paupers, anarchists and thieves.*

## IMMIGRATION FEARS

1 Read Source G. What did White accuse Jewish people of being?

2 What do you think 'professional pauper' means?

3 Read Source H. Why did Morrison think that crime would not be cured by giving people better housing and more money?

**Source H** From *Crime and its Causes*, by W.D. Morrison, published in 1891.

*Very often crime is but the offspring of degeneracy and disease. A diseased and degenerate population no matter how favourably circumstanced in other respects will always produce a plentiful crop of criminals.*

## Practice questions

### Exploring the sources

1 Describe two features of:
   a) lodging houses in Whitechapel
   b) conditions in workhouses
   c) the effect of drink on crime in Whitechapel.

2 How useful are sources A and B on page 125 for an enquiry into the problems of housing and overcrowding in Whitechapel? Explain your answer, using Sources A and B and your knowledge of the historical context.

3 How could you follow up Source B on page 128 to find out more about the causes of crime in Whitechapel? Use the following headings:
   • Detail in Source B I would follow up
   • Question I would ask
   • What type of source I could use
   • How this might help my question

# 1.4 The working of the Metropolitan Police

In the early part of the nineteenth century there was a feeling that crime had increased in London. There were local watchmen and other types of police force throughout London, but they were variable in their effectiveness. Poorer places like Whitechapel could not afford to pay for enough watchmen to protect people from crime. Sir Robert Peel, who was the Home Secretary between 1822 and 1830, decided that London needed one police force that was under central control.

## What was the public attitude towards the Metropolitan Police?

When the Metropolitan Police was set up in 1829, it was paid for by local London authorities, but controlled by the Home Secretary. Before this each local area had employed its own 'watchmen'. Many worried that a centrally controlled police force could be used by government to spy on ordinary Englishmen and women, and interfere with their liberty. In 1833 a coroner's jury decided that the stabbing of a policeman at a riot had been justifiable homicide because of the tactics of the police force in controlling the crowd. Did the reputation of the police improve as time went on?

---

### A QUICK HISTORY OF THE METROPOLITAN POLICE ❓

1 Read the boxes on the next page. Produce a living graph like the one here to record how good the reputation of the police would have been at different times, in your view.

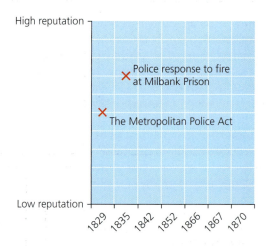

2 Focus on the professionalism of the force.
   a) Identify three changes which aimed to improve the quality of recruits and the workforce.
   b) Identify three improvements to police organisation or investigation techniques.
3 Discuss with a partner and divide this timeline into different phases, such as times when things seemed to be going better or worse.

---

**1829**

The Metropolitan Police Act, drafted by Sir Robert Peel, set up the Metropolitan Police. Sir Charles Rowan and Richard Mayne were the first **Commissioners** (see page 134). By 1830 there were 3,300 policemen in the force.

**1835**

Newspapers praised the quick response by the police to a fire at Millbank Prison, which prevented any escapes or trouble among the prisoners.

**1842**

Detective Branch formed (see page 134). Some worried that police **detectives** would be used to spy on ordinary people. **Plain-clothed policemen** were ordered to reveal their identity in confrontations with the public.

**1852**

Sir Charles Rowan died. There were now 5,700 men in the force.

**1866**

3,200 policemen were used to control a riot in Hyde Park – Commissioner Mayne was injured, and the army was called in to control the crowd.

**1867**

Irish 'Fenians', who wanted independence for Ireland, planted a bomb in Clerkenwell. The police ignored warnings of the attack.

**1870**

New Commissioner Edmund Henderson introduced rules to increase the quality of recruits and to raise standards of reading and writing in the police. He relaxed rules about **drill** (see page 134).

**1877**

A court case revealed corruption among senior officers at the Detective Branch in an international gambling fraud conspiracy. This 'Trial of the Detectives' was closely followed and reported in the newspapers. The following year, Sir Charles Vincent reformed this branch into the Criminal Investigation Department (CID).

**1885**

Only a year after a 'Special Irish Branch' was set up to infiltrate Irish terrorist cells, **Fenian** bombs exploded at the Houses of Parliament and the Tower of London.

**1886**

A protest in Trafalgar Square got out of hand and houses were damaged. Henderson resigned as Commissioner. Sir Charles Warren replaced him.

**1887**

Warren resigned after seeming to criticise the Home Secretary following another riot in Trafalgar Square. James Munro was appointed in his place.

**1888–89**

The Whitechapel Murders were carried out – five were thought to be the work of one man: Jack the Ripper. The Ripper was not caught.

**1894**

New system for identifying suspects was put in place – using physical measurements, photographs and 'the **mug shot**'.

**1895**

New rules for recruitment. Applicants had to be between 21 and 27, able to read and write well, and be taller than 5'9''.

**1901**

Fingerprint identification introduced.

**1902**

Medals, time off and a bonus was paid to all policemen to repay them for extra duties during the coronation of Edward VII.

# Police Commissioners and the Home Secretary

Between 1870 and 1900 there seemed to be a crisis at the very top of the police force, with two Commissioners being forced to resign from their jobs. Their experiences allow us to explore people's attitudes to the police – why were people suspicious of them and were they doing an effective job?

## BULL'S EYE ON BOBBY.

Mr. Bull (takes Policeman's lantern). "THANK YOU. I'LL JUST HAVE A LOOK ROUND MYSELF. STRIKES ME THE PREMISES AIN'T AS CLEAN AS THEY MIGHT BE!"

▲ **Source A** A cartoon published in *Punch* magazine in 1877 during the Trial of the Detectives. Sir Edmund Henderson is shown as a normal constable. A policeman's light is being shone in his face by John Bull – a symbol of Britishness. The words 'detective branch' are on the door.

**Source B** From *The London Daily News*, 17 December 1880.

*Nothing could well be stronger than the language in which Mr Justice Stephen [the judge who tried the case] condemned the conduct of the CID. He will, we think, have the general body of public opinion with him in saying that 'the employment of spies to go and tell a parcel of lies was a proceeding that must be deprecated [condemned] by all'.*

## Commissioner Edmund Henderson

Edmund Henderson, who was appointed as Commissioner in 1870, was forced to resign in 1886 following a string of scandals. Henderson was accused of having relaxed police discipline – he had allowed officers to grow beards, and reduced the amount of military drill practice they had to do. His critics often ignored the action he had taken to raise the standard of reading and writing in the force, and his expansion of the Detective Branch.

In 1877 a scandal called 'the Trial of the Detectives' was uncovered involving corruption in the Detective Branch (see page 143), and suspicion of the police continued throughout the time Henderson was in charge. In the case of Thomas Titley in 1880 some thought that the police had made Titley break the law. They had posed in plain clothes as customers wanting to buy a chemical in order to bring on an abortion. On 17 December 1880 *The London Daily News* wrote that the case had been 'manufactured' in an 'extraordinary manner'. The jury found Titley guilty but recommended a lenient sentence 'on the ground of the provocation by the police inducing him to the crime'. The following year 3,800 people signed a petition against Titley's eighteen-month sentence.

Following this, in 1884 and 1885, Irish Fenian terrorists exploded a series of bombs, including two that damaged the Houses of Parliament (see Source C). This was especially humiliating as the Special Irish Branch, which had been set up in 1883, had failed to stop the plot. Finally, following a riot in Trafalgar Square which had got out of control, Henderson was replaced by Charles Warren in January 1886.

## THOMAS TITLEY ?

1 How might the Titley case have made people suspicious of the police?

2 Look at Source A. Why is 'John Bull' shining a light in this cartoon?

▼ **Source C** The front page of the *Graphic Newspaper* from January 1885, showing a drawing of the damage done to the chamber of the House of Commons.

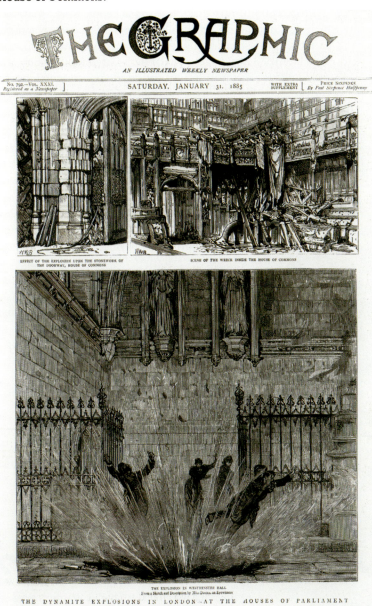

## Commissioner Charles Warren

Unfortunately for Warren, he was appointed just before a change in Home Secretary. The new Home Secretary, Henry Matthews, got his position just six months after the appointment of Warren as Commissioner. Matthews made no secret of his dislike for Warren's approach and made it clear that he would have preferred to promote James Munro, Warren's deputy. Monro himself undermined Warren by complaining that Warren did not support the CID with enough men or money. Neither Monro, Matthews nor Warren were easy to work for – all three were stubborn and did not listen to advice.

## SIR EDMUND HENDERSON, 1821–1896

Henderson was an adventurer and soldier before settling down to the job of Commissioner of the Metropolitan Police. He carried out surveys of British territory in Canada and was in charge of the **prison colony** in Western Australia. He became Commissioner in 1869. Henderson made several reforms, including allowing policemen to vote in elections and setting up a charity to look after widows and orphans of policemen killed in service. He also created a 'register of Habitual Criminals' which was supposed to allow the police to keep records on people who kept committing crimes. Henderson resigned in January 1886.

## SIR CHARLES WARREN, 1840–1927

Warren had an amazingly varied life – and could have been written into novels as a heroic Victorian. He went to train as an army officer aged fourteen and joined the Royal Engineers aged seventeen. During his army career he served in Gibraltar, the Middle East and South Africa, returning to England when he was seriously wounded in the Kaffir War. In 1882 he was sent to find out what had happened to an archaeological expedition to the Sinai Peninsula in Egypt. Warren discovered that the team had been murdered, so he tracked down the killers and arrested them. He was the Commissioner of the Metropolitan Police between 1886 and 1888.

## ACTIVITIES

1 Look up 'corruption' and 'incompetence' in the dictionary and summarise the definitions.

2 Write your notes about Sir Edmund Henderson's time as police commissioner. Make sure you note down evidence of corruption and incompetence.

3 Were there other reasons why Sir Edmund Henderson's reputation was not a good one?

### Reactions to Warren's approach

Warren's approach to his job was to try to raise standards. He issued orders to increase the military drill practice, and tightened up the rules for recruitment – he also brought more ex-soldiers into the force. Warren's focus on military discipline made people worry that the force was becoming an army which would be used to control the people. The press reacted badly when, in November 1887, another protest in Trafalgar Square was put down with what seemed like excessive force. In late 1888, when Jack the Ripper started to kill women in Whitechapel (see page 151), he seemed to be running rings round the police, who looked incapable of catching him.

**BLIND-MAN'S BUFF.**

*(As played by the Police.)*

" TURN ROUND THREE TIMES, AND CATCH WHOM YOU MAY ! "

▲ **Source D** A cartoon published by *Punch* magazine when the panic over the Ripper murders was at its height. The policeman's blindfold is stopping him from catching the criminals who are taunting him.

In November 1888, at the height of the Ripper crisis, Warren wrote an article that was published in *Murray's Magazine*, a popular news magazine.

> It is to be deplored that successive Governments have not had the courage to make a stand against the more noisy section of the people representing a small minority, and have given way before over [protests] which have exercised a terrorism over peaceful law abiding citizens.

Warren was reacting to accusations that his police force had used too much force in controlling a protesting crowd in Trafalgar Square in 1887, and criticisms that he was turning London's police into a military organisation. His biggest mistake, however, was in not getting this article approved by the Home Secretary, Henry Matthews. Warren's criticism of the Government looked like criticism of Matthews. When Matthews wrote to Warren in November 1888 to rebuke him for writing the *Murray Magazine* article, Warren offered his resignation in anger, and Matthews accepted it at once.

### ACTIVITIES ?

1  Make notes on Sir Charles Warren's time as commissioner, focusing on corruption and/or incompetence.

2  Were there other reasons for Sir Charles's resignation?

3  Write a paragraph which explains why there was a crisis at the head of the Metropolitan Police in the years 1870–1889.

# 1.5 The organisation of policing in Whitechapel

The Metropolitan Police was split up into different 'divisions' – each was responsible for policing a different area of London. Whitechapel came under 'H' Division. In 1886, H Division was extended eastwards, which gave it the territory set out on the map below. Each division was run by a Superintendent Constable, who had a hierarchy of policemen working under him.

## Recruits

New constables were recruited by the headquarters of the Metropolitan Police, which from 1890 was at Scotland Yard. Once the recruits were accepted and trained they were sent out to divisions that needed new men. Applicants filled out a form, giving details of their lives and experiences, and which gave the addresses of people who could act as character references.

---

**Source A** Requirements for applicants, from the application form for new recruits.

*He must not be under 21 years, nor over 32 years of age*

*He must not be less than five feet nine inches in height without his shoes*

*He must not have more than two children*

*He must not carry on any trade, nor will his wife be permitted to keep any shop*

*He must read and write legibly*

*He must produce satisfactory testimonials as to character*

*He must be certified as physically fit [...] by the Surgeon of the Police Force*

---

Successful applicants were given two weeks' training in military drill exercises (marching to order) followed by one week of 'beat' duty alongside a more experienced constable in B or C Division (see map below). They were then assigned to the division that they would work in.

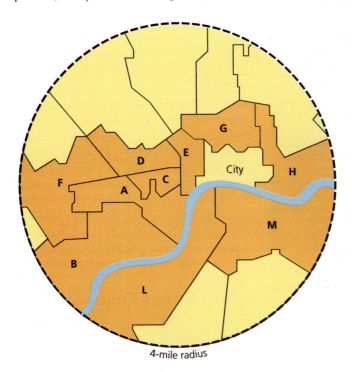

4-mile radius

▲ A map showing the different divisions of the Metropolitan Police. B Division is Chelsea and C Division is Mayfair and Soho. H Division included the Whitechapel area.

## Who were the recruits?

Recruitment of the right kind of candidate was very important. It was thought that the best policemen were men who had been brought up in the countryside, as they would be bigger and healthier than those from London. Character was thought to be very important. Recruits would have to show that they had good 'discipline' – that they would take orders and not break rules and regulations. The 1871 *Instruction book for Candidates and Constables*, a handbook for new police recruits, is very clear about the qualities the police were looking for (see Source B).

> **Source B** Extracts from the *Instruction Book for Candidates and Constables* (1871).
>
> *He is to speak the truth at all times and under all circumstances and when called upon to give evidence to state all he knows [...] without fear or reservation.*
>
> *Perfect command of temper is indispensable. A [constable] must not allow himself to be moved or excited or by any language or threat, however violent. The cooler he keeps himself the more power he will have over his assailants.*
>
> *A constable must act with energy, promptness and determination, for if he wavers, or doubts the thief may escape or the opportunity to render assistance may be lost.*

The police offered a steady job in an age when work was usually poorly paid and temporary. Right from the start of the Metropolitan Police it was decided that senior jobs would be given to serving policemen – so good policemen who stayed in their jobs could expect promotion. After 1860, a pension was given after 30 years in the service. The police even set up sports clubs for those who wanted to play cricket or football, and awards for good service or bravery.

A survey of recruits in 1874 suggested that 31 per cent of new recruits came from the countryside around London – many were farm labourers and 12 per cent came from the military. The historian Haia Shpayer-Makov's research suggests that the more wealthy or skilled the recruit, the less likely they were to stay in the police for their whole careers – perhaps because they had other options to earn money.

## H Division

▼ A map of Whitechapel and surrounding areas.

In 1885, *Dickens's Dictionary of London* listed 19 inspectors, 44 sergeants, and 441 constables in H Division. This made a force of 505 policemen to cover Whitechapel's population of about 176,000 people. The numbers of H Division's forces went up and down, but even at its peak during 1888 there were only around 575 police officers, including both constables and detectives. This meant that there was one policeman for every 300 people living in Whitechapel in normal times. Across the whole of London the force was 14,000 for a population of about 5.5 million people, about one policeman for every 390 people. To compare, the population of London in 2015 is around 8.6 million and there are approximately 32,000 police officers – about one policeman for every 268 people who live in London.

## Leman Street Police Station

Just north of the place where the Peabody Estate would be built (see page 127), but south of the Whitechapel Road, is Leman Street and the main police station for H Division, and the Whitechapel area. In 1891, it was moved to specially built premises on the site of a theatre that had been demolished a few doors down. Most of the records of this station for our period have not survived, but we can get an idea of the work of the policeman from other sources.

For instance, we could use information in the Census returns for Leman Street. In 1881, the Census records list two sergeants and 42 police constables as staying there on the night of the Census. It also records six prisoners as well as one 'destitute' person sleeping on the street outside. The 1901 Census, taken when the station had moved to a new and bigger building, lists 63 police constables, seven prisoners, eight police families and interestingly, three sergeants and five inspectors. Inspectors were not mentioned at all on the earlier Census record from 1881.

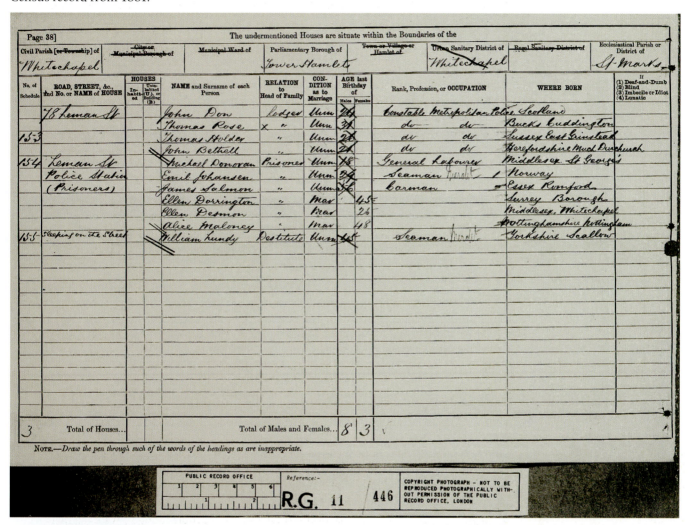

▲ **Source C** A digital scan of the Census record for Leman Street in 1881. Each entry was copied by hand from the Census return filled in by the residents, or, in this case, probably a police sergeant on duty that night at the station.

## LEMAN STREET

1 What do the numbers of people living and being held in Leman Street Police Station between 1888 and 1901 suggest about how H Division was changing?

2 Why might the entering, copying and recopying of names from returns to registers make research more difficult for historians?

3 See if you can identify on the 1881 return (Source C) what the prisoners normally did for a living, and the places they were born.

4 What might the birthplaces of those staying in Leman Street on the night of the Census tell you about the population of Whitechapel?

## SOURCES AND PROBLEMS

Add a few more ideas to the list of sources that you started on page 118. In particular, can you think of things that the Census might tell you, as well as some of its drawbacks?

## Thames Police Court

If we want to find out more about the kinds of things that constables did as part of their work we could look at reports of cases that were taken to the Thames Police Court, which was the court for the whole area of Whitechapel down to the Thames. It heard thousands of cases relating to crimes that could be tried without a jury.

Crimes of forgery, assault, attempted drownings in vats of wine, and others can be found in these reports. The most serious cases of murder or attempted murder and other crimes that the magistrate felt needed harsher punishments were sent to the Old Bailey. Here there was a jury, and the judge could impose more serious sentences, but the dividing line between these serious crimes and those that stayed at the Police Court was not clear.

Though there are no official records detailing what was said at these cases, the court register for the year 1888 has survived. This document lists the cases, defendants and the crimes they were charged with. The historian Drew Gray has studied the register to find out the proportion of the different crimes that were committed (see Source D).

**Source D** Hearings at the Thames Police Court, January 1887–December 1887, from the court register. From Drew Gray, *London's Shadows*, published in 2010.

| Type of offence | Male | Female | Total |
|---|---|---|---|
| Property | 381 (85%) | 74 (16%) | 455 (27%) |
| Violence | 352 (84%) | 65 (16%) | 417 (24%) |
| Disorderly | 337 (62%) | 208 (38%) | 545 (32%) |
| Regulatory* | 244 (85%) | 44 (15%0 | 288 (17%) |
| Total | 1,314 (77%) | 391 (23%) | 1,705 |

\* These tended to be crimes such as breaking the rules of the Workhouse by running away, driving a cart dangerously or running away from the army.

> Using what you already know about what Whitechapel was like, can you explain why crimes of 'disorderly behaviour' might be the most common?

Source D tells us a lot about the types of crime, and proportion of crimes that the H Division constables would have faced. So, the most common type of crime was disorderly behaviour, but this was only slightly more frequent than crimes against property (which means theft, or fraud) and crimes of violence.

### COMBINING INFORMATION FROM SOURCES

One of the problems with sources like the register, and tables based on them, is that each category covers a very large range of crimes. Violence could mean anything from the threat of violence, or fear of being hurt, right up to attempted murders, stabbings and beatings. If I want to know more about the kinds of crimes and difficulties that the Whitechapel police faced, I need to look at more than one source, and learn from them together.

# The role of the beat constable

The role of the constable was to prevent crime by being an obvious presence, and to arrest those caught committing a crime.

## Uniform and equipment

The **beat constable**'s uniform was woollen trousers and jacket, both a deep blue-black colour, with shiny buttons and (until 1863) a top hat. This uniform was meant to stand out in the crowd, because one of the jobs of the policeman was to be seen. A truncheon was carried to help defend a constable under attack, and handcuffs or 'come along' cuffs were used for bringing unwilling citizens back to the station. The oil-fired bulls-eye lamp – the 'dark lantern' – gave heat as well as light, which was especially welcome on cold nights. The flame could be hidden from view in order to help the officer creep up on suspected criminals.

The initial 'stovepipe' top hat didn't give enough protection from blows to the head, so, from 1863, a new design of the helmet, called the custodian, was introduced. The design of this helmet was supposed to deflect a downward blow to the side.

## The beat

There are lots of mentions in the records of the Old Bailey, and in the newspaper reports from Whitechapel, of policemen being called by witnesses to a crime, or happening to come across a crime in progress. This wasn't just luck. Without radios, CCTV, computer surveillance or motor patrols, the main tactic for preventing crime was 'the beat'. This was a specific area that each constable would have to patrol, using a route that had been given to him by his sergeant. The beat was timed precisely – and the constable would be expected to reach certain places, and to be at the end of the beat, at specific times so that his sergeant could meet him or contact him when necessary. In the days before radio, this was the only way in which a sergeant could track his constables, and the only way he could get messages and instructions to him. As you can see from Source E, the instructions about the speed of his walking were very precise.

> **Source E** From the *Candidates and Constables Instruction Book*, 1871.
> *He is to walk at a gentle pace, about 2½ miles an hour, keeping the outer or kerb side of the street by day, and walking close to the houses by night. He must not loiter or stand in an idle and listless manner, or gossip. He is not on any account to receive drink from any one. If he requires refreshment, he can obtain the permission of his Sergeant to purchase it.*

## THE BEAT ?

1 How did policemen's uniform help them in the prevention of crime?
2 Can you come up with two possible reasons why?
3 Why was the beat timed so precisely?

## The 'beat' routine

At the start of the day's duty a squad of policemen would leave their station in single file, each peeling off at the start of their beat.

During the day the beat was about half an hour. At night the beats were made half as long – so that the route was walked every fifteen minutes. This meant that burglars and thieves had less time to carry out crimes during the cover of night. Each shift would last nine hours – eight of which would be spent walking in boots made with wooden soles! In the hour before their beat began, officers would study their orders of the day, which listed wanted criminals or crimes that had happened in the shift before theirs, and put on the black and white striped armband which showed that they were on duty.

Policemen usually travelled the beat alone, unless they were working in a particularly dangerous area. They were expected not only to learn the route of their beat, but to know the shops, warehouses, pubs and other businesses and the people who worked there, as well as the alleyways, yards and squares that led off their routes. After a month a policeman would be moved on to another beat. This was to prevent corruption between officers and locals – it was often the case that shopkeepers might give a constable a cup of tea, in return for being extra vigilant when walking past their shop, or in case there was trouble from customers in the future. The landlord of a pub might leave a pint of beer on the window for a constable as he walked past, in return for a good word from the officer when the application to renew the pub's licence came up. Officially this was frowned upon, but sergeants and inspectors saw that the constable needed to get to know the people on his beat. They were encouraged to share a cup of tea with the watchmen (today we might call them security guards) who patrolled larger commercial buildings like warehouses, so that they could share information on suspicious persons and potential suspects.

## Disadvantages

The obvious downside to the beat system was that, after watching each policeman for a little while, a criminal would be able to work out the route, and commit his crime when the policeman was on another section of the beat. The constable would try to alter his beat a little on each route, or might sometimes walk it the other way round, so that his position was less predictable. This was not the only complication. At night, constables were expected to check doors and downstairs windows of the premises that they walked past. Some would use tricks like leaving strips of paper wedged in the doors of places that might be targeted by thieves. If they walked by again and noticed that the paper had gone, they could then investigate further.

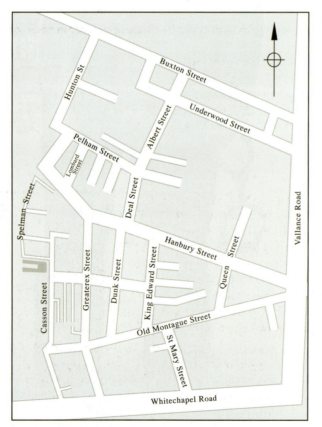

▲ **Source F** A redrawn map from one of the 'beat books' for H Division. This one is from the 1930s but the beat system had not really changed since the end of the 1800s.

> ### THE BEAT
> 1 What were the advantages and disadvantages of the beat system?
> 2 Why were the beats shorter at night?
> 3 How do the beat system and the uniform of the constable suggest that the job of the police was mainly to prevent crime?

# The development of the Central Investigation Division (CID)

From the first days of the Metropolitan Police in 1829, people were suspicious of the idea of detecting crime – it seemed too much like snooping. So a detective force wasn't set up until 1842, but even then this was only a small unit which worked the Metropolitan Police's headquarters at Scotland Yard. In 1870 Commissioner Henderson decided to recruit more detectives, but also to move them out to the divisions, so that they could work with the constables and use their local knowledge.

These detectives didn't perform very well. There were cases of mistaken identity which led to arrests of the wrong person. In 1877, a group of detectives were found guilty of accepting bribes in return for protecting a gang which had stolen thousands of francs from French gamblers in an international betting scam. This 'Trial of the Detectives' led to a reorganisation of detectives in London. They were brought back under the control of a new single organisation called the Criminal Investigation Division or CID, based at Scotland Yard in Westminster.

Howard Vincent was given the job of leading the CID – and he set out new ways of working. He centralised control of the CID, and increased the pay of detectives in order to attract the best constables. He also encouraged detectives to do more plain-clothes operations, and to investigate crimes that they suspected might happen – rather than wait for them to be reported.

However, detectives still worked in local divisions so that they knew their patch, its people and policemen well. One example is Inspector Reid. He worked his way up from constable to the role of detective in Bethnal Green, and was very experienced in policing the East End, before being given the job of inspector (an inspector was a more experienced policeman who oversaw the work of several sergeants and his constables) at H Division. He replaced Inspector Frederick Abberline, who had spent most of his career in Whitechapel, and was promoted to a role at CID in Scotland Yard (before being sent back to work with H Division during the Whitechapel murder investigation).

> ## CHARLES EDWARD HOWARD VINCENT (1849-1908)
>
>
>
> - He had travelled widely in Europe and then trained as a lawyer.
> - He spent the whole of 1877 studying Parisian police detective techniques.
> - Head of the CID between 1778 and 1884.
> - Was given the job of reforming the CID after the 'Trail of the Detectives.'
> - Published the first Police Code in 1889, which set out guidelines for collecting evidence and detecting criminals.

# The day-to-day work of the detective

Detectives often worked in plain clothes, so that they could 'shadow' suspects – follow them to observe their activities or make arrests. Each day they would receive a report from the chief inspector in each division, which listed the unsolved crimes and ongoing investigations in each area. In addition, from 1878, they also had to look out for 'habitual criminals' – those who repeatedly committed crime. Details of these criminals were kept in a 'Register of habitual criminals' at Scotland Yard, where the CID's headquarters were. Detectives also had the job of supervising prisoners who had been released early for good behaviour. These men had to visit a police station at least once a week, and were given a 'ticket of leave' which explained their crime, and which they had to produce if asked by a policeman.

The detective's main job was to observe and gather information. As we'll see, however, before 1900 there were few forensic investigation techniques. Detectives were starting to use photography, but there was no reliable way of gathering fingerprint evidence. The analysis of fibres or DNA matching was unimagined, and the most usual method of getting evidence was to gather descriptions and witness statements, take casts of footprints, or to get a tip from an informant.

> ## ATTITUDES TOWARDS DETECTION **?**
>
> 1 Describe the attitude towards detective work during this period.
>
> 2 Describe the role of a detective policeman during this period.
>
> 3 In what ways did the detective's role develop during the period?

143

# Following up a source

**Source H** From a report in the *Graphic Newspaper*, 28 December 1895, Issue 1361.

*So, I grabbed the brother who was kicking out at my shins. I got a good hold of his neck with my right hand ... I thought that as I was alone among a rare lot of 'em, men and women, pushing and crowding and cursing, and the nearest ones beginning to get me wedged in, I had better blow my whistle; and no sooner did the other brother see both my hands busy than he came straight for me with a knife.*

**Source I** Details from PC William Short's entry in the H Divisional Register.

*Collar No: 615*

*Warrant No: 70668*

*Occupation: Farm Labourer*

*From: Parkham Bideford, Devon*

*Age: 22*

*Date of joining: 11 May 1885*

*Height: 6'1/4"*

*Transferred to: A Division 8 February 1890*

▲ **Source G** A picture published in 1895 in the *Graphic Newspaper* which shows a scuffle described to a journalist by PC H615 when he stepped in to stop a fight.

This looks like an interesting story – and I would like to know more about it! To do that I need to work out which details in the source I can follow up, and where and how I might search for more information. The most obvious person to focus on is the police officer. I know that he worked in H Division in Whitechapel (because of the H on his collar number). The collar number is useful as these were given when a constable joined a particular division. Like numbers on a football shirt, they were re-used and given out again as people joined and left the division. This means I can search the H Divisional Register, which will tell me who used that collar number.

Not all of the Divisional Registers have survived, and they are in paper form – they have not (yet) been digitised, so they have to be searched by hand. I was lucky because the Heritage Centre of the Metropolitan Police agreed to do the search over the phone – otherwise I would have to have visited in person. The Divisional Register had one person using that collar number between 1885 and 1890, then another person using that number from 1911. That was great for me, because the incident I was investigating happened before 1895 (that's when the story was published). So, it looked like William Short used the collar number in the picture. From the Divisional Register I learned several interesting things about PC William Short (see Source I).

## RECRUITMENT

**1** Look back at page 138 then at William Short's record in Source I. What made Short the ideal candidate to join the Metropolitan Police?

**2** Look back at the picture on page 144. Considering Short's age and height in the divisional record, does the picture seem like an accurate image of him?

Warrant numbers were given to each new recruit as he was accepted into the force and he kept this number, even if he moved between divisions. Now that I have a warrant number, I can search the Attestation Ledgers and Joining and Leaving Ledgers. These were handwritten record books of when people joined and left the force. They have been digitised and are searchable online at the National Archives. They tell me a little more about Short – he left H Division in 1890, five years before the publication of the story in the *Graphic*. If it is Short in the news article, perhaps he left Whitechapel because of incidents like this one. He stayed in A Division for another 21 years, leaving in 1911 – when he would have had a full police pension after such long service.

In this case the ledgers can't tell me much more. But I have more details from the picture (Source G) that I might want to follow up. In the background I can see a police station. I can use a map, and the details that I have from the article to find more information.

Short (if it was him) says that the incident took place near Pearl Street, and near a public house and a police station. Source J shows the station as being on a fairly sharp corner – the building narrows at the corner quite a lot. It is also across the road from a pub (in the left-hand corner). The junction of Commercial Street and Elder Street has a pub nearby and a police station on the corner, and it is very near Great Pearl Street.

▼ **Source J** A recreation of the 1894 street map, showing the Commercial Street Police Station, the public house on the corner of Wheler Street, Great Pearl Street and Commercial Street.

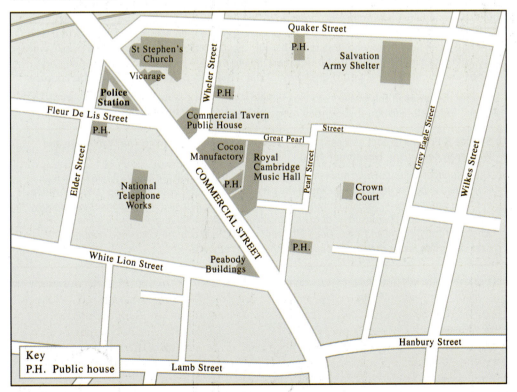

## KEY ITEMS

How could each of these items be useful for following up a source?

- Attestation ledger
- Joining and leaving ledger
- Warrant number
- Collar number

## THE INCIDENT IN SPITALFIELDS

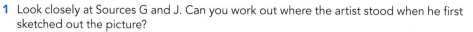

1 Look closely at Sources G and J. Can you work out where the artist stood when he first sketched out the picture?

2 Source G is not a photograph, but a drawing of the events. How does this change the way that you might use it as evidence?

Now I have the warrant number and name I can use these details to follow up searches of newspaper reports. One of the most important sources for crime at this time is newspaper reports. Newspapers often printed short items about criminals and victims appearing at the Police Court. It looks like the event recorded in the *Graphic* happened at least five years before the publication date of 1895, because by this time Short was in A Division in Westminster, a long way from Great Pearl Street. However, the details of when he joined and left Whitechapel Division help me narrow the newspaper search down even further.

Unfortunately in our case I cannot find any reference to the fight that is mentioned in the story in the *Graphic*. This doesn't mean that it didn't happen, just that it didn't get into the papers at the time. The story seems to match with the details on the ground, and PC615 was serving in the Whitechapel area around the time of the *Graphic* story. In fact, there are local newspapers that I could search in local museums and libraries that might have details of this story, so there's still more following up that I could do. The search was not a waste of time either – browsing through these stories and sources I started to get a picture of the work of the police and some of the problems they were facing in Whitechapel.

## SEARCHING THE ARCHIVES

Looking in old editions of some newspapers is much easier than it used to be, because many have been digitised. However, what we're able to look at online may not give us the whole picture, as these reports only represent a small fraction of court cases. The newspapers tend to cover the more surprising cases, or the most interesting details – like the charges against a woman who dressed as a man in order to follow her husband, in the hope of discovering his affair, or the case of a warehouse man accused of cruelty to a dog – he had been seen throwing it as far as he could by its front legs. The reading public were very interested in the crimes that happened in less wealthy areas like Whitechapel, and stories about crime there would often re-appear in newspapers up and down the country.

Some of the cases in the papers are very odd – like this one in Source K, which tells us about a loud interruption to a Sunday religious service.

> **Source K** From a report of a case at the Thames Police Court from *The Watchman and Wesleyan Advertiser*, November 1860.
>
> *The defendant did unlawfully molest, let, disturb, vex, and trouble the said Thomas Dove, a clergyman in holy orders, ministering in the parish church of St. George, during the celebration of divine service. He occupied a pew near the reading-desk, and said the responses very loudly. Mr. Churchwarden Thompson went to him and requested him not to make so much noise, when he turned round and said, 'Don't interrupt me, sir,' and continued his loud reading. The Churchwarden then called in the police, and had him removed.*

# 1.6 Difficulties of policing Whitechapel

Large parts of Whitechapel were slums at the start of the period and this remained the case despite work done by charities such as the Peabody Trust. The layout of the streets and the buildings themselves made policing difficult. Criminals could hide from the police in the rookeries, and use the alleys and yards as places from which to watch for victims, hide after committing a crime, or to run criminal activities from. However, there were other difficulties which the police faced in Whitechapel. In this section we're going to study these.

## RECORDING YOUR RESEARCH

Use a table like the one below to record information from pages 147–150 about the difficulties to policing caused by life in Whitechapel.

| Issue | What difficulties did it cause? | What did the police try to do about this issue? |
|---|---|---|
| Alcohol and pubs | | |
| Gangs | | |
| Prostitution | | |
| Violent demonstrations and attacks on Jews | | |

## Alcohol

As we have already seen (see page 129), alcohol played a large part in the work of a policeman. It made some people more vulnerable to becoming victims of crime, like John Watson, who, according to a report on 22 July 1870 in the *Clerkenwell News*, had fallen in with a couple of young women in a pub in Gowers Walk, Whitechapel. He became 'intoxicated' and the women were caught relieving him of his watch in the street by Constable Deddnould from H Division.

The case of William Froomberg reported in the *East London Observer* on 3 May 1879 (see Source A) shows that alcohol could also make small disputes much worse, and that it could also make work harder and more dangerous for policemen. Froomberg was shouting at a watchman in front of the Sailors' Home (a place for sailors to sleep when their ship was in dock). The watchman of the Sailors' Home blew his whistle, summoning PC Gallagher, who was off duty and enjoying a drink in a local pub, but arrived when he heard the whistle. At the same time PC Gunter also arrived. Froomberg did not co-operate. Though 'no more violence was used than was absolutely necessary to get [Froomberg] to the police station',

he made two complaints. The first was that he had been assaulted by the policemen, and the second was that both constables had been drinking. Gunter admitted that he'd had half a pint, in a shop doorway, but denied that he had been in the pub with Gallagher.

Drink also had a large part to play in many of the cases of violence and abuse within families – like the case from June 1878 of Henry Seigenberg of Cable Street, whose drunken father beat him so badly that the injuries, when shown in court, 'caused quite a groan of execration to run through the Court'. The case was so serious that it was committed for a full trial at the Old Bailey.

## Pubs

Making sure that landlords of pubs did not break the terms of their licences was also an important part of the work of the police. Policemen would check that landlords were closing their pubs on time, and that they were not allowing gambling or illegal boxing to take place on their premises. After 1870 it was illegal to serve alcohol to someone who was already drunk. As the period went on it was harder and harder for landlords to keep their licences if they had broken the law, and as a result most landlords worked hard to make sure that they were on the right side of the police.

### JUST A DRINK?

1 What problems did alcohol cause for the police in Whitechapel?
2 Why was the allegation against Gunter so serious?
3 What details in the report about Henry Seigenberg's beating could you follow up?

**Source A** From *East London Observer*, 20 October 1877.
*Sergeant Singer 13H said that on the 11th he visited the [Prince of Denmark Public House]. There were two or three men and some women in front of the bar. One of the men, a sailor, was staggering about drunk. … For the defence the defendant and two other witnesses said that they did not believe that the man was drunk, he was merely excited. [The] Defendant said that he wanted to get the man out of his house, but he would not go.*

### SAILING INTO TROUBLE

1 Look at the map on page 138. Why do so many Whitechapel reports mention sailors?
2 Why were sailors attracted to Whitechapel?
3 Why might men far from home in London be more likely to get into trouble?

# Gangs

Alcohol was also involved in some of the racketeering that went on in Whitechapel – illegal pubs and unlicensed boxing matches being some of the most common rackets. Some were run by well-organised gangs. In 1935 W.G. Cornish, who had been a detective in the Whitechapel area in the later 1800s, wrote in his memoirs about 'Bessarabian' gangs that ran protection rackets which threatened the owners of Jewish businesses. The immigrants that the gang preyed on were already scared of the authorities – as many of them had come to London to escape persecution by the army and secret police in Russia. They tended to try to pay up, or to sort out their problems without getting the police involved. This means that they have left very little evidence behind. An 'ex-detective Sergeant Leeson' did publish some memoirs and stories during the 1930s when he retired, which contained references to these immigrant gangs (see Source B).

> **Source B** From *An East End Detective* by B. Leeson, published in 1936.
>
> The 'Bessarabians', or the 'Stop-at-nothing' gang, were the greatest menace London has ever known. The public little guess how much they owe to the Metropolitan Police for the fact that London to-day is free from a terror that made it – in the early days of this century – almost as dangerous a place as … Chicago … at its wildest.*
>
> * Early in the 1800s Chicago had a reputation similar to Whitechapel's – it was seen as a place of prostitution, gambling, theft and murder.

## GANGS OF LONDON?

1 From the tone and content of Source B, what evidence can you find that Leeson might be exaggerating the danger of the Bessarabian gang?

2 What do you know about these gangs that would tell us how much of a threat they were to different kinds of people living in Whitechapel?

It is very hard to get much evidence to back up these stories. Most reports about gangs in the newspapers seem to be about small groups of younger people getting into fights, or taking opportunities to rob and steal. A typical report is that from *Lloyd's Weekly* in 1888 during the Jack the Ripper murders, which describes a gang of women and bullies who robbed 'a young woman who had been spending the evening with a sea captain', after which she had taken up with a well-dressed man. This man had drawn her into a side court where the other members of the gang were waiting. This report also shows us how difficult it is to know what is happening, because the papers didn't always write in plain language about the people of Whitechapel. The reference here to the woman spending part of the evening with a sea captain and then taking up with another man is meant to signal to us that she was a prostitute, without directly saying so.

Many of the problems that the police had with young people were much less dramatic than this – the *Standard* from 15 July 1884 tells of the arrest of a group of young men who had created a disturbance in a street near Regent's Canal at the far end of Whitechapel Road. This group were gambling, bathing and 'running about the towing path in a nude state'!

# Prostitution

Prostitution was not in itself a crime – though after 1885 keeping a brothel was illegal. It is sometimes called 'the oldest profession', but for many women in Whitechapel it wasn't a job, but a necessity in really desperate situations, or when their lives were affected by alcoholism. For instance, all of the victims of Jack the Ripper had sold sex in order to pay for lodgings or alcohol, but they had all done other work before, and sometimes after, they had started to work as prostitutes.

The case of Emily Warder illustrates the way that prostitutes were dealt with in newspaper reports and the ways in which they could end up in trouble with the police.

> Emily Warder, 28 was charged … with being drunk and disorderly outside the Sailors' Home, Half Street Whitechapel. The prisoner had been found by a constable dancing about at night outside the home in a suit of men's clothes, belonging to a young sailor who was staying with her.

Julia Le Fair, one of the few women actually referred to directly as a prostitute in the newspaper records of the Thames Police Court, shows how this work could lead to involvement in crime, as well as making the women very vulnerable in other ways (see Source C).

## PROSTITUTION

1 What links between drink, crime and prostitution can you see in the case of Julia Le Fair?

2 What attitude towards prostitutes can we detect in the newspaper report (see Source C) and in the charges against Le Fair?

**Source C** From a report in the *East London Observer*, 22 September 1877.

*SHOCKING ASSAULT ON A SAILOR – Julia Le Fair 32, a prostitute, was charged with feloniously [seriously] cutting and wounding a sailor, named Jackson ... It appears that on Tuesday night last, the prisoner and the injured man were in one of the low lodging houses in the vicinity of Wellclose-Square. A quarrel broke out between them in the course of which ... they then had a struggle and fell on the ground together, knocking over a paraffin lamp. The prisoner is then said to have caught hold of the lamp and struck the man on the side of the head with it ... causing him to lose a great deal of blood.*

# Immigration

As we have seen, tensions also came from the presence of Jewish and other minority communities in Whitechapel. The stories in the archives often focused on stereotypes of the greed or dishonesty of Jewish criminals – so there are tales of Jewish bigamists and false doctors defrauding young Jewish women of all their money. In one article in the *Derby Telegraph* Mr Montague Williams (who had been a magistrate at the Thames Police Court) described how difficult he found it to decide cases where each side was Jewish (see Source D). Jewish shopkeepers and tailors were in competition with other traders and workers. Suspicion and anti-Semitism also caused problems for Jewish people living in Whitechapel. In turn, especially more recently arrived Jewish immigrant communities tended to try to police their own problems. They were in fact unlikely to go to the police if they were victims of crime, because they were treated so badly by the police in their homelands of Russia and Poland.

The police themselves were made nervous and suspicious by the presence of many eastern European Jews in Whitechapel. In 1904 the Superintendent of Whitechapel Division wrote to the Home Office to ask for funds to pay for language lessons in Yiddish, a language often spoken by Jewish immigrants (see Source E).

## IMMIGRATION

1 Which words and phrases from Source D tell us that there was prejudice against Jewish people?
2 What things meant that many immigrants did not mix with other people living in Whitechapel?

## Visible learning

### Thinking carefully about sources

When you use a source, there are three stages to think about:

1 What is it telling you about the subject of the enquiry – either directly or through what you can infer?
2 What does the information about the author or speaker, and details such as the date, suggest about how reliable or useful the source is for the enquiry?
3 How does your knowledge of the topic help you decide how useful the source is? For example, from your knowledge, does an account seem typical of other accounts of the same topic?

1. What valuable information does each report give me?

2. Does Williams [Source D] seem well-informed and does his evidence agree with other sources?

3. Does my knowledge of how Jewish people were treated suggest these sources are useful evidence?

**Source D** An extract from a news article published in 1889 reporting the words of Mr Montague Williams, a magistrate at Thames Police Court.

*[Jews] thought no more of taking an oath to a lie than they did of drinking a glass of water. He often felt bewildered in the attempt to decide disputes between the foreign Jews living in [Whitechapel], and it was quite certain that if one side told half a dozen lies in their cases, witnesses [for the other side] would be forthcoming to tell as many lies.*

**Source E** From a Letter to the Home Office from the Superintendent of Whitechapel Division, 1904.

*Bills and circulars in this language are distributed and posted all over the division, but police know nothing of their [meaning]. As it is known that a number of these people are members of Continental Revolutionary Societies it would be very desirable to have members of the service who could speak this language.*

So, just before the Whitechapel murders the MET seemed to be in chaos. Two chief inspectors had resigned in little more than two years following corruption scandals and riots that had been too lightly controlled and protests which had been too violently put down. James Monro, the head of the CID had resigned just before the first Ripper murder, and his replacement was on a long holiday in Switzerland. Combined with their inability to prevent the Ripper's killing spree, these events made the MET look ineffective.

## Political demonstrations and strikes

The politics of some of the new Jewish immigrants, and their reaction to the low wages and long hours they had to work, also caused problems for the police. This can be seen in the report of a riot which followed a protest on 16 March 1889. This protest march had set off from the International Workers' Association headquarters in Berner Street towards the Chief Rabbi's synagogue in Aldgate. The protestors wanted the rabbi to preach against their low wages and long hours – he refused. When the protestors returned to Whitechapel, the police raided the IWA on Berner Street, and arrested the leaders of the march. They were found guilty of assaulting police officers during their arrest, and one was given three months' hard labour as well as a £40 bond for good behaviour afterwards. That autumn there was a strike of 10,000 sweatshop tailors, which was more successful than the protests in March. They demanded, and got, a maximum twelve-hour working day.

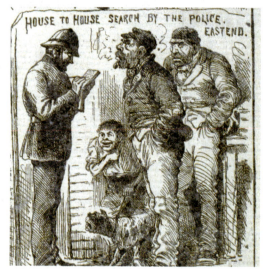

▲ **Source H** From *Illustrated Police News* 27th October. This image was taken from the front page in 1888, showing how those living outside Whitechapel saw the immigrant communities who lived there.

## Attacks on Jews

Newspaper reports also contain stories of crimes and attacks carried out against Jewish people. In most of these cases the victim's religion was not the cause of the assault, which often happened during robberies. However, some Jews were targeted because of their religion (see Source F).

### CONFLICT BETWEEN JEWS AND CHRISTIANS

There were sometimes reports of conflict between people because of their religious differences. In October 1878, an article in the *East London Observer* covered a disturbance outside St Mary's (see Source G). There is a tradition in some forms of Christianity that Jesus will return to earth when the Jews have converted to Christianity. St Mary's was well-known as a place which preached to the Jews. It is clear that not all Jewish people living in Whitechapel appreciated the attempt to convert Jews to Christianity, and policing these tensions was one of the difficulties that H Division faced. The police had to bring this crowd under control, but it seems that they had another problem. Mr Lushington, a magistrate at the Thames Police Court who was not known for letting people off lightly, dismissed the evidence against the three Jewish defendants – and he noted in particular that one policeman's story was very different from the others, which suggests that Lushington had detected anti-semitic bias in the testimony of at least one of these constables.

# 1.7 How did the police try to capture the Ripper?

Between 31 August and 9 November 1888 five women were murdered in strikingly similar and gruesome ways – as we can see below. There was a frenzy of coverage in the press, and a large number of letters from hoaxers to the papers and to the police, claiming to be the murderer – one of whom signed himself as 'Jack the Ripper'. This nickname stuck – it highlighted the brutal way that the killer opened the bodies of his victims, often taking body parts as 'souvenirs'. The crimes got grizzlier as they went on – until they suddenly stopped after the terrible murder and mutilation of Mary Kelly in November 1888. There

had been women murdered before in Whitechapel, and there were others afterwards, but only these five have been conclusively linked to the Ripper.

As we will see, the failure of the police to capture the killer made them seem incompetent. Cartoons and newspaper articles (see page 158) presented them as helpless, perhaps even clueless, in their response to the Ripper. In reality, the police worked extraordinarily hard, and tried a number of ways to capture the killer, though none were successful. There is even evidence that the police improved their use of some techniques as the case went on.

## THE RIPPER'S VICTIMS

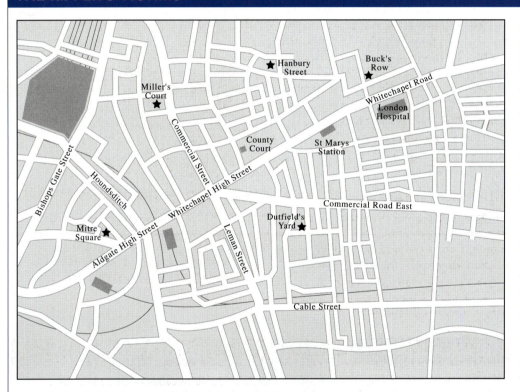

### Elizabeth Stride and Catherine Eddowes, 30 September

Stride was found first, at Dutfield's Yard, outside the theatre where Jewish socialists had been meeting in Berner Street. Stride's throat was cut – but nothing else was done to her, possibly because the killer was interrupted. Eddowes' body, found hours later in Mitre Square, was badly mutilated and disembowelled. This time the killer had cut at the face – taking a part of her nose and part of one ear. Later that morning, part of her apron was found at Goulston Street. These killings became known as the 'double event'.

### Mary Nichols, 31 August

Nichols was the first victim whose death seems to match the Ripper's methods. She was found in Bucks Row, to the north-east of Whitechapel. Her throat had been cut. It wasn't realised that her abdomen had been cut open until she was examined at the mortuary.

### Annie Chapman, 8 September

Chapman was found near some steps in George's Yard off Hanbury Street, near Commercial Street to the north of the Whitechapel Road. There were signs that she had been strangled before her throat was cut. Some of her intestines had been pulled out of her body.

### Mary Kelly, 9 November

Kelly's body was the most badly 'ripped', perhaps because unlike the other killings, her murder had taken place inside her room at Miller's Court in Dorset Street. Her injuries were terrible {-} parts of her body were cut completely out and strewn around the room. The policeman who first saw the body through a broken window said that it was 'indescribable'.

## INVESTIGATIVE TECHNIQUES

We are going to study the following techniques:

- careful observation
- autopsy
- photography and sketches
- interviews and following up clues
- identifying suspects.

Create six note cards so that you can record what you learn about each of

these techniques. For each technique you need to record a few sentences about:

- how the police used this technique
- things that made this technique more or less effective
- ways in which this technique was developing.

**?**

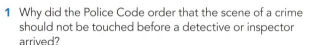

Careful observation

The police used observation to help them gather clues and evidence.

• Inspector Chandler made a note of how the blood from Annie Chapman splashed on a nearby fence …

## Careful observation

The Police Code, written by Howard Vincent, set out what constables were supposed to do when they came across the scene of a crime. Mainly, this was keeping the area clear of onlookers so that evidence wasn't disturbed before an inspector or detective arrived. The job of the inspector was to make a careful note of the scene, so that this could be used for investigating the crime and identifying the criminal.

**Source A**
A mock-up of the cover of the Police Code – a set of instructions designed by the head of CID to improve the way the police collected evidence. It was used from the early 1880s.

▶

A
POLICE CODE
AND
General Manual of the Criminal Law
FOR THE BRITISH EMPIRE

BY
C.E. HOWARD VINCENT, ESQ., C.B., M.P.,
*Late Director of Criminal Investigation*

SIXTH ABRIDGED EDITION

PRECEDED BY
*ADDRESSES ON POLICE DUTIES*

BY
THE HON. SIR HENRY HAWKINS
THE COMMISSIONER OF POLICE OF THE METROPOLIS

### THE IMPORTANCE OF OBSERVATION

The record of the bruises and marks on the bodies of the Ripper's victims were very important in helping decide how he killed them. There was never any blood on the front which suggests that they were on their backs when their throats were cut. The bruises on their faces and necks perhaps tell us how this was done – it seems they were strangled, either to death or to unconsciousness beforehand. They were dead before they were cut open.

This observation of the scene wasn't always possible, as Inspector Spratling's report from the night of Mary Nichols' murder shows. Instead of waiting for the arrival of an inspector, the doctor had called for an 'ambulance' (really a kind of wheeled stretcher) to take the body to the mortuary (a place where bodies are examined and stored before burial). However, it was Spratling who noticed that

the body had been disembowelled, and his report contains a detailed record of what Nichols was wearing. At the scene of Annie Chapman's killing, Inspector Chandler made a very detailed observation which included noticing the pattern of blood spots on the fence and floor next to her neck.

## MAKING OBSERVATIONS

**?**

1 Why did the Police Code order that the scene of a crime should not be touched before a detective or inspector arrived?

2 Explain two important observations that the police made during the Ripper investigation.

3 How accurately were police able to estimate times of death?

4 What similarities were there between these crimes which made the police think they were looking for one suspect?

▲ **Source B** The outside of Mary Kelly's lodging house at 13 Miller's Court taken the day after her murder. The arrow on the picture shows the broken window through which Bowyer made his discovery.

# Photography and sketches

The Metropolitan Police made limited use of photographs during our period. Photographs were commonly taken of bodies before and after a post-mortem, although they were used for identification of the victim rather than to help solve the crime. We might argue that, during the Ripper investigation, the Metropolitan Police seem to have developed their use of photography (as we will see when looking at the Mary Kelly murder scene) – possibly because they worked more closely with the City of London Police, which had made much more use of this technology. However some historians think that even the photographs taken at the scene of Kelly's murder were actually taken by a photographer from the City of London Police, which would suggest that the use of photography by the Met was still limited.

## SKETCHES OF A KILLER

The newspapers produced several pictures of Jack the Ripper, like Source C. However, these were never part of the official investigation, and it is not clear on what information the sketches were made, other than descriptions given at coroner's inquests or perhaps in statements like the one that Matthew Packer gave (see Source H).

## Sketches

Today when we think of a police sketch we might think of an identikit drawing from a witness statement. This technique was not used by the police until the mid-1890s, years after the Ripper killings stopped. The City of London Police did collect detailed drawings of Mitre Square and the doctor called to Catherine Eddowes' crime scene made a sketch of the position and condition of her body before she was moved. The City Police also asked Frederick William Foster to make drawings of the position of her body in Mitre Square, for the inquest.

When Mary's Kelly's body was discovered on the morning of 9 November 1888, the room in which she was lying was not opened for more than two hours after her body was spotted through a broken window by her landlord's servant. The inspector on the scene was hoping that bloodhounds could be brought to use to track the murderer and did not want to confuse them by disturbing the scene. At the same time a photographer was called to document it. Pictures were taken from outside, through the broken window, and then of inside the room and Mary's body. These pictures are horrible, but they did record the crime scene, and have been used since by criminologists and historians studying the case.

## SKETCHES OF THE RIPPER ?

1 Why did the papers publish sketches like the one in Source C even though they had no clear description of the Ripper?

2 In what ways did the Metropolitan and City Police differ in the way they recorded a crime scene?

3 How accurate do you think the estimates of the time of death of each victim were?

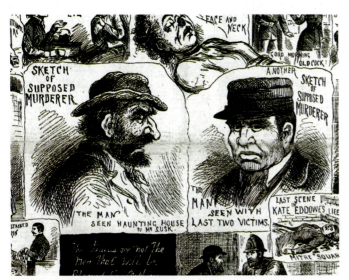

▲ **Source C** Sketches of Jack the Ripper, from *Illustrated Police News*, 20 October 1888.

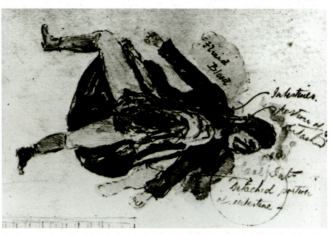

▲ **Source D** A sketch by the police surgeon of the City of London Police of Catherine Eddowes' body at Mitre Square.

## Autopsy

Post-mortem or autopsy examinations (looking at and inside the body of the victim) have been happening since classical times. We read about Lucy Fisher's autopsy on page 120, and all the Ripper's victims had autopsies, the details of which were given to the police. From the start the police thought that they were looking for a left-handed murderer, from the way that the bodies were injured.

### CORONER'S INQUESTS

Coroner's inquests are official meetings at which the coroner, someone given the job of investigating suspicious deaths, makes a decision about whether the person has been killed or has died naturally. Most of the original coroner's papers have not survived. So, how do we know about what happened at coroner's inquests? Fortunately, because inquests were public meetings, newspapers reported them.

**Source E** A report of the coroner's inquest on Mary Kelly's body from the *Morning Post*, 13 November 1888.

*Thomas Bowyer, 27, stated that he was a servant to Mr McCarthy and served in his chandler's shop. At a quarter to eleven on Friday morning he was ordered to go to 'Mary Jane's' room, No. 13 to get the rent which was in arrears. He knocked at the door but received no answer. He knocked again, and, as there was still no reply he went round the house and where there was a broken window he … pulled the curtain aside, looked in and saw two lumps of flesh lying on a table close by the bed. The second time he looked he saw a body lying on the bed and blood on the floor.*

### BODY TEMPERATURE: TIME OF DEATH

One of the most important observations that could be made was the temperature of the body. Using thermometers, in 1868 two doctors at Guy's Hospital had produced tables that showed how quickly bodies lost heat, so that the time of their death could be calculated. However, this was a very new technique, and the common practice in the police at the time was to feel the arms and legs to see if the ends of them had cooled down. PC Lamb 252H, who took control of the scene of Elizabeth Stride's murder on the night of 30 September, felt that her face was still warm. This, and the fact that although her throat had been slit, she had not been 'ripped', made the police think that she had not been dead for very long. They also thought it likely that the killer had been interrupted before he could start to cut open her body.

## Interviews and following up clues

The police went to houses and businesses in the areas around where each of the bodies were found. After the murders of Elizabeth Stride and Catherine Eddowes on 30 September 1888 (known as 'the double event' – see page 151), they made a full-scale search of lodging houses in the Whitechapel area, in the hope of finding evidence that would lead them to the killer. This led to them questioning more than 2,000 people, with a focus on butchers and slaughter-men. The Metropolitan Police also printed handbills and posters to be displayed and handed out in Whitechapel.

# POLICE NOTICE.

## TO THE OCCUPIER

On the mornings of Friday, 31st August Saturday, 8th, and Sunday, 30th Sept. 1888, Women were murdered in or near Whitechapel, supposed by some one residing in the immediate neighbourhood. Should you know of any person to whom suspicion is attached, you are earnestly requested to communicate at once with the nearest Police Station.

Metropolitan Police Office,
30th September, 1888

▲ **Source F** The words on one of 80,000 handbills that were handed out in the days after 30 September 1888.

### Practice questions

1 Describe two features of:
   a) the use by the police of photographic evidence
   b) the use by the police of sketches
2 How useful are Sources A (on page 152) and D (page 153) for an enquiry into how the police investigated the Ripper crimes? Explain your answer using Sources A and D and your knowledge of the historical context.
3 How could you follow up Source C on page 158 to find out more about how the public felt about the Ripper investigation? Use the following headings:
   a) Detail in Source C that I would follow up
   b) Question I would ask
   c) What type of source I could use
   d) How this might help answer my question.

## Witness statements

Howard Vincent's Police Code, which was in use from 1881, set out the way in which statements should be recorded by the police. The statement was written using only the words of the witness, and then read back to them. Errors were corrected by crossing out so that the error should still be seen, after which each page was signed. Statements were also taken at coroners' inquests. A witness statement was given by a Mr Hutchinson after the death of Mary Kelly (see Source G).

> **Source G** An extract from George Hutchinson's witness statement. Hutchinson thought he saw Kelly talking to a man in Commercial Street just before her murder.
>
> *I heard her say alright to him and the man said you will be alright for what I have told you, he then placed his right hand around her shoulders. He also had a kind of a small parcel in his left hand, with a kind of a strap around it. I stood against the lamp of the Ten Bells Queens Head Public House, and watched him. They both then came past me and the man hid down his head, with his hat over his eyes. I stooped down and looked in the face. He looked at me stern.*

## Following up clues

Inspector Chandler was sent to follow up clues such as a scrap of paper in Annie Chapman's possessions, which had come from an army regiment in Hampshire. Inspector Abberline went to Gravesend in Kent to arrest a delirious ex-pub landlord who matched the description of a man who had been seen at Chapman's murder. According to the historian Neil R. A. Bell, after house-to-house enquiries after 'the double event' the police then followed up 300 lines of enquiry and arrested 80 people across London for further investigation and questioning. All these clues and leads came to nothing, but they show how active the police were in tracing them to the end.

> ### WERE THERE ENOUGH POLICEMEN?
>
> #### Plain-clothed and extra officers
>
> As early as 29 September 1888, orders were given for more constables to work in plain clothes – six in total. This had grown to more than twenty by the end of October. This was in addition to the approximately 50 constables who were transferred temporarily to Whitechapel to work on the Ripper case, and to help keep order as the public began to panic.

# Identification techniques

The main identification technique available was for police to take notes from the descriptions given by witnesses. A good example is that of Matthew Packer, who claimed that he had seen Elizabeth Stride in Berner Street, just before she was murdered.

> **Source H** An extract from Matthew Packer's statement, summarised by Carmichael Bruce, who was still standing in as head of CID.
>
> *On Sat night about 11pm a young man from 25–30 – about 5.7 with long black coat buttoned up – soft felt hat, kind of Yankee hat rather broad shoulders – rather quick in speaking, rough voice … He had a frock coat on – no gloves. He was about 1 1/2 inch or 2 or 3 inches – a little higher than she was.*

As you can see, this is quite a detailed description. The only problem with it is that it was probably made up, as we will see. The police realised that Packer was not a reliable witness. So, descriptions like these were only helpful if they were based on real information, and they took time to note down as well as to follow up.

The art of identification sketches was only just developing and was not used in the Ripper investigation. The ideas of a Frenchman, Alphonse Bertillon, were taken up as official policy in the 1890s – the use of mug-shots and facial measurements to reconstruct sketches of suspects from descriptions. However, this was not available to the police investigating the Ripper murders. Similarly, the idea of using fingerprints had been suggested, but it wasn't until the early years of the twentieth century that they were actually first used in criminal investigations.

>
>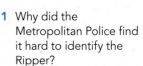
>
> ## IDENTIFYING CRIMINALS
>
> 1 Why did the Metropolitan Police find it hard to identify the Ripper?
>
> 2 What improvements were taking place in the methods of investigation and detection that the police had?
>
> 3 What evidence is there that the Metropolitan Police could have made better use of some of these techniques?

**Identity parades** were used from the beginning of the Whitechapel murder investigations, but without success, although they were useful in ruling out suspects such as Jack Pizer or 'Leather Apron', whose nickname was circulated in the press (see page 158).

## ABSTRACT OF
## THE ANTHROPOMETRICAL SIGNALMENT

1. Height.
2. Reach.
3. Trunk.
4. Length of head.
5. Width of head.
6. Right ear.
7. Left foot.
8. Left middle finger.
9. Left forearm.

▲ A diagram explaining Bertillon's system for photographing criminals, from a book published in 1896 in the USA as a guide for American police.

## Criminal profiles

The Ripper investigation was the first documented use of a criminal profile. These involve using the evidence gathered about the criminal and from the crime scene to work out the type of person that the police should be looking for. Following the murder of Mary Kelly, Dr Thomas Bond was asked to prepare a profile of the killer. Bond was a **police surgeon** at the scene of Kelly's murder, and had carried out her autopsy. He was then given the papers and records of the other four killings in order to write a report on the case as a whole.

> **Source I** From Dr Bond's report on the murderer.
>
> *The murderer in external appearance is quite likely to be a quiet inoffensive looking man probably middle aged and neatly and respectably dressed. I think he must be in the habit of wearing a cloak or overcoat or he could hardly have escaped notice in the streets if the blood on his hands and clothes were visible … he would probably be solitary and eccentric in his habits, also he is most likely to be a man without regular occupation, but with some small income or pension. He is possibly living among respectable persons who have some knowledge of his character and habits and who may have grounds for suspicion that he is not quite right in his mind at times.*

## INTERVIEWS AND CLUES

1 What evidence is there that the Metropolitan Police were working hard to catch the Ripper?

2 Explain how the police make witness statements as accurate as possible.

3 Why did the questioning focus on butchers and slaughtermen?

## BLOODHOUNDS

One development that was not carried through was the use of bloodhounds. The Met Commissioner Charles Warren had ordered a trial of their use and a pair bred by Mr Edwin Brough, who had a reputation for breeding excellent dogs, were brought down from Scarborough in Yorkshire. The trial at the start of October went well, and the next stage in the plan was to use the dogs at a murder scene. However, there was a lull between the 'double event' and the murder of Mary Kelly – and Mr Brough took the dogs back to Scarborough on 1 November, frustrated at the delays.

# 1.8 How did the press make it more difficult for the police to investigate the Ripper case?

During the Whitechapel murders those in charge of the police seemed to be in chaos. Two chief inspectors had resigned in little more than two years, after corruption scandals and riots, which the papers reported in great detail. James Monro, the head of the CID, had resigned just before the first Ripper murder, and his replacement was on a long holiday in Switzerland. This seemed to leave the CID without a leader at a crucial point. The fact that they could not capture 'the Ripper' seemed to confirm that the police could not do their jobs properly. However, as we have seen, the police on the ground were working very hard to find the killer – but they didn't seem to get any credit for this work in the press.

The papers themselves were full of criticism, as well as suggestions from those who thought that the police should be doing more than they were. The Reverend Samuel Barnett, a vicar from a nearby church, wrote to *The Times* claiming that the murders were partly caused by the failure of the police to revoke the licences of 'criminal haunts' – pubs in which criminals and prostitutes mixed. Other letters suggested that the police should use bloodhounds, or even set up a team of policemen disguised as prostitutes so that they could trap the Ripper.

▲ **Source A** A cartoon from the news magazine *Punch*, October 1888 – the posters are advertising newspapers filled with horrible details of the murders.

## CORNELL NOTES

You need to record the information in this section so that you remember how the press affected the Ripper investigation. You can use a 'Cornell Notes' Knowledge Organiser to help you do this. Split your page into three, as shown in the diagram below. As you read through pages 157–161 you should make notes, as you might do normally. When you have done this read through your notes, and in the wider margin on the left write some questions that are answered by your notes. For instance, you might write 'Published Matthew Packer's story that he sold grapes to "Jack" and Elizabeth Stride' when you are first making notes, and then 'How did the press encourage false stories?' when you come back to review these notes. In the bottom box you can write further questions that you'd like to find out the answers to, or make a note of anything that confuses you.

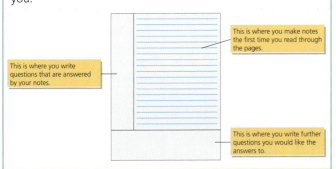

This is where you make notes the first time you read through the pages.

This is where you write questions that are answered by your notes.

This is where you write further questions you would like the answers to.

## ACTIVITY

1 Try to remember why the Met was in trouble in 1881. Make a list of events that suggest the Met was in crisis. Looking back over pages 132–136, have you missed anything?

2 Why were people so worried and fascinated with crime in Whitechapel? Make a list of all the reasons and then check back over pages 128–131 to see if you have remembered everything.

## Sensational Stories

The Ripper murders were an opportunity for the newspapers to sell copies. There was fierce competition between the thirteen morning and nine evening daily papers being sold in London. This led to stories that sensationalised the details of the murders – and witnesses even made things up.

### SENSATIONALISM

We often find references in newspaper sources to seven, eight and even ten, eleven or more victims of the Ripper. The papers were adding to the list victims of murders that happened before the first Ripper killing of Mary Nichols on 31 August. They continued to add other murder victims after the killing of Mary Kelly on 9 November – despite the fact that they did not match the very unusual methods used to murder the 'canonical' victims.

TWO PRIVATE DETECTIVES ON THE TRACK OF THE ASSASSIN.

WHERE HE BOUGHT THE GRAPES FOUND BESIDE THE MURDERED WOMAN.

MATTHEW PACKER'S STORY.

INTERVIEW WITH THE MAN WHO SPOKE TO THE MURDERER.

▲ **Source B** Headlines from the *London Evening News*, 4 October 1888.

The police did not give very much information about the murders – beyond the details that might help identify the victims. Journalists had to rely on speaking to people that gathered when the body had been found in order to get a description. This led to the press printing many details and stories that weren't true or exaggerated. Annie Chapman's rings had been ripped from her fingers, and were never found – but in some stories the journalist claimed that they had been arranged at the feet of the body.

## The press and the reputation of the police

As the newspapers filled with apparent witnesses and descriptions of the murderer it made it seem even more incredible that the police had not caught the killer. Cartoons which presented the police as incompetent made this feeling even worse. On 1 October, the *Pall Mall Gazette*, which had been a critic of Charles Warren even before the Ripper attacks, gleefully reported on a demonstration in Victoria Park in Bethnal Green at which speakers called for Warren's resignation (see Source C).

**Source C** From a report on a public demonstration in Bethnal Green, published in the *Pall Mall Gazette*, 1 October 1888.

*After several speeches upon the conduct of the Home Secretary and Sir Charles Warren, a resolution was unanimously passed that it was high time both officers should resign and make way for some officers who would leave no stone unturned for the purpose of bringing the murderers to justice, instead of allowing them to run riot in a civilised city like London.*

Warren did not help matters. In early October the Board of Works (a kind of local council for London) published a statement which called on the police to do more to stop the Ripper. Warren published a reply which claimed, 'Statistics show that London, in comparison to its population, is the safest city in the world to live in' and went on to suggest that the Board should provide more street lights to make it harder for criminals like the Ripper.

### LEATHER APRON

The rumours that the newspapers published also led to dead ends, and to suspects going into hiding. One such suspect was John Pizer – a Jewish cobbler known as 'Leather Apron'. Pizer was a strange and violent man who had threatened prostitutes. A suspect with his nickname was reported in the paper, and Pizer was then arrested hiding at the home of a family member. It became clear that Pizer had a good alibi for the murders and he was released.

# The Ripper Letters

The press also published many of the letters that they received from people claiming to be Jack the Ripper – in fact it was one of these letters, signed by 'Jack the Ripper', that gave the killer his nickname. The first two were published at the request of the police – in the hope that they might lead them to the identity of the killer. They were in the same handwriting, and made references which made them convincing.

> **Source D** A letter received by the Central News Agency on 27 September, and passed on to the police on 1 October 1888.
>
> *Dear Boss,*
>
> *I keep on hearing the police have caught me but they wont fix me just yet. I have laughed when they look so clever and talk about being on the right track. That joke about Leather Apron gave me real fits. I am down on whores and I shant quit ripping them till I do get buckled. Grand work the last job was. I gave the lady no time to squeal. How can they catch me now. I love my work and want to start again. You will soon hear of me with my funny little games. I saved some of the proper red stuff in a ginger beer bottle over the last job to write with but it went thick like glue and I cant use it. Red ink is fit enough I hope ha. ha. The next job I do I shall clip the ladys ears off and send to the police officers just for jolly wouldn't you. Keep this letter back till I do a bit more work, then give it out straight. My knife's so nice and sharp I want to get to work right away if I get a chance. Good Luck.*
>
> *Yours truly*
>
> *Jack the Ripper*

> **?** Look back at page 151 and the description of 'the double event'. Why might Catherine Eddowes' murder make this letter (Source D) seem more likely to have come from the killer?

# The Whitechapel Vigilance Committee

George Lusk, a builder from Whitechapel, felt not enough had been done to catch the killer and set up the Whitechapel Vigilance Committee. The Committee hired two private detectives to investigate the killings. These were the two who questioned Matthew Packer after his press interviews led him to claim that he had talked to the killer and sold grapes to Elizabeth Stride just before she was murdered. They also took Packer to the mortuary to identify Stride's body. Packer's story (which as we've seen was probably false) caused a great deal of interest in the papers and added to the panic on the streets of Whitechapel.

The Committee also published posters offering a small reward. They offered this reward after petitioning the Home Secretary, Matthews, to offer an official reward. The Government refused to do this, as neither the Home Secretary nor Charles Warren thought that it would produce useful information. In the past rewards had seemed to create lots of allegations made on suspicion or even made up completely. It was feared that these would take up police time, so an official reward was never offered.

Lusk became very well-known, and started to receive hoax letters from people claiming to be the Ripper. On 16 October Lusk received a parcel containing a human kidney and a letter with the address 'From Hell'.

> **Source E** A transcription of the 'From Hell' letter.
>
> *From Hell.*
>
> *Mr Lusk,*
>
> *Sor*
>
> *I send you half the Kidne I took from one woman and prasarved it for you tother piece I fried and ate it was very nise. I may send you the bloody knif that took it out if you only wate a whil longer*
>
> *signed*
>
> *Catch me when you can Mishter Lusk*

Lusk had the kidney examined by a Dr Openshaw at the London Hospital who confirmed that it was a human kidney preserved in wine. He confirmed it was human, but suggested that it could have been taken from any of the numerous bodies that turned up in London autopsies in normal times. Along with the dramatic letter, this seemed to be a joke, possibly by a medical student.

> ## Practice questions
>
> 1  Describe two features of:
>    a)  the treatment of the Ripper story by the newspapers
>    b)  the development of the CID.
> 2  How useful are Source F (page 154) and Source I (page 156) for an enquiry into the techniques used by police to identify suspects? Explain your answers using Sources F and I and your knowledge of the historical context.
> 3  How useful are Sources C (page 158) and E (page 159) for an enquiry into the attitude of Londoners to the police? Explain your answer using Sources C and E and your knowledge of the historical context.

# 1.9 Did the City and Metropolitan Police work well together?

We have already seen that rivalry and personality clashes meant that James Munro, the man in charge of CID, resigned just before the Ripper murders (see page 150), and that criticism of Warren (as well as a bad working relationship with the Home Secretary) forced him to resign just before the murder of Mary Kelly (see page 136). This made it look as if the top of the police force was in chaos – and accounts for some of the bad press that the police received.

However, on the ground the different types of police force and the different divisions of the Metropolitan Police, worked very well together. The other divisions helped by sending men to patrol the beat in Whitechapel. It was hoped that this increased manpower would make it more likely that the Ripper would be caught in the act. PC Long, who found the piece of Eddowes' apron on the night of 30 September, had been drafted in from A Division in order to increase the number of policemen on the streets, and is a good example of this kind of co-operation.

> **Source A**: A transcription of the graffiti seen above where the piece of Eddowes' apron was seen – written by Commissioner Charles Warren at the scene.
>
> *The Juwes are*
> *The men that*
> *Will not*
> *be Blamed*
> *for nothing*

In general there was also co-operation between the City and Metropolitan Police forces. Donald Swanson, who was in charge of the Whitechapel investigation at Scotland Yard, worked well with Inspector James McWilliam, who was in charge of the City's detectives. For instance, Swanson's reports comment on how 'cordial' the relationship was.

However, during the investigation there was a point at which the co-operation broke down – from the top down. On the night of 'the double event' – the night that both Elizabeth Stride and Catherine Eddowes were killed – there

was some anti-Jewish graffiti in chalk (see Source A) above the piece of Eddowes' apron covered in blood on Goulston Street, which PC Alfred Long found.

Eddowes' murder had taken place in Mitre Square, within the City Police's territory. The City of London Police were a separate and independent police force and not under Charles Warren's control. Two City detectives did see the chalk writing, and insisted that a photographer record the words. However, many people had decided that the crimes against women were being carried out by a Jew, and attacks on Jewish people had increased during the crisis. Warren decided that the risk of an anti-Semitic riot was too great to wait for a photographer to arrive and so he made a copy of the graffiti, and ordered that the writing be washed from the wall. This did cause problems, and criticism from the press. Warren had to write to the Home Office to explain his actions.

> **Source B** From a report written by Charles Warren and sent to the Home Office on 8 November 1888, shortly before his resignation.
>
> *It was just getting light, the public would be in the streets in a few minutes, in a neighbourhood very much crowded on Sunday mornings by Jewish vendors and Christian purchasers from all parts of London … The writing was visible to anybody in the street … after taking into consideration the excited state of the population in London generally at the time the strong feeling which had been excited against the Jews … I considered it desirable to obliterate the writing at once, having taken a copy.*

This seems to be the only point at which relations were strained. It could even be argued that H Division learned lots from the City of London Police during the investigation. Mary Kelly's murder scene was preserved and photographed. If we compare this to the way that the earlier Ripper crime scenes were handled then we could see this as evidence that H Division had learned from the City Police's handling and recording of the Mitre Square site where Catherine Eddowe's body was found.

## Practice questions

1 Describe two features of the co-operation between the City and Metropolitan police during the Ripper murders.

2 How useful are Sources A and B for an enquiry into cooperation between the Metropolitan and City police forces? Explain your answer using the sources and your knowledge of the historical context.

3 How could you follow up Source A (above) to find out more about the Goulston Street graffiti? Use the following headings:
   a) Detail in Source A that I would follow up
   b) Question I would ask
   c) What type of source I could use
   d) How this might help answer my question.

# 1.10 Conclusions

## What have I learned about crime and policing in Whitechapel?

When I first started looking at this period I had an outline of the topic in my head. I expected to find lots of poverty, and a violent society. My view of this part of London at that time was definitely dominated by what I thought I knew about the crimes of Jack the Ripper. I was convinced that Whitechapel was positively dangerous. My view of policing at the time was dominated by the idea of the detective – a Victorian hero, perhaps modelled on Sherlock Holmes who used clues and logic to solve crimes. Writing this book has meant that I have been able to read lots more about the topic, and to learn that the reality was **much** more complicated.

I have learned that Whitechapel was not just filled with a violent or thieving underclass of people desperately taking from each other what they could. Instead I found out it was a mixed area, with some very poor people, often immigrants from Russia, Ireland or elsewhere. Not all of these people trusted the police. Poor people often lived in crowded 'rookeries' but only a few streets away middle class families lived much more comfortably.

I learned that the conditions in which people lived, their low wages and the fact that they often lost work without any warning, meant that committing a crime was a way of surviving. The first case we looked at, the death of Lucy Fisher, made me think a lot about what would drive a mother to take a sick child out on a cold night so that she could use her for begging.

People turned to drink in response to their harsh lives. Some became alcoholics, which meant they were more likely to get involved in crime – in violent fights perhaps, or by becoming victims of crime like the women murdered by the Ripper.

I learned that many middle-class and wealthy Victorians were worried about poverty and crime. This led to investigations like Charles Booth's or the clearance of slums and the building of new model places to live like the Peabody Estate.

I have learned that the police were a relatively new force, and that the tools they had to use to combat crime were limited. Detection was viewed suspiciously – people were worried that the police were snooping into their lives.

I learned that crime was big news – people across London read avidly about the work of the police in newspapers, and that this interest became a frenzy in 1888 during the Ripper crisis.

Finally, I learned that the police had a tough job in catching the Ripper, because they didn't have many of the forensic tools that we might use today.

## What next?

One of the reasons I chose to study and to teach history is that it is never 'done'. There are always new questions that can be followed up, and often there are new books, or new pieces of research to read, or even more sources to consider and fit into the jigsaw. The questions I would like to explore next are:

1 Is there any record of how women in Whitechapel felt about and reacted to the Jack the Ripper crisis?

2 What was the impact of slum clearance on crime in Whitechapel in the longer term?

3 What patterns over time can we see in the types of crimes that were committed during the period? Did types of crime change as the types of people living in Whitechapel changed?

4 What did H Division policemen think of the way the Metropolitan Police handled the Ripper crisis?

5 Did the reputation of the Metropolitan Police recover quickly?

To find out the answers I need to think about what kinds of sources might help me. Here are some possibilities.

| | |
|---|---|
| housing and employment records | photographs |
| council records | London newspapers |
| Census returns | national newspapers |
| local police records | Old Bailey records of trials |
| coroner's reports | *Punch* cartoons |

### ACTIVITY: WHAT NEXT?

Which of these records and documents would help me answer the five questions above?

# 1.11 Visible learning: Review and revise

## Thinking about sources

This activity will help you practise asking questions and choosing sources. We have done a lot of work already in this unit to prepare you for questions 1 and 2 in paper 1 of your exam. You can also find more guidance on the specifics of tackling these questions on pages 168-169. This page is designed to help you with question 2b in paper 1 of your exam. Question 2b will look like this:

2(b) How could you follow up Source B to find out more about the problems in (a topic will be identified)? In your answer, you must give the question you would ask and the type of source you could use. Complete the table below. (4 marks)

> Detail in Source B that I would follow up:
>
> Question I would ask:
>
> What type of source I could use:
>
> How this might help answer my question:

The focus is, therefore, on asking questions, identifying sources that would be relevant to the topic and would help you answer the questions you ask, and on using your knowledge of the topic. You can find more guidance on this question on page 170 but this activity will help you practise asking questions and choosing sources.

> 1 Choose one of the topics in the *purple box* below. Write down at least two questions you want to ask about it to deepen your knowledge.
>
> 2 Look at the sources in the *blue box*. Select one source that might help you answer your questions, and then explain how it might do this. You could choose different sources for each question.
>
> 3 Repeat these steps for at least one more topic.

## Topics to find out more about

| 1 Types of crime and criminals | 2 Workhouses | 3 Poverty and causes of crime |
|---|---|---|
| 4 Lodging houses | 5 Jewish immigration | 6 Irish immigration |
| 7 Political activism | 8 Recruitment to H Division | 9 The role of the constable on the beat |
| 10 Improvements in detection techniques | 11 Newspapers and crime | 12 The development of the CID |

## Sources you could use

| A Housing and employment records | B Council records | C Census returns |
|---|---|---|
| D Charles Booth's survey | E Workhouse records | F Local police records |
| G Coroner's reports | H Photographs | I London newspapers |
| J Old Bailey records of trials | K *Punch* cartoons | L CID records |
| M Home office papers | | |

# Cementing your knowledge

In your examination you will be asked three questions (see pages 164–165). These questions will be about the sources we use to find out about crime and policing in Whitechapel and will also test your skills in enquiry, such as asking questions. To do well in all the questions you also need a good level of knowledge about the topics you have studied in this unit. Examiners will be looking to see how much you know and how you use that knowledge in your answers. Therefore it is important that you make that knowledge stick in your brain.

## 1 Test yourself!

The more you identify what you're not sure about, the more chance you have of filling those gaps and doing well in the exam. How many of these can you get right?

| | | |
|---|---|---|
| 1 What kinds of trials took place at the Old Bailey? | 2 Where was the most notorious 'rookery' in Whitechapel? | 3 Explain what 'having money for doss' means. |
| 4 What was the name of the man who gave money to help build better housing in Whitechapel? | 5 Why did prostitutes visit pubs frequently? | 6 Which immigrant groups had been moving into Whitechapel? |
| 7 Explain the differences between the Workhouse and the Casual Ward. | 8 Why did many people in Whitechapel turn to crime? | 9 What evidence is there that Victorians were worried about poverty? |
| 10 When was the first and last Ripper murder? | 11 Explain the beat system. | 12 What was the Whitechapel Vigilance Committee? |

## 2 Asking questions

We have provided some answers below, but it is your job to come up with suitable matching questions. Try to make each question as detailed as possible so that you are using your knowledge to help you word it.

| | | | | |
|---|---|---|---|---|
| 1 Lodging houses | 2 Sailors | 3 Rookery | 4 Bessarabian gang | 5 Alphonse Bertillon |
| 6 Sarah Fisher | 7 The Old Bailey | 8 Commercial Street | 9 William Short | 10 Sir Charles Warren |

## 3 Telling stories

The tasks in 1 and 2 above focus on individual pieces of information, but you also need to have an understanding of the stories at the heart of this unit. Take each of these questions and prepare an answer that will take you a minute or two to explain aloud. Explaining it aloud will help to cement it in your brain.

1    Why was Whitechapel a place with lots of criminal activity?
2    How did the reputation of the Metropolitan Police change during the period?
3    What steps were being taken to make Whitechapel a better place to live?
4    How was policing organised in Whitechapel?
5    How did the newspapers make it more difficult to investigate the Ripper murders?
6    What steps did the police take to catch the Ripper?
7    What were the aims of the beat system?
8    Why weren't bloodhounds used in the Ripper investigation?
9    How did methods of identifying criminals and investigating crime improve during the period?
10    How well did the Metropolitan Police co-operate with the City of London Police and the CID during the Ripper crisis?

# PART 3: Writing better history

## Introducing the exam

Simply knowing a lot of content is not enough to achieve a good grade in your GCSE History exam. You need to know how to write effective answers to the questions. Pages 164–178 give you an insight into the exam and provide guidance on how to approach the different questions. This page and page 165 introduce the structure of Paper 1 of your exam.

The guidance on page 166 helps you approach your exam with confidence.

Paper 1 is divided into two sections. Section A covers the **study of a historic environment** on Whitechapel, c.1870–c1900. Section B covers the **thematic study** of crime and punishment in Britain, c.1000–present.

---

### Paper 1: Thematic study and historic environment

**Option: Whitechapel, c.1870–c.1900: Crime, policing and the inner city**

**Time**: 1 hour 15 minutes
**You must have:**

**(1)** Source Booklet (enclosed)

**Instructions**

**(2)** • Answer Questions 1 and 2 from Section A.

**(3)** • From Section B, answer Questions 3 and 4 and then **EITHER** Question 5 **OR** Question 6.

**Information**

• The total mark for this paper is 52.

**(4)** • The marks for each question are shown in brackets.

#### SECTION A: Whitechapel, c.1870–c.1900

**Answer Questions 1 and 2.**

**1.** Describe two features of housing in Whitechapel between 1870 and 1900.

**(5)** Feature 1

Feature 2

**(Total for Question 1 = 4 marks)**

**2.** (a) Study Sources A and B in the Source Booklet.

**(6)** How useful are Sources A (Source D on page 154) and B (Source A on page 158) for an enquiry into the problems the police faced when investigating the Ripper murders?

Explain your answer, using Sources A and B and your own knowledge of the historical context.

(8 marks)

**(7)** (b) **Study Source B**

How would you follow up Source B to find out more about the types of crime committed in Whitechapel in this period?

In your answer, you must give the question you would ask and the type of source you could use.

Complete the table below:

(4 marks)

| Detail in Source B that I would follow up: _____ |
|---|
| Question I would ask: _____ |
| What type of source I could use: _____ |
| How this might help answer my question: _____ |

**(Total for Question 2 = 12 marks)**
**TOTAL FOR SECTION A = 16 MARKS**

**SECTION B: Crime and punishment, c.1000–present**

Answer Questions 3 and 4. Then answer EITHER Question 5 OR 6.

**8** → **3.** Explain one way in which trials in medieval England were similar to trials in the seventeenth century.

(4 marks)

**9** → **4.** Explain why there were changes to policing in the period between 1700 and 1900. (12 marks)

> You may use the following in your answer:
> * the growth of London    * increased taxation
>
> **10** → You **must** also use information of your own.

**Answer EITHER Question 5 OR Question 6.**

**Spelling, punctuation, grammar and the use of specialist terminology will be assessed in this question.**

**EITHER**

**11** → **5.** 'The role of the Church was the most important factor affecting law enforcement during the Middle Ages.'

How far do you agree? Explain your answer. (16 marks)

> You may use the following in your answer:
> * benefit of the clergy    * tithings
>
> You **must** also use information of your own.

**OR**

**6.** 'The main purpose of punishment during the period c.1000–c.1700 was to deter people from committing crimes.'

How far do you agree? Explain your answer. (16 marks)

> You may use the following in your answer:
> * corporal punishment    * the introduction of transportation
>
> You **must** also use information of your own.

**12** → (Total for spelling, punctuation, grammar and the use of specialist terminology = 4 marks)

(Total for Question 5 or 6 = 20 marks)

# Timing tip

It is important to time yourself carefully. One hour and fifteen minutes sounds a long time but it goes very quickly! Some students run out of time because they spend too long on Section A, thinking that it is worth spending half their time on this Section. However, Section A is worth 16 marks whereas Section B is worth 36 marks. The final two questions of Section B are worth more marks than all the other questions put together. This shows the importance of having a time plan and sticking to it.

Look at the plan on the sticky note to the right. You could use this plan or develop your own and check it with your teacher.

> Questions 1 and 2 approx. 25 minutes
>
> Questions 3 and 4 approx. 25 minutes
>
> Either Question 5 or 6 approx. 25 minutes

# Planning for success

### 1 THE SOURCE BOOKLET

The exam paper on pages 164 and 165 gives you an idea what your exam will look like. We have not included the Source Booklet. For practice use the sources and activities in Part 2 of this book (pages 114–163). Make sure you spend time reading and annotating the sources before you attempt Question 2 in the exam.

### 2 FOLLOW INSTRUCTIONS CAREFULLY

Read the instructions very carefully. Some students miss questions they need to answer while others waste time answering more questions than they need to answer. Remember to answer **both** parts of Question 2 and to choose between EITHER Question 5 OR 6. You will also see that for Question 1 you need to describe **two** key features whereas with Question 3 you only need to explain **one** way in which people's reactions were similar.

### 3 THINK CAREFULLY ABOUT WHICH QUESTION YOU CHOOSE

After Questions 1, 2, 3 and 4, you need to decide whether to answer Question 5 or Question 6. Do not rush your decision. Think carefully about which question you will perform best on. Plan your answer – it is worth 16 marks, nearly a third of the total marks for the paper.

### 4 SPEND TIME DE-CODING QUESTIONS

The marks for each question are shown in brackets. This gives you an idea of how much you need to write, as does the space for your answer on the exam paper. However, do not panic if you do not fill all the space. There will probably be more space than you need and the quality of your answer is more important than how much you write. The most important thing is to keep focused on the question. If you include information that is not relevant to the question you will not gain any marks, no matter how much you write!

Read each question carefully before you to start to answer it. Use the advice on de-coding questions on page 167 to make sure you focus on the question.

### 5 DESCRIBING KEY FEATURES

The first question asks you to describe two features of an aspect of the historic environment you have studied. Headings on the exam paper help you write about each feature separately. Advice on how to gain high marks is on page 168.

### 6 EVALUATING THE USEFULNESS OF A SOURCE

This question asks you to evaluate how useful two sources are for a specific enquiry. Use the Source Booklet to annotate the sources. Make sure you use your own knowledge to place the source in its historical context. This is a challenging task. Page 169 explains how to approach this question.

### 7 FOLLOWING UP A SOURCE

This question has four parts. You need to fill in the table on the exam paper. Page 170 provides advice on this question.

### 8 EXPLORING SIMILARITIES AND DIFFERENCES BETWEEN PERIODS

This is the first question that tests you on your knowledge and understanding of crime and punishment in Britain from c.1000 to the present. It will ask you to explain a similarity or a difference between the key features of two different periods. Page 171 explains how to answer this question.

### 9 EXPLAINING WHY CRIME AND PUNISHMENT PROGRESSED (OR STAYED THE SAME)

Questions such as this test your ability to write effective explanations. You may be asked to explain why crime and punishment progressed so quickly or why there was little change during a period. Pages 172–173 help you write a good answer to this question.

### 10 USING THE STIMULUS MATERIAL

When you attempt Question 4 and either Question 5 or 6 you will have bullet points as stimulus material to help plan your answer. You do not have to include them but try to use them to get you thinking and to support your arguments. You must bring in your own knowledge too. If you only use the stimulus material you will not gain high marks for your answer.

### 11 MAKING JUDGEMENTS

This question carries the most marks and requires a longer answer that needs careful planning. You will be provided with a statement. It may be about the pace of change in a period (for example Question 5) or the significance of an individual or a discovery (for example Question 6). Pages 174–175 provide advice on answering this question.

### 12 CHECKING THE QUALITY OF YOUR WRITING

Make sure you leave five minutes at the end of the exam to check your answers. If you are short of time check your answer to the final question first as spelling, punctuation, grammar and use of specialist terminology are assessed in this question. You can gain 4 additional marks on this question – page 176 provides advice on what to focus on. However, remember that the accuracy of your spelling, punctuation and grammar is important in all questions as it affects the clarity of your answer.

# De-coding exam questions

The examiners are not trying to catch you out: they are giving you a chance to show what you know – and what you can do with what you know. However, you must stick to the question on the exam paper. Staying focused on the question is crucial. Including information that is not relevant or misreading a question and writing about the wrong topic wastes time and gains you no marks.

To stay focused on the question you will need to practise how to 'de-code' questions. This is particularly important for Section B of the exam paper. Follow these **five steps to success**:

**Step 1** Read the question a couple of times. Then look at **how many marks** the question is worth. This tells you how much you are expected to write. Do not spend too long on questions only worth a few marks. Remember it is worth planning the 12- and 16-mark questions.

**Step 2** Identify the **conceptual focus** of the question. What is the key concept that the question focuses on? Is it asking you to look at:
- the **significance** of a discovery or individual
- **causation** – the reasons why an event or development happened
- **similarities** – between the key features of different periods
- **change** – the extent of change or continuity, progress or stagnation during a period?

**Step 3** Spot the **question type**. Are you being asked to:
- **describe** the key features of a period
- **explain** similarities between periods or why something happened
- **evaluate** how useful a source or collection of sources is
- reach a **judgement** as to how far you agree with a particular statement.

Each question type requires a different approach. Look for key words or phrases that help you work out which approach is needed. The phrase 'How far do you agree?' means you need to weigh the evidence for and against a statement before reaching a balanced judgement. 'Explain why' means that you need to explore a range of reasons why an event happened or why the pace of change during a period was fast or slow.

**Step 4** Identify the **content focus**. What is the area of content or topic the examiner wants you to focus on?

**Step 5** Look carefully at the **date boundaries** of the question. What time period should you cover in your answer? Stick to this carefully or you will waste time writing about events that are not relevant to the question.

Look at the exam question below. At first glance it appears this question is just about punishment. This shows the danger of not de-coding a question carefully. If you simply describe what punishments there were you will not get many marks as you are still not focusing on the actual question.

*The conceptual focus is change and continuity – you need to reach a judgement on how far deterrence was continuously the main reason behind punishments throughout the period, or whether other reasons played a greater part at times.*

*The date boundaries for the question are c.1000 and c.1700. If you include references to events in the eighteenth and nineteenth centuries you will waste time and not pick up any additional marks.*

6. 'The main purpose of punishment during the period c.1000–c.1700 was to deter people from committing crimes.' How far do you agree? Explain your answer.

(16 marks)

*16 marks are available – this means the question requires an extended answer. It is definitely worth planning this answer!*

*The content focus is more than just punishments that deterred. It is exploring a wider theme – the purpose of punishments and so includes other purposes.*

*The phrase 'How far do you agree?' means that this question requires you to reach a judgement about the statement in quotation marks. This means (with examples) how punishments were used to deter crime throughout the period. It also means weighing the importance of deterrence against other reasons for punishments used c.1000–c.1700 (to humiliate, reform or remove the criminal).*

## PRACTICE QUESTIONS

Look at the other questions in Section B of the exam paper on page 165.

Break each question down into the five steps and check you have de-coded the question effectively.

# Describing key features of a period

'Describe' questions only carry 4 marks so it is important to get to the point quickly so you do not waste precious time that is needed for questions that carry 12 or 16 marks.

Look at the question below.

> **1.** Describe two features of housing in Whitechapel between 1870 and 1900.
>
> (4 marks)
>
> Feature 1: _____
>
> Feature 2: _____

## Tip 1: Stay relevant to the question

One major problem with 'Describe' questions is that students write too much! They include details that are not relevant to the question. Make sure you stick to the question – describe housing in Whitechapel in this period.

You do not need to:

- include more than two features (extra features will gain you no more marks)
- evaluate and reach a judgement as to which was the worst or most important feature of housing in Whitechapel.

If you write too much you could run out of time later in the exam when you are answering questions that are worth a lot more marks and need longer answers.

## Tip 2: Keep it short and simple

You can get 2 marks by simply identifying two features of the housing in Whitechapel.

For each feature you identify add a sentence that adds further detail and develops your answer.

Look at the example below. Then practise your technique by tackling the examples in the practice question box.

**Key feature 1 identified**

Housing in Whitechapel was often of very poor quality.

 1 mark

**Answer developed**

In rookeries like those in Flower and Dean Street whole families would rent one room to live in.

 1 mark

**Key feature 2 identified**

Housing was changing because of slum clearance.

 1 mark

**Answer developed**

The Peabody Trust knocked down rookeries and lodging houses and built new houses with better ventilation, shared kitchens and bathrooms.

 1 mark

## Practice questions

1. Describe two features of an Old Bailey trial.
2. Describe two features of the organisation of policing in Whitechapel.
3. Describe two features of the effect of alcohol on crime in Whitechapel.
4. Describe two features of immigration into Whitechapel.
5. Describe two features of the difficulties of policing Whitechapel.
6. Describe two features of the police investigation during the Ripper murders.

### REMEMBER

Stay focused and keep it short and simple. Four sentences are enough for 4 marks.

# Evaluating the usefulness of sources

In Section A of the exam you will be asked to evaluate the value of a source for a specific enquiry. Look at the example below.

> **2.** (a) Study Sources A and B. How useful are Sources A and B for an enquiry into the problems the police faced when investigating the Ripper murders? Explain your answer, using Sources A and B and your own knowledge of the historical context. (8 marks)

You should annotate the sources in the booklet before you start to write your answer. Also, to evaluate effectively we need to use criteria. Use the criteria opposite to help you.

▼ **Source A** Part of a picture printed on the front page of the *Illustrated Police News*, October 1888.

**Source B** From a report on a public demonstration in Bethnal Green, published in the *Pall Mall Gazette*, 1 October, 1888.

After several speeches upon the conduct of the Home Secretary and Sir Charles Warren, a resolution was unanimously passed that it was high time both officers should resign and make way for some officers who would leave no stone unturned for the purpose of bringing the murderers to justice, instead of allowing them to run riot in a civilised city like London.

## REMEMBER

The question is asking you how useful the sources are, not how useless they are. There will not be any sources that are completely useless. Try not to get bogged down telling the examiner just what is wrong with a source. Look at the strengths of each source as well as considering any limitations. Try to begin and end your answer positively. Start your answer by highlighting how each source *helps* us with this enquiry.

## ☐ Criteria 1: Consider the content of the source

Highlight or underline useful information for the enquiry in both sources. Make sure you judge how useful it is for the enquiry specified in the question. For this question the sources need to help us understand some of the failings that people accused the police of, as well as the frenzy that the murders caused in the press. Start your answer by highlighting how each source helps us with this enquiry.

## ☐ Criteria 2: Consider the provenance of each source

Look at the captions provided above the sources. Think carefully about the following key questions and the impact that this might have on how useful the source is.

■ **What is the nature of the source?**
What type of source is it? How does this affect its utility? For example, a private letter or diary can be useful because the person usually gives his or her honest view.

■ **What are the origins of the source?**
Who produced it? Are they likely to have a good knowledge of the events they talk about? Are they likely to give a one-sided view?

■ **What is the purpose of the source?**
Why was it produced? How might this affect the reliability of the source? For example, a politician's speech or a newspaper report might be produced for propaganda purposes – to make people more angry with the police. The *Pall Mall Gazette* often criticised Sir Charles Warren, for instance.

## ☐ Criteria 3: Use your own knowledge of the historical context to evaluate the source

Compare the information and key messages contained in the source with your own knowledge of the enquiry topic. Do the **CAT test**. Ask yourself these three key questions:

■ How **comprehensive** is the source? Does it have any limitations? What does it miss out?

■ How **accurate** is the source? Does it 'match' what you know about the topic?

■ How **typical** is the source? Were the problems and feelings described common or unusual? Were there any other such problems or are they unusual and untypical of what went on for the majority of the time?

## Practice questions

You can find sources with practice questions on pages 131, 159 and 160.

# Following up sources

One of the key aims of this book is to help you understand how we use the enquiry process to research history. As we said on page 116, asking the right historical questions is a crucial part of enquiry and historical research. Exam questions like the one below provide you with the opportunity to show the enquiry skills you have been developing throughout the book.

2.  (b) How could you follow up the table of crimes on page 118 to find out more about the types of crimes committed in Whitechapel? In your answer, you must give the question you would ask and the type of source you could use. Complete the table below.

    (4 marks)

    - Detail in the source that I would follow up: _____
    - Question I would ask: _____
    - What type of source I could use: _____
    - How this might help answer my question: _____

The key tip with this question is to make sure that the four different parts of your answer link together.

**Step 1: Link the detail to the enquiry**

Start by identifying the focus for the enquiry – in this case the types of crime committed in Whitechapel. Make sure that the detail you say that you would follow up is linked to this enquiry. For example, if the source mentioned how often alcohol was involved in crime, you could identify this as a detail that you would follow up as this is linked to the main enquiry.

**Step 2: Link the question to the detail**

The question you choose must be linked to the detail you are following up from the source. Do not simply choose an interesting question unrelated to the enquiry! If we were following up the detail about violent crime, we could use 'What types of violent crime were committed?' as our question.

**Step 3: Link the type of source to the question**

You now need to choose a type of source that would be useful for following up that question. Look at the list in the box opposite. Make sure you choose a source that would help with the question. For example, in this case, newspaper articles about trials in the Police Court might give us a useful insight about the crimes that were committed.

**Step 4: Link this with your own knowledge**

Do not forget to explain the advantages of using this type of source and link it to the enquiry. The source type mentioned above would be particularly useful because the records of the trials themselves have been lost or destroyed, and the newspaper reports are often the only details that we have left.

**Different types of sources**

**National records**

- national newspapers
- records of crimes and police investigations
- Old Bailey records of trials
- Punch cartoons.

**Local records**

- housing and employment record and council records
- census returns
- Charles Booth's survey
- workhouse records
- local police records
- coroners' reports
- photographs
- London newspapers.

# Exploring similarities between the key features of two different periods

Question 3 is the first question that tests your knowledge and understanding of the thematic study on crime and punishment in Britain, c.1000–present. Remember this is where de-coding questions comes in useful. Look at the question below.

This is an 'explain' question. However, as it is only worth 4 marks, you only have to explain one similarity.

This question has a very specific content focus. To save time make sure you stay relevant – only write about trials during the time periods mentioned. There is no need to mention punishments or policing.

**3.** Explain **one** way in which trials in medieval England were similar to trials in the seventeenth century.

(4 marks)

The date boundaries are crucial. You must focus on the right case studies, trial by ordeal c.1000–1215, witch-hunt 1645–47.

The conceptual focus of this question is 'similarities and differences' – the ability to compare different periods of history. In this case the focus is on similarities.

The first thing to notice is that the question is only worth 4 marks. It is important that you are clear on the focus of the question so that you can keep your answer short and to the point.

## Explaining similarities between time periods

As this is an 'explain' question you must do more than simply identify a similarity. You will need to support your answer with specific details – a good motto is 'prove' don't 'say'. Would your explanation convince the reader that there was a similarity between the ways that trials were conducted in the Middle Ages and the seventeenth century?

For example, you might 'say' that one similarity between trials in the Middle Ages and the seventeenth century was that there was some kind of ordeal used to decide guilt or innocence. However, this would not get you high marks. Instead you need to prove your big point about the use of ordeal by providing supporting information **and** 'killer evidence'.

- **BIG POINT** – With a question only worth 4 marks do not spend time on an introduction. Start your answer with your 'big point' – in this case an ordeal was used to decide guilt or innocence.

- **SUPPORTING INFORMATION** – You need to develop your initial 'big point' or argument. You could explain how in both periods a form of trial by cold water was used.

- **KILLER EVIDENCE** – You now need to prove that this was the case by providing specific examples from each time period. For the Middle Ages you could refer to the use of trial by cold water. The accused was tied with a knot above their waist and lowered into the water on the end of a rope. For the seventeenth century you might talk about the 'swimming' test used to decide whether the accused was guilty of witchcraft. It was believed the innocent would sink and the guilty would float. If they floated, the accused would be examined for the 'Devil's marks' as a final proof of witchcraft.

### Practice questions

You can find further practice questions on pages 131, 159 and 160.

### REMEMBER

You should only be spending around five minutes on this question. Keep your answer focused on explaining **one** way in which people behaved or reacted in a similar way. Do not list lots of similarities.

171

# Tackling 12-mark explain questions

Look at the question below.

**4.** Explain why there were changes to policing in the period between c.1700 and c.1900.

(12 marks)

You may use the following in your answer:
- **the growth of London**
- **increased taxation**

You must also use information of your own.

This question is different in two ways from Question 3 on page 171. Firstly, the conceptual focus is different – in this case the key concept is causation (explaining **why** an event took place or explaining the pace of change). Secondly, this question is worth 12 marks. The examiner will expect you to give a range of reasons **why** there were changes to policing in the period between c.1700 and c.1900.

It is important to spend time planning this question during your exam. Follow the steps below to help you plan effectively and produce a good answer.

## Step 1: Get focused on the question

Make sure you de-code the question carefully. Note that the content focus is on policing so you do not need to explain about changes to punishment or crime.

## Step 2: Identify a range of factors

Try to cover more than one cause. If your mind goes blank always go back to the key factors that influence change in crime and punishment (see page 10). The stimulus bullet points can also help you. For example, in the question above, the reference to increased taxation shows how 'Goverment' played a key role in changing policing methods. The reference to the growth of London shows how 'Towns' were another important factor.

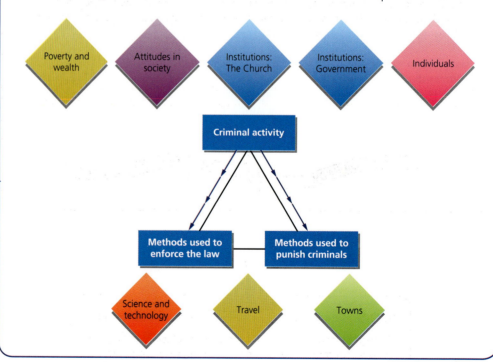

### Step 3: Organise your answer using paragraphs

Do not worry about a long introduction. One or two sentences are more than enough and you can use words from the question. Look at the example below. Note how the student has built a short introduction into the first paragraph which focuses on the growth of London.

*One important reason for the changes in policing was the growth of London which significantly increased the need for a full-time professional police force.*

Aim to start a new paragraph each time you move onto a new factor that caused change. Signpost your argument at the start of the paragraph. For example, you could start your next paragraph like this:

*The actions of government also played an important role in influencing developments in policing.*

### Step 4: Do not 'say' that a factor was important – 'prove' it was

Remember that a list of reasons why policing changed will not get you a high-level mark. You need to **prove** your case for each factor. This means developing your explanation by adding supporting information and specific examples (killer evidence).

This is where your work on connectives will come in useful. Look again at the advice on page 30 and remember to tie what you know to the question by using connectives such as 'this meant', 'this led to' and 'this resulted in'. For example, you may want to build on the opening to your first paragraph by using the examples of how the population increased rapidly and the problem of closely packed houses and streets. Look at how the student below starts to prove a point.

*The growth of London caused changes in policing because there were too many people, crammed into closely packed streets and houses. This made the job of watchmen and parish constables more difficult as there were plenty of places for criminals to commit crimes and to escape. It soon became clear that old systems of policing were no longer up to the job.*

WHAT YOU KNOW — WHAT THE QUESTION ASKS

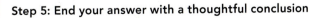

### Step 5: End your answer with a thoughtful conclusion

Keep your conclusion short. A good conclusion makes the overall argument clear – it is not a detailed summary of everything you have already written! Make it clear which factor played the most important role. You may want to show how it links to other factors.

## Practice questions

You can find further practice questions on pages 131, 159 and 160.

## REMEMBER

Do not try to cover too many factors that led to change. Select which factors you can make the strongest argument for. Remember in the exam you would have approximately 15 minutes to answer this question.

# Making judgements – tackling the 16-mark question

The last question on the exam paper carries the most marks and requires a carefully planned, detailed answer. You will be provided with a statement in quotation marks and be asked to reach a judgement about **how far you agree** with it. The phrase 'how far' is important as it is unlikely that you will totally agree or disagree with the statement. The examiner will be looking for you to show that you can weigh the evidence for and against the statement.

Look at the example below.

---

5. 'The role of the Church was the most important factor affecting law enforcement during the Middle Ages.' How far do you agree? Explain your answer. (16 marks)

   You may use the following in your answer:
   • benefit of the clergy
   • tithings

   **You must also use information of your own.**

   (Total for spelling, punctuation, grammar and the use of specialist terminology = 4 marks)

   (Total for Question 5 = 20 marks)

---

## Step 1: Focus

The content focus is important – you have to reach a judgement on the role of the Church in law enforcement in medieval England. This includes information about the religious basis of trial by ordeal, claiming sanctuary, benefit of the clergy and Church courts. The conceptual focus is on causation. You have to evaluate the extent to which the role of the Church was the main factor affecting law enforcement c.1000–c.1500?

## Step 2: Identify

In 16-mark questions you are required to reach a judgement on a statement. In order to do this effectively you need to identify **clear criteria** for reaching that judgement. Just as you need to cover a range of factors in 'explain' questions, you need to **cover a range of criteria** in 'judgement' questions.

Possible criteria for reaching a judgement:

- If you are judging the importance of an event or development you could analyse and evaluate the immediate impact, the short-term impact and the long-term impact.
- If you are judging the extent of change you could analyse and evaluate how many people were affected (was everyone affected by the role of the Church or was it mainly churchmen?).

In this example, you are being asked to reach a judgement on role of the Church in medieval England, so you could use the following two criteria:

- What role did the Church play in influencing policing methods or the trial system?
- What other influences (the King, local communities) affected policing methods and the trial system during this period?

## Step 3: Organise

There are two ways of organising your answer.

**Approach 1: Write about one criterion in each paragraph:**

- Paragraph 1 – Evaluate the extent to which policing was influenced by the Church or by other factors (weigh the evidence for and against).
- Paragraph 2 – Evaluate the extent to which trials were influenced by the Church or other factors (weigh the evidence for and against).
- Paragraph 3 – Your final conclusion – weigh the evidence – how far do you agree with the statement?

**Approach 2: The simplest is to plan 'for' and 'against' paragraphs:**

- Paragraph 1 – Evidence to **support** the statement (make sure that you use the criteria – the role of the Church was the most important factor affecting law enforcement during the Middle Ages)
- Paragraph 2 – Evidence to **counter** the statement (once again use the criteria)
- Paragraph 3 – Your final conclusion – weigh the evidence – how far do you agree with the statement?

## Step 4: Prove

Remember to tie what you know to the question. Do not include information and think that it will speak for itself. Some students think that simply dropping in examples to the right paragraphs is enough. One of the stimulus points refers to the benefit of the clergy. The following statement from a student could be further developed and gain more marks.

*The use of benefit of the clergy had a big impact on law enforcement because churchmen could be tried in Church courts.*

This does not **prove** that benefit of the clergy affected law enforcement. To gain more marks, the student would need to go on to explain that benefit of the clergy affected law enforcement because those tried in Church courts avoided the death penalty and could expect more lenient treatment than in royal courts.

# Step 5: Conclude

Your conclusion is a crucial part of your answer. You have been asked to reach a judgement on a statement. You need to clearly state how far you agree with it and your reason why. It would be easy to sit on the fence and avoid reaching a final conclusion. But sitting on the fence is a dangerous position. Your answer collapses and you lose marks.

Instead of sitting on the fence, you need to be confident and reach an overall judgement. Imagine that you have placed the evidence on a set of scales. How far do they tip in favour of the statement or against it?

You can then move on in your conclusion to explain your judgement. Do not repeat everything you have already written. Think of the scales – what are the heaviest pieces of evidence on each side? Build these into your conclusion in the following way:

| | |
|---|---|
| JUDGEMENT – Start with your judgement – try to incorporate words from the question into this sentence. | To a large extent, I disagree that the role of the Church was the most important factor affecting law enforcement in the medieval period. |
| COUNTER – Show that you are aware that there is some evidence to counter this and give the best example. | The Church did have some influence over the trial system, especially trial by ordeal. |
| SUPPORT – Explain why, overall, you have reached the judgement you have. Give your key reason or reasons why. | However, local communities were the basis of nearly all punishment methods and local juries sat in judgment of most cases. |

## Practice questions

You can find further practice questions on pages 131, 159 and 160.

## REMEMBER

Leave enough time to **check your answer** carefully for spelling, punctuation and grammar.

Four crucial marks are available (this is as much as your answer to Question 1, 2b or 3).

- You will be marked for the accuracy of your spelling and punctuation.
- You will also be marked for your grammar – does your work make sense? Are your arguments clear?
- Finally, the examiner will consider your use of 'specialist terms' – have you used a wide range of historical terms?

# What are the key ingredients of effective writing in GCSE history?

The language you use to express your ideas is very important. One of the ways to get better at history is to be more precise with your use of language. For example, rather than simply saying that you *agree* or *disagree* with a statement you can use language that shows whether you agree to *a large extent* or only *to some extent*. Look at the different shades of argument below and experiment with using some of the phrases. Use them when you are debating or discussing in class.

## Thinking carefully about the language you use

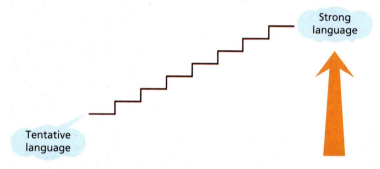

| Varying your language to show how far you agree with a statement: | Varying your language to show how important a factor/cause is: |
|---|---|
| I totally/entirely/completely/absolutely agree with … | … was by far the most important reason why … |
| I substantially/fundamentally/strongly agree with … | The key/crucial/essential factor was … |
| I agree to a large extent with … | … was the main cause of … |
| I mainly/mostly agree with … | The most influential cause was … |
| I agree to some extent with … | … played a significant/important/major role in … |
| I partially/partly agree with … | … was of some importance in … |
| I only agree with … to a limited/slight extent | |
| **Varying your language to show the significance or importance of an individual, discovery, event or development:** | **Varying your language to show the extent of change:** |
| … made the most important/significant contribution to … | … was revolutionised in … |
| … had a crucial/major/highly significant impact on … | … totally changed during … |
| … had an important/influential impact on … | … was transformed during … |
| … was of some importance/significance | … there was fundamental change in … |
| … only made a limited/partial/slight/minimal contribution to … | The period saw significant/important progress in … |
| | … saw some changes in … … saw some progress in … |
| | … saw limited/slight/minimal progress in … |

## Helpful phrases and sentence starters

| When you want to explore the other side of an argument: | When you want to highlight similarities: | When you want to make an additional point to support an argument: | When you want to show that an individual, event or discovery was important: |
|---|---|---|---|
| On the other hand … <br><br> However … <br><br> Alternatively, it could be argued that … | In the same way … <br><br> Similarly … <br><br> This is similar to the way that … <br><br> Likewise … | Also … <br><br> Additionally … <br><br> In addition … <br><br> Moreover … <br><br> Furthermore … | … was a crucial turning point in … <br><br> … acted as an important catalyst for … <br><br> Without this event/ development/ discovery … would not have happened. <br><br> This had an immediate impact on … <br><br> In the short term this transformed/revolutionised … <br><br> In the long term this had a lasting impact on … |
| **When you want to link points or show that one thing led to another:** | **When you want to refer to evidence in a source:** | **When you want to give examples to support a point:** | |
| Therefore … <br><br> Due to … <br><br> Consequently … <br><br> One consequence of this was … <br><br> This caused … <br><br> This led to … <br><br> This resulted in … <br><br> This meant that … | Source A suggests/implies/ indicates that … <br><br> According to Source B … <br><br> Source A shows/illustrates/ demonstrates that … | For example … <br><br> For instance … <br><br> This can be seen when … <br> This is clearly shown by … <br><br> This is supported by … <br><br> This is proven by … | |

You can use the **progression grid** below to get an idea of what getting better at history looks like. This is designed to give you a general idea of what you need to do to produce good answers in the exam. It focuses on the four key things in the coloured squares on the bingo card (page 178).

## The History progression grid

| | | Question focus | Organisation | Line of argument | Supporting information |
|---|---|---|---|---|---|
| **High level** | | The answer is consistently focused on the question. | The answer is structured very carefully and explanations are coherent throughout the answer. | The line of argument is very clear and convincing. It flows throughout the answer. | Supporting information has been precisely selected, and shows wide-ranging knowledge and understanding. |
| | | The answer is mainly focused on the question. | The answer is well organised but some parts lack coherence. | The line of argument is clear, convincing and generally maintained through the answer. | Supporting information is accurate and relevant, and shows good knowledge and understanding. |
| | | The answer has weak or limited links to the question. | Some statements are developed. <br><br> There is some attempt to organise the material. | The line of argument is partly convincing but not maintained through the answer. | Supporting information is mainly accurate and relevant, and shows some knowledge and understanding. |
| | | The answer has no real links to the question. | The answer lacks organisation. | The line of argument is unclear or missing. | Supporting information is limited or not relevant. |

# Self-assessing and peer assessing your work

It is important that you check your own work before you hand it to your teacher to be marked. Sometimes you may be asked to assess the work of someone else in your class. In both cases you need to know what you are looking for. What are the key ingredients of great writing in history?

You can use the **bingo card** as a checklist – get competitive and try and show that you have covered all the squares and got a full house of ingredients!

| | | |
|---|---|---|
| The answer starts with a **clear focus on the question** (there is no long introduction).<br><br>Key words from the question are used during the answer.<br><br>For longer answers, each paragraph is linked to the question. | Statements and arguments are fully developed and explained – showing good knowledge and understanding.<br><br>Arguments are **well supported** by accurate, relevant and well-selected evidence. | **Connectives** are used to help prove arguments and show significance/impact.<br><br>Look for phrases like:<br><br>*this led to …*<br><br>*this resulted in …*<br><br>*this meant that …* |
| There is a **clear line of argument** at the start of each paragraph – think of it as a signpost for what follows. The rest of the paragraph supports this argument.<br><br>The line of argument flows throughout the answer building up to a clear conclusion. | Paragraphs have been used to provide a **clear structure**.<br><br>Each paragraph starts with a different cause/factor<br><br>(12-mark explain questions)<br><br>or<br><br>a different theme/criteria<br><br>(16-mark judgement questions). | The answer shows **wide-ranging** knowledge and understanding.<br><br>It considers a range of factors/causes (explain questions) or explores the evidence for **and** against a statement (judgement questions). |
| The language used helps to construct very precise arguments – showing how important the writer thinks a cause/factor, event or individual is.<br><br>A good range of specialist **historical vocabulary** has been used. | There is a **clear conclusion**.<br><br>For explain questions factors/causes are prioritised or linked.<br><br>For judgement questions there is a focus on 'how far' the writer agrees with the statement. | The answer has been **carefully checked** for spelling, punctuation and grammar.<br><br>The meaning is always clear throughout the answer. |

# Glossary

**Abscond**  Leave or escape to avoid arrest.

**Absolute poverty**  When a person lacks the basics (food and shelter, etc.) needed to survive for any length of time.

**Alibi**  A claim to have been elsewhere when a crime was committed.

**Anarchism**  A belief that opposes all forms of state government in favour of government on a voluntary, co-operative basis.

**Arrest warrant**  Permission from a Judge or magistrate to make an arrest.

**Assize judges**  Royal judges who travelled around the country hearing serious cases. See Quarter Sessions.

**Beat constable**  The lowest rank of police officer whose usual duty is to walk 'the beat'.

**Benefit of the clergy**  The right to be judged in a Church court.

**Black market**  The illegal buying and selling of goods.

**Blood feud**  The early Saxon right of a murder victim's family to track down and kill the murderer in revenge.

**Bloody Code**  Harsh laws, introduced in late seventeenth and eighteenth centuries that made even minor crimes punishable by death.

**Board of Works**  A kind of council for London, but with very limited powers and money.

**Borstal**  A type of prison set up especially for young offenders in the early twentieth century. Abolished in 1982.

**Capital crime**  A crime punishable by death.

**Capital punishment**  The death penalty.

**Castration**  Removal of the testicles.

**Chief inspector**  The person in charge of a division or in charge of the CID.

**Colliers**  Coal miners.

**Compensation**  Money paid to the victim of crime or the victim's family.

**Compurgation**  The oath taken during the Middle Ages by witnesses or people known to the accused in support of his or her innocence.

**Coroner**  An official responsible for investigating violent or suspicious deaths.

**Coroner's inquest**  A legal hearing which investigates causes of death.

**Corporal punishment**  A physically painful punishment.

**Counterfeiting**  Making illegal copies or forgeries.

**County Assizes**  See Quarter Sessions.

**Criminal Investigation Department (CID)**  A department in the police force that employs detectives to investigate crimes.

**CS gas**  A powerful form of tear gas that creates a burning sensation in eyes, nose and throat.

**Curfew**  A time at which people must be at home, not on the streets or elsewhere.

**Custody**  Being locked up.

**Customs officers**  Officials who ensure nothing illegal is brought into the country and that the necessary taxes are paid on any legal goods entering the country.

**Debtor's prison**  An early type of prison where debtors were locked up until they paid back what they owed.

**Detecting**  Investigating crime.

**Deterrence**  To scare/warn people from committing a crime.

**Disembowel**  To cut open and remove the guts.

**DNA matching**  Using DNA to help trace victims and criminals.

**Drug crime**  Includes possessing, consuming, selling or smuggling illegal drugs.

**Fenian**  Committed to establishing an independent Irish Republic in the nineteenth century.

**Forest Laws**  Norman laws that banned ordinary people from hunting or gathering wood in the King's forests.

**Fraud**  A deliberate act of deception that results in personal gain.

**French Revolution**  Overthrow of the monarchy in France in 1789. Nobles and landowners lost their power and privilege. Became increasingly bloody by 1793, creating much fear in England.

**Gamekeepers**  People paid to patrol private land to protect game (animals for hunting) from poachers.

**Gold rush**  The rapid influx of people hoping to make their fortune once gold is discovered in an area.

**Hard labour**  Being made to work hard as a punishment while serving a prison sentence. This included pointless work such as the crank and the treadmill.

**Heresy**  The crime of holding religious beliefs different to those of the monarch.

**Highway robbery**  Stopping a coach and robing the passengers.

**Hoaxers**  People who make things up in order to make money or to fool the police.

**Home Rule**  The right to local self-government.

**Home Secretary** Minister responsible for the internal affairs of England and Wales, including police and prisons.

**Horse patrol** A mounted patrol to deter highway robbers.

**Horsewhip** A whip used to control horses or for corporal punishment.

**Houses of Correction** An early type of prison where vagabonds and prostitutes were whipped and made to work before being sent back to their parish. Also used to hold petty criminals awaiting trial.

**Hue and cry** Raising the alarm (by means of loud shouts or cries) when a crime has been committed. Everyone within hearing distance was expected to join the hunt for the suspect.

**Hulks** Old ships, often in derelict condition, used to house prisoners in the nineteenth century.

**Identity parades** A way of identifying a criminal in which a witness picks out a person they think they have seen from a line of people.

**Inspector** A more senior policeman in charge of a station or a group of sergeants.

**IRA** Irish Republican Army – terrorist group wanting an independent Ireland that joined Northern Ireland with Eire.

**Irons** Fetters or chains.

**Justices of the Peace (JPs)** Local magistrates appointed to keep the peace, hear minor legal cases, and ensure the Poor Laws were being maintained.

**Knuckle-duster** A metal guard worn over the knuckles in fighting to increase the effect of blows.

**Legal highs** Legal highs contain one or more chemical substances which produce similar effects to illegal drugs. Little is known about their long- or short-term effects on health.

**Lock down** A security or safety measure in prisons that confines all inmates to their cells.

**Lodging house** A building converted into many rooms in which people could pay a small fee – 4 or 5 pence – to sleep the night in.

**Lord Chief Justice** The top judge in the country.

**Lunatics** Mentally disturbed people.

**Magistrate** See Justices of the Peace (JPs).

**Manor courts** Local medieval courts that dealt mainly with minor crimes.

**Market regulations** Laws relating to the buying and selling of goods in a market.

**Mass** A Catholic Church service.

**Metropolitan Police Force** The official name of the police force responsible for London. Established in 1829.

**Moral offences** An action that offends the moral standards of the majority of society.

**Mortuary** A building or facility where bodies are stored.

**Mug-shots** Photographs of faces, which started to be used by the police as way of recognising people.

**Murdrum fine** Norman law that made the whole community pay a heavy fine if a Norman was killed.

**Neighbourhood Watch** An organisation set up in the early 1980s to prevent crime in local communities.

**Non-custodial** To do with an alternative to being locked up in prison.

**Ofsted** An organisation that inspects the quality of education in schools, nurseries and prisons.

**Open prison** Prisons for low-risk category prisoners. Open prisons allow prisoners freedoms such as day release and work placements in the community.

**Opportunistic thief** A thief who acts on the spur of the moment when the opportunity arises.

**Pamphleteers** People who printed and sold cheap news stories or tales of crime.

**Parish constables** Men from every village or town who were appointed to uphold law and order. This was part-time and unpaid work.

**Penal reform** Reforms to the prison system.

**Pepper spray** A spray that irritates the eyes.

**Pillory** A wooden frame with holes in it that held the head and hands of a convicted offender. Intended to publicly humiliate the criminal.

**Poaching** The illegal hunting of animals.

**Police surgeon** A police officer with medical training, often qualified as a doctor.

**Poor rates** A tax paid by the wealthier members of a parish to provide relief for the poor.

**Posse** A group of men called upon by the sheriff to track down a criminal.

**Prison colony** A settlement in a remote location used to exile and separate prisoners from the general population.

**Prison warders** Prison guards.

**Probation officer** A person who manages offenders in order to protect the public and reduce the chances of re-offending.

**Protection racket** A system of taking money from people in exchange for agreeing not to hurt them.

**Quaker** A person of religious belief characterised by a total rejection of violence.

**Quarter Sessions** Courts, held four times each year, used to hear serious cases. See Assize judges.

**Race crime** A crime motivated by racial prejudice.

**Reformation** A period of violent change in religion, especially in northern Europe, when Protestant Christians rejected the Roman Catholic Church.

**Repeal** When a law is withdrawn.

**Residuum** A word meaning the lowest possible class of person – literally the 'dregs' of humanity.

**Retribution** Revenge.

**Rookeries** Overcrowded and poor-quality housing in slum areas.

**Sanctity of life** The belief that all life is sacred and therefore must be protected.

**Sanctuary** A safe place within a church or cathedral. Once a person claimed sanctuary they could not be removed by force.

**Scribe** A person who writes books or other documents by hand.

**Serial killer** A killer who has committed a number of murders.

**Sheriff** The chief law officer in each county during the Middle Ages.

**Slum clearance** A process begun in the late 1800s, and not completed until after the Second World War, which saw destruction of unhealthy or dangerous housing.

**Smuggling** Bringing goods into the country illegally or not paying tax on legal goods entering.

**Snares** A form of trap used to catch animals.

**Social crime** An illegal act that many people do not regard as a crime.

**Socialism** A political and economic system in which most forms of property and resources are owned or controlled by the state.

**Sociological research** Studies of the way that people live, using observation and by taking notes and measurements.

**Solitary confinement** Being locked up on your own and totally separate from other people.

**Stagecoaches** Horse-drawn coaches that would stop at intervals or 'stages' to refresh the horses or allow rest for passengers.

**Stocks** A wooden frame with holes in it that held the feet of a convicted offender. Intended to publicly humiliate the criminal.

**Sweatshops** Workshops, often making clothes or shoes, where people were paid low wages (often only receiving a small sum for each item they finished).

**Thief-takers** People who made money from collecting the rewards offered for the return of stolen goods or the capture of criminals.

**Tithings** Groups of ten men who were responsible for each other's behaviour. If a member of the tithing broke the law then the others had to bring him to justice or face a fine.

**Trade union** An organisation of workers set up to defend their interests and campaign for improvements in their working conditions.

**Transportation** Sending convicted criminals overseas.

**Treason** Disobedience or disloyalty to the monarch (or the government).

**Trial by combat** A type of trial by ordeal. Guilt is decided if the participant is defeated in combat.

**Trial by ordeal** A trial, held in or near a church, in which God judges the accused with a sign of guilt or innocence.

**Tribunal** A panel of people brought together to settle some type of dispute. Tribunals were sometimes used to decide on the cases of conscientious objectors.

**Vagabondage** The crime of being a wandering beggar. Also known as vagrancy.

**Welfare state** The system by which the government provides support for the poorest and most vulnerable in society. This includes health care, unemployment relief and other benefits.

**Wergild** A form of compensation paid to victims of crime in Saxon times.

**Witchcraft** The crime of using magic to cause harm to a person or their property.

**Young offenders' institutions** Secure units for young offenders that are run along the same lines as adult prisons.

## Answers to crime survey on page 3

1c; 2d; 3d; 4c; 5b; 6c; 7d

# Index